A Way of Life

Healing Animals

Mary Bromiley

Edward Gaskell
Devon

Edward Gaskell publishers
Old Gazette Building
6 Grenville Street
Bideford
Devon
EX39 2EA

First published May 2014
Reprinted July 2014

ISBN 978-1-906769-52-9

© Mary Bromiley

A Way of Life
Healing Animals

Mary Bromiley

Typeset, printed and bound by
Lazarus Press
Caddsdown Business Park
Bideford
Devon
EX39 3DX
www.lazaruspress.com

Besides Edward Gaskell, editor, proof reader, and publisher who took a jumble and made a book there are many people and even more animals who deserve my thanks, too many to mention individually. Most thanks are due to my children, particularly my two daughters Penelope and Rabbit. Also grandchildren, all of whom, without too much obvious irritation, have not only helped me, but by doing so have enabled me to pursue the idiosyncratic, possibly slightly selfish existence, associated with a pioneering idea, physiotherapy for animals, resulting in an amusing, albeit varied, way of living.

Edward Gaskell *publishers*
DEVON

Contents

Prologue.   7

Early Life.   11

A Malayan Interlude.   51

Home Again.   95

Downs House Created.   137

Exmoor Relocation.   231

WWW.LAZARUSPRESS.COM

Prologue

It was a bitterly cold morning in November 2010. Porridge and coffee consumed I gazed out of the kitchen window: the sky was a flat grey, unusually cold looking. Across the valley a group of Red Deer Stags were scavenging under a hedge, the bird table in the garden was already empty. Resignedly I realised winter really was here - depressingly early for the West Country.

The dogs began to bark suggesting an arrival. I opened the backdoor to find the postman who despite the ice - the remains of an earlier snowfall - had nobly slid down our near vertical, quarter mile track from the lane. Over a cup of coffee he imparted a rather gloomy report on the state of the roads and expected weather.

Thanking him as he left and before closing the door I looked outside. Obviously all the outside water troughs would have frozen over and the ice would need to be broken so the sheep, cattle and horses could drink.

Struggling into another layer of clothing I quickly scanned the daily pile of letters and junk mail noticing, with some irritation, an official looking white envelope. Printed boldly across the top I read: 'On Her Majesty's Service', suggestive of DEFRA or the Tax Office. Unlikely to be a pre Christmas cheque from either: what on earth did officialdom want now; what had I forgotten I wondered. The letter could certainly wait, probably best opened in the evening with a fortifying whiskey to hand.

Heavy snow started to fall as I went out. My daughter, who by now had already dealt with the iced-up troughs drove the Land Rover to the top of the drive, where fortunately there are additional farm buildings including the large barn housing the stables. I followed, through the deepening snow, driving the 'Yellow Peril', a type of low gear biscuit box on wheels; chilly to drive, as although it has a roof and windscreen, there are no side doors. However its wheels, shod with deep-tread tyres, grip on the most hazardous surfaces - unlike my warm comfortable RAV4.

Leaving the *Peril* in the barn and changing to the Land Rover, I negotiated the two miles to the village shop to stock up with milk and bread. We were snowed in by lunchtime and the efforts of farm living rather took over and it was at least two days before I remembered that the OHMS envelope had not been opened. Searching I found the pile of mail and looking with more care at the envelope I read, in the bottom left hand corner: 'Urgent Personal' and below that: 'Cabinet Office', the latter underlined. This text, which I had previously missed, suggested the contents were probably *not* a Tax Demand.

To my astonishment the letter read as follows:

The Prime Minister has asked me to inform you, in strict confidence, that having accepted the advice of the Cabinet Secretary and the Main Honours Committee, he proposes to submit your name to The Queen. He is recommending that Her Majesty may be graciously pleased to approve that you be appointed a Member of the Most Honourable Order of the British Empire (MBE) in the New Year 2011 Honours List.

I read the page again: why me? what on earth for? Close scrutiny of the remaining pages informed me the Citation would read:

For Services to Equine Sport and Equestrian Physiotherapy

Amazing. Childishly I have always felt that Honours should really only be given following deeds of chivalry: the Slaying of Dragons by Knights of the Realm, unsurpassed Acts of Bravery and the like.

To me pioneering the transposition of physiotherapy techniques from human to animal patients and subsequently proving it could be as useful in the treatment of animals as it was in their human counterparts was not in that league.

My natural inclination was to say, 'No thank you,' because doing something I had enjoyed did not seem worthy of such recognition, but after discussion with my four children without whose help and backing - particularly that given by my two daughters - had enabled success I was persuaded to fill in the form stating, 'Yes, I would be delighted to have my name put forward.'

Since the Honours List announcement many people have been kind enough to enquire about physiotherapy for animals. Why did you start? How did you get it accepted? Have you ever considered writing about it?

The interest has resulted in my attempting to try to chronicle a little of my life in an attempt to describe the path that led to an award I had never expected; never even dreamed of.

My mother on her preferred mode of transport

1

Early Life

My childhood seems, looking back, to have been very different from that experienced by children today. Born into a strata which now, would I suppose, be called upper middle class, I was a child in the days when 'upper' people enjoyed servants thus early days passed in a safe, regulated, nursery environment.

My mother had been brought up in Sussex, the family background averse to girls being educated at school or trained for a career.

The youngest of three sisters she was taught, at home, by a governess. These lessons were interspersed by trips to Europe to visit relatives of her mother's extended family: spells in both France and Germany ensured a lasting fluency in both languages.

She was in England at the start of World War One and enrolled, with no training, as a voluntary nurse. After the War ended she started on the usual round of 'visits' like many other career-less girls, luckily for her she was not curtailed to the European Tour, as were many of her contemporaries, but was able to travel to both India and Ceylon to stay with her married sisters.

My father had qualified in Edinburgh as both veterinary surgeon and doctor of medicine, I believe one of the first, if not *the* first, to achieve this distinction, practicing both professions simultaneously throughout his working life. When he met and married my mother he was attached to the Colonial Medical Service.

Following a honeymoon on Exmoor the newlyweds set off for Nigeria where the approved method of travel was by horse, unfortunately the area of my father's new posting, Northern Nigeria, abounded with tsetse fly whose bite can make a horse seriously ill, even cause death. With no other form of transport available this meant my parents had to walk from one native settlement to another, their household goods and his medical equipment carried on the heads of a train of native porters trotting behind them, often up to 120 men, clad only in scanty loin cloths. Photographs depict a pretty primitive existence and without realising it, certainly with no pre-arranged trek in mind, my mother became the first white woman to walk across Northern Nigeria. Photographs show her unsuitably clad wearing hat, dress and shoes that would have graced an attendance at Ascot Races.

I was not conceived for several years and suspect my mother, discovering she was 'with child' was anything but overjoyed particularly as she was shipped home to sit out the pregnancy in Edinburgh. To add to her misery, just before I was born my father had to have his left leg amputated. He had been operating on a man who had been savaged by a crocodile, during the operation his dresser had handed him the wrong end of a scalpel, the blade cutting through his surgical glove and pricking a finger, unfortunately this gave entry to poison from the infected wounds of the patient. There were no antibiotics around in the 1930s and what started as a simple infection in a finger became a generalised septicaemia and he nearly died. Luckily he pulled through but the bone in his left leg remained infected necessitating a haunch removal.

As a one-legged doctor he was no longer fit for active service overseas and my parents moved to North Devon where I was brought up. They settled, in 1931, at Venn, a moderately sized house with gardens and paddocks just outside the village of Instow on the North Devon coast; the venue chosen because a friend owned the house and was willing to let. In hindsight the family probably fled South to escape matriarchal confines

Above: My father with his medical staff: The dresser who caused him to lose his leg is on the right.

Below: Venn, where my parents settled in 1931. A moderately sized house with gardens and paddocks just outside the village of Instow on the North Devon coast. As a one-legged doctor my father was no longer fit for active service overseas. This was where I was brought up.

imposed by my father's mother on all family members, and I understand in order to sooth ruffled feelings, it was diplomatically suggested, that following his operation my father would not tolerate the cold of Scotland, his birthplace. Venn was a fortunate choice resulting in over 70 years of occupancy.

Both grandmothers were widows: the paternal ruling the house in Edinburgh whose inmates included other widows or widowers taken in if they were a close family member following the departure of their other half. There were also several spinster aunts: marriage denied them due to the carnage that almost wiped out the males of their generation during the First World War. These ladies spent a great deal of their time 'doing good works', one deeply involved in the Earl Haig organisation which she had helped found.

There were also a number of aged retainers who cooked, cleaned, and coped with all the household tasks, in fact it was probably due to their efforts, rather than orders from my grandmother, that ensured the smooth running of the establishment.

The maternal resided adjacent to the Downs, near the seaside town of Eastbourne cared for by a resident couple. She lived alone apart from two permanent animal companions: a grey parrot and a black Scottie dog; the Scotties must have died and been replaced occasionally, but the resident one was always named Don.

The Parrot, who outlived her, was unfriendly and if allowed free range hid under chairs waiting for some unfortunate visitor to seat themselves when it would bite their ankles. I have no idea why this was tolerated but no one ever seemed to complain, far too frightened of losing face I suppose although I seem to remember several incidents of tea spillage, these necessitating a mopping up operation performed by a kneeling parlour maid.

I was christened twice, for there was a definite North/South family divide: a Hamilton Miller family gown in Edinburgh, Presbyterian faith, venue St Giles Cathedral; a Howden family gown in the South with an Anglo Catholic service. Down the years the Southern family had vacillated between the doctrines of Rome and those imposed by Henry VIII.

Both households, North and South, lived by the word of God perhaps neither entirely certain, when enrolling me into the Christian community which method of worship was superior: their uncertainty necessitating, in my case, the dual approach.

I experienced something similar many years later on discovering that the Chinese who wore white when in mourning always, in case they had got the colour wrong, pinned a square of black to their clothes and black mourning garments were similarly adorned with a square of white.

From as far back as I can remember, prior to the Second World War, life seemed to involve a series of visits. The telephone, considered an expensive luxury, was rarely used and calls were short for after three minutes a piping sound intervened: a signal to indicate that the cost of the call was rising steeply.

Information was exchanged by letters, those that survive providing a rich source of the social history of the time. Recently, searching through countless papers to verify dates, I found a note sent by balloon from a family member confined during the siege of Paris in 1870: the writer bemoans the fact that the Spring Fashion Shows had been cancelled but, '. . .luckily the peasants came through the lines daily bringing fresh foods into the city so that Froufrou [a Pekinese] was able to have her normal diet of chicken'. Unfortunately the art of letter writing has all but disappeared, replaced by seemingly incomprehensible *texts* and *tweets*.

The time required for even a short a journey during my childhood must seem incomprehensible when considered to-day and inter-family stays were lengthy: no weekend visits then, the trains were slow although always on time! No 70mph cars, no motorways, and few aeroplanes.

Train was usually the mode of travel although the car, ridiculous though it must seem, was often sent on ahead to be waiting when we arrived. The parents travelled first class, bone china and real linen in the Restaurant Car, nanny and I went second - or was it third? The current dog sat with our luggage in the guards van, often in company with rows of boxes containing homing pigeons, these were to be loosed by porters or the guard at a pre-arranged site, even if it meant stopping the train between stations. A stamped addressed post card filled in with time and place of release was sent to the owner of each loft from the next station following the loosing of the birds.

Lunch for nanny and I, delivered in a cardboard box, but with linen napkins, came on at Salisbury, always thin buttered slices of brown bread, railway fruit cake, and delicious cold chicken which tasted like no other.

We travelled to Scotland joining the Flying Scotsman in London to see father's family or went to the South Downs to join mother's family, this was a tolerable visit for as I grew older my pony and my father's horse sometimes travelled with us so we could ride over the Downs; they were loaded in a coach arranged as stalls all beautifully built of wood. The coach would be waiting in a loading bay at the departure station, every stall deep in straw, each had a manger and wooden water bucket, these checked by a porter at every stop. When the horses were loaded their coach was attached to the rear of the train.

Trains chugged slowly, no concept of travelling at 100mph! It was a very safe, stress-free way of travel for a horse. If accompanying us horse and pony were collected at Eastbourne station to be stabled with Sybil Smith who became not only a very noted Pony Judge but also the riding instructress to the then Princesses, Elizabeth and Margaret Rose. She summered in Sussex with some of her father's horses for groups were moved out of London to give them summer break.

Her family had for several generations been the premier livery and hireling yard in London. My great grandfather who always drove a pair of Blue Roans kept his carriage horses with Sybil's grandfather.

The Isle of Jersey was home to a favourite Aunt: it was often a somewhat fraught journey as the Jersey aerodrome did not exist, the occasional plane did land on the beach at St Ouen's at low tide but more often than not, due to head winds, arrived when the tide was up and had to return to England or if fuel was low fly to the coast of France to land.

A sea crossing was the only reliable method of travel, the voyage often lengthy due to endless sea fogs necessitating that the ferry hove to for hours off the lighthouse at Corbiere as it boomed out its warning, no radar to guide them into the Port of St Helier, it had not been invented!

Memories of life on Jersey is of a series of picnics, collecting Ormers - a large shell fish - delicious when baked, catching lobsters, surfing down sand dunes, and racing sand yachts. It rarely seemed too wet or too cold to picnic but if it was, as a group, we children spent hours making model aeroplanes out of balsa wood, little did we anticipate that in the not so distant future the eldest of the plane-making group, would help to design the Spitfire.

As I grew older I began to dread Sundays if staying in either of the grandmotherly establishments, it was dour in both. In Scotland Presbyterian ethics demanded the entire day was devoted to God, this necessitating attendance at two if not three services, no games, no toys, a State Tea in the drawing room attended by the Minister, and woe betide a spillage.

The Anglo Catholic South was equally regulated, lengthy prayers followed grace at breakfast, then dressed in one's best off to 11 o'clock Matins. During the sermon, often an hour long, the Sunday school teacher marshalled all children attending into a side Chapel. Religious books were handed out to keep us quiet. Rather as Lenten rings depicted Church attendance pre-Easter in the middle ages, regular attendees were given a small sticker illustrating some notable Christian event, and these needed to be much licked before being put into a Record of Attendance booklet. Not being a regular I was often denied a sticker, this rankled, however there was nothing to do but accept, even at an early age, that very often life seems unfair. I remember the licking released a unique aroma after which every one seemed to become temporarily stupefied: were we perhaps sniffing glue?

A formal roast at lunch, reading religious stories filled the afternoon then evensong for adults, in my case 'high tea' followed by early bed time.

Stays in Edinburgh were enlivened by visits to the Zoo. I adored the Elephant, begging to be allowed to feel the softness of the tip of its trunk as it moved gently toward proffered food; these early experiences, meeting such huge animals without fear I am certain enabled me to work later in life with the exotic animals I met when they were injured. I am not certain how it came about, but on one of these Zoo visits I was a guest at the Chimp's tea party, not a happy experience. Other, apparently envious children, stared through the bars surrounding the cage as my disapproving nurse handed me over to their keeper. I was led to the chimp's table, invited to sit on an empty chair. Three adult chimps, already seated, ignored my presence and got on with the business of peeling and eating their bananas. A younger one suddenly leapt down from above, obviously I was sitting in his chair, climbed onto my lap, peed, gave a hideous shriek, then grasping a branch above the table, swung off through the branches to the tree house.

I have never really felt an affinity for monkeys since but must admit to being moved by hearing of the plight of wild Gorillas from John Aspinall while I was repairing him. The loving playfulness displayed when he interacted with a Gorilla he'd helped rescue resulted in several severe arm and shoulder injuries. He persisted in his rescue missions and was to become famous for both his Zoo and gambling empire.

My father was not often present at family visits, sensibly he usually abandoned his family removing to his London Club or, as a fanatical fisherman, when we went north he continued onward to fish the Spey.

I think he may have been discouraged, even banned, from the establishment of grandmother South, for early in his marriage he had, by smoking, set the bed on fire. Smoking was regarded as a disgusting habit and forbidden in her house despite the presence of a smoking room.

I suspect I was nearly banned after what was described 'as a deeply shaming incident'. Pre the Second World War calling on friends was an integral part of life, each household within a circle of acquaintances allocated a day when the lady of the house would be 'At Home'.

Afternoon tea consumed guests' expected entertainment, possibly a game of cards, even music provided by the hostess if she could play or sing, any resident or visiting child was expected to recite. At one of these ordeals when staying with grandmother South, I was parked in the drawing room doorway by nanny. Having curtseyed (obligatory) I proudly began to recite, 'Hark the Herald Angels Sing', the early part of the rendition, greeted by sighs and murmurs of appreciation that one so young should be displaying such an early religious bent, changed to scandalised shrieks, as I continued, 'Mrs Simpson's pinched our King'. I can still remember the feeling as nanny grasped my sash and I flew backward.

The longed-for treat in the South was a visit to the Pier at Eastbourne. Grandmother South had a pay phone installed when all three of her daughters married men whose work took them overseas, realising no doubt that they would become dependent upon her hospitality when on home leave. Prior to a Pier visit, the coin drawer of the telephone was unlocked and with due ceremony six pennies extracted. These were sent below stairs, later to be returned bright and shining, having been scrubbed in the scullery, by some luckless kitchen maid lest they carried germs. The awful decision on arrival at the Pier was how to spend? Which of the wonderful attractions held most promise? The hen that laid a tin egg containing a piece of jewellery was a favourite, but to which delight should I treat Nanny? I longed to put her in the hall of mirrors but realised this was probably an unwise choice as she was not blessed with good looks.

I do not remember exactly when 'a girl' replaced Nanny, but it was probably due to an ebb of cash flow; unfortunately my father never submitted a bill if he did not cure a patient be it human or animal; naturally patients, once they realised this foible, rarely reported successful treatment outcomes. How my mother managed I have no idea as he also gambled on horses, at cards, and on football results: this meant our financial situation was often pretty precarious.

With 'the girl' a small, skewbald Shetland pony arrived to graze the paddocks. Jess was the mascot of the North Devon Regiment. When needed for a ceremonial event she was washed by the gardener, collected in the bread van, then driven away to lead the parade. She served me as a mobile conveyance for it was the era of long afternoon walks, if made to walk my short legs grew tired as the routes taken were through Devon lanes where the rutted surfaces were often too rough and the hills too steep for a pram to be easily pushed.

The confines of the nursery began to recede and I became an adept escapee catching Jess and going off to explore the country near home, or riding down to the beach. On wet days, if I could sneak into the consulting area, I amused myself by trying to match up the bones of varied animals for there were a mass of skeletons housed in drawers. Seemingly an odd occupation for a small child but I was an 'only': dolls held no interest, my mother was usually too busy gardening, playing tennis or visiting friends to worry while my father actively encouraged me.

On one unforgettable day I had climbed into the car to lie down and fantasise, stretched out luxuriously on the back seat. The car was huge, an Armstrong Siddeley, then the only model built with a clutch on the steering wheel, a necessary adaptation for a driver minus a left leg. Hearing footsteps approach I lay low, and my father got in, slammed the door, and started the engine. The car, for once missing the sides of the garage entrance, shot down the drive with the usual multiple variation in forward progression. His driving was erratic - a result of his general irritation and impatience, rather than the poor quality of available artificial limbs.

Once the main road was safely reached we sped along and I stayed where I was, remaining silent and only emerging, to make my presence known when the car had stopped.

Looking out I saw we had arrived at Wicketts' farm, nothing could be done about my presence, no time to take me home for we were met by Sid Wicketts the farmer and greeted with the news: yes his wife was in labour but a cow, also in labour, was more important. His words being, 'cum quick Doc. the coo 'er be bad; the ol umman, er kin wait.'

I tagged along to the shippen where a miserable-looking cow was obviously in a bad way. I dragged buckets, spread straw, and was exhilarated as, half an hour after our arrival, the two

Above: Jess was the mascot of the North Devon Regiment.

Left: Off parade.

Right: Jess, my mobile conveyance.

men pulled off a live heifer calf. During the calving my father had fallen over several times, his artificial leg was not reliable, and he was covered in shit, blood and general cow filth. Listening intently throughout, I'd learned a number of new and exciting words to share with the gardener's boy (the source of the unfortunate reference to Mrs Simpson).

Calf delivered, Sid and my father calmly stripped off and washed under the yard pump, then remembered Mrs Wicketts. She had during the calving, assisted by 'aunt,' delivered herself of a bouncing baby boy, son number four, and was making tea in the kitchen by the time we reached the house. The drive home was even more erratic due to the whiskey drunk to toast the safe arrival of both calf and baby.

Looking back I suppose the events of that day might possibly have implanted a seed which manifested in later life as a fascinating career associated with trying to repair those sick or injured. Such work is never boring or routine as no two cases are ever identical, each arising from varied circumstances with many differing yet associated complexities.

As well as riding I loved the sea, and to celebrate my sixth birthday my father, aided by Bill Valentine, a retired Colonel from the North Devon Regiment brought up in the boat-building village of Appledore, had built a small, pram shaped dinghy. I named her *Seagull*, proudly flying a pennant embroidered with a seagull from her broomstick masthead.

With the Valentine children I spent many happy hours aboard *Seagull* until a violent gale, coupled with a September equinox tide, drove her against the Marine Slip and smashed her to matchwood. I was so distraught that Bill Bailey was hired to teach me to sail: an elderly man from Appledore he was one of the ferrymen rowing passengers from Instow to Appledore at high tide. Prior to becoming a ferry man he had worked in whaling. He always wore his hair just off his shoulders, the somewhat greasy locks kept in place by a battered grey bowler. I had no idea why he sported this head gear until he told me he'd lost his ears and the tips of several fingers to frost bite when he had worked as harpoon man on a whaling ship. The whales were harpooned from an open rowing boat in his day, the boat crew were lucky he explained, and kept warm rowing as it was hard to catch up with the whale. The harpoon man meanwhile just stood waiting in the bow, getting colder and colder.

There was nothing Bill did not know about the estuary named Bideford Bay, a tidal area on the North Devon coast where the waters of the twin rivers, Taw and Torridge, meet and race outward to merge with the Atlantic Ocean with nothing to check them other than Lundy Island the only place between Lands End and South Wales where ships can find shelter from Atlantic storms. Formed by a table of granite three miles long, half a mile wide, the Island which stands some 400 feet above sea level has a chequered history. Sited outside territorial waters there is evidence of early visitors, with Hubba the Dane said to have pillaged from there, and a Roman settlement has been excavated. There are tales of smuggling, pirates, and drug-running; life now rather more peaceful, a few humans co-existing with feral ponies and puffins.

Bill taught me in his own boat, a local design known as a dipping lug. She was a single sailed vessel about 18 feet long, no cabin, her square canvas sail attached to a long pole or gaff suspended from a metal ring surrounding the mast. It took time to learn to haul up the gaff ring, sail furled, move aft unfurling the canvas, then pick up the wind. He taught me to shoot tides, read the leading marks sited on the hill behind Appledore village, lining them up correctly in order to cross the estuary safely, no matter the state of tide in order to beach either at the Lifeboat Station or main slipway. From him I learned to tie the sailing knots he considered essential, read the sky to predict the weather, to appreciate and never to underestimate the natural forces created by wind and tide. These last have stood me in good stead when sailing in unknown waters all over the world.

Along with learning to ride and sail, formal education involving the three Rs started at the village school. PE took place each morning before prayers, no matter the weather. Snow, rain or sun Miss Beattie Saxton stood and commanded as we raised and lowered our arms, star jumped, skipped on the spot in the concrete yard that served as gym, sports field, and play-ground.

Sometimes everyone wore coloured bands to divide the class into teams for running and touch games, competition was fierce, and the seniors swung Indian Clubs. We infants longed for the day when we too would become club-wielders. Sometimes an infant was honoured by being allowed to carry a club and put it away in the wooden hut that served as a store.

Daily, at break time there was a third of a pint of milk to be consumed, this from a glass bottle. In winter the cream turned to ice crystals spilling out of the top of the bottle, in summer the milk had often turned sour but we still had to drink it. No health, safety or hygiene rules, no one worried about the bottles being glass, we rinsed them under the yard tap, loaded them into crates, and they reappeared next day after being filled straight from the cooler at the local farm. Everyone drank raw milk, no pasteurisation; my generation who have survived these unhygienic conditions seem to be living to a ripe old age!

I only went to Instow village school for a short time, probably due to grandmother interference and the era of governesses began, these varied in both teaching ability and ferocity. The worst was a Miss Hope Hearson: arithmetic, tables, basic maths no problem but I simply could not spell. For years afterwards, if I had a temperature, I had nightmares about my spelling book, and this horror certainly related back to her.

Dyslexia had not been heard of but all the associated difficulties now identified suggest it must have been my problem, there was no let up in the daily ruler-rapping of knuckles, even being forced to write each misspelled word again and again and again made no difference. Lessons were usually held in the house of the Symonds family to which I could ride on Sheila, a replacement Shetland for the by-now outgrown Jess. Sheila had been bought for £2:10 shillings as we were in funds after Golden Miller had won the Grand National!

Sometimes we had to go to Miss Hearson's house in Westleigh village; there she lived with, and cared for, her widowed mother. Lessons took place in their dining room where we were seated around a vast table covered in a deeply dark green cloth.

Sheila had replaced Jess at a cost of £2 10shillings.
Don, supposedly a gun dog, looks on.

Aged 5, with Sheila on Instow beach. My cousin Ronnie Traill is holding my father's horse.

A useless memory, of no educational value whatsoever, remains vivid: I can still picture hanging on one wall, a huge oil painting depicting a very small ship being squashed between two gigantic icebergs.

The room was dark, the house eerily silent apart from the tap, tap, tapping of old Mrs Hearson's stick. I should think she probably had Alzheimer's as she was very unpredictable, sometimes bringing milk and biscuits, but often charging into the room waving her stick attempting to frighten us in an effort to make every one get up and leave the house.

I became so miserable I was taken away and joined a Miss Cress who was tutor to, and in hindsight probably carer for, a boy my age called John L. Life became much easier as he was even less apt than I; beside being taught the conventional three Rs, we kept nature note books and in these we recorded the weather, drew, painted and logged by date the flowers, animals and bugs we found on our rambles through the countryside, these excursion all in the guise of education.

When it was wet natural history was delightfully replaced by stories read aloud, Pilgrims Progress, Gulliver's Travels, Piers Ploughman's History. I also recollect books describing the life of twins, a boy and a girl living abroad, the series titled *The Twins in.* . . followed by the name of their country, Austria, Russia, India, China. These books described and illustrated the way the varied children lived, the clothes they wore, their food, explained their religious beliefs and described festivals, inaugurating an early appreciation and basic understanding of the differing cultures present throughout the world.

Later, when in Malaya, I remembered the significance to the Chinese Twins, of Chinese New Year. We employed Chinese servants and the knowledge I had gained all those years previously was invaluable, ensuring there were appropriate gifts correctly wrapped, time off was arranged and there was appreciation of their requirements at other important festivals, religious or otherwise, in order that The Ancestors were not neglected.

A French girl was produced to aid Miss Cress and French was added to the curriculum. I can still visualise the French book, the cover was green and the story described the lives of a humanised mouse family, *Monsieur et Madame Souris qui reste dans un petit maison, avec leur deux enfants Yovonne et Yevette*. They had many adventures including the near demise of Yovonne when on a fishing expedition. Not much use really, somewhat reminiscent of books designed at the time of the Grand Tour when one of the phrases, translated into the language of all the countries to be visited, was, *'the postillion has been struck by lightning'*, however not all was lost as the mice did, much later, have an amazing influence on my life and career.

One not quite so useful result was my accent: after much verbal repetition mine became irreproachable and I am still left with the problem that if I need to speak in French it is assumed I must be fluent.

Looking back it was a formative period, for it was Miss Cress who began to train my eye, teaching appreciation of shape in three dimensions, creating an improved sense of touch by making us first feel objects then, with eyes shut describe the sensation, were they were soft, hard, rough? Her relentless requirement for acute observation has been invaluable. I have often wondered if her unusual approach, in the guise of education, might possibly have utilised brain paths latent as a result of dyslexia?

When working with patients animal or human I look at body shape imagining I am going to draw or sculpt what I see, then associate the shape to the development of the underling muscles, have these developed correctly, incorrectly? Muscle development tells you a lot about movement, likewise incorrect movement directs you to muscles.

After two years this happy time ended abruptly, for one day when being collected by grandmother South she unfortunately arrived early and discovered John and I playing in water. It had been a wonderfully hot day and there was a large pond at the bottom of the orchard belonging to John's family. It was nothing new that we should be exploring pond life, what shocked grandmother South was the fact we were both naked.

The explanation given by Miss Cress was that only thus - by mimicking them in their natural habitat - could we experience the lifestyle of a tadpole, frog, newt or fish and that she was teaching us how wrong it was to try to change a way of life by, in the case of a tadpole for example, confining it in a glass jar. The reasoning was summarily dismissed.

Perhaps Miss Cress was 'before her time' appreciating that the changes, about to be thrust upon an unwilling world, would create only misery and chaos: Hitler had just begun to round up the Jews.

The War
I vividly remember the day war was declared, it was a glorious day, bright sunshine bathing the amazing, panoramic view, across the Taw and Torridge estuary to Appledore then onward toward Hartland Point etched stark against a blue, blue sky.

Normally everyone would have been outside, a picnic or sailing trip planned, but we were all indoors: a strange group gathered in the sitting room, father, mother, visiting aunt, grandmother South, the cook, gardener, and the house-maid all waiting for the 'news'. At 11 o'clock Mr Chamberlain announced 'England was at war'.

The elderly wireless with its fretwork face and rechargeable wet battery crackled slightly throughout his speech, distorting his sombre tones. Suddenly the Church bells from Appledore sounded across the full tide, the volume of their chimes as they rang the death toll completely overshadowed his voice.

I have no idea why I burst into tears. Grownup solemnity at a level never before experienced? Perhaps a subconscious, fearful realisation that life was about to change forever.

Immediately following the declaration of war telephone calls heralded the impending arrival of the first family of cousins, the Hughes Reckitts. They were being removed from the danger zones of the south coast and London and due to arrive parentless, their father and mother had already volunteered and were involved in patriotic War Work: he in the War Office, she a Colonel in the ATS.

The vanguard consisted of Nanny Strickland who enforced the strict part of her name throughout the entire war; she was accompanied by her 'last' baby, 3 year old Patrick, the nursery maid, the necessary luggage to enable her to arrange a suitable nursery, also that required for Elizabeth and John the two older children who would be the next to arrive after being uprooted from their respective boarding schools. To house them my mother had rented rooms in a small private hotel.

Nanny emerged from the train stiffly starched and disapproving followed by the nursemaid who, on handing over Patrick, began to wrestle with the mountain of luggage. I remember I was wearing a blue short sleeved aertex shirt, grey flannel shorts and sandals: not up to Nanny's standards. 'Undisciplined child, no chauffeur, what have I come to,' she sniffed, her nose raised as she regally entered the car. The private hotel did not suit, and she rapidly found and rented Instow House, then took over, not only running her children but sweeping me up as well.

On every visit involving a meal I had to take my share of rations; when butter was rationed to one ounce per person per week she would draw lines on the pat that appeared for nursery tea, itself looking slightly lost on a dish capable of holding a pound lump, the lines divided it into six squares, one square for herself, one each for Liza, John and I, a full width at one end for Pat, he always got double ration! None of us ever dared complain and as Pat began to realise our resentment he played on this, 'Darling Nanny my toast is simply oozing butter, do look'.

She had not been in charge for very long before a Great Uncle and Aunt accompanied by sit-up-and-beg bicycles turned up. This amazing couple, both in their seventies became proxy parents to nine children whose ages ranged from 2 to 16 years: myself, three Hughes Reckitts and five Cornells.

Nanny and the Greats relied on a Victorian code of conduct embracing punctuality, politeness and cleanliness. Good manners were required at all times: 'Manners Maketh Man', along with other timeless adages were commonplace. While many of their rules would be considered harsh by today's standards they were actually a source of comfort and reassurance in a world suddenly turned topsy turvey.

My father began to organise the village First Aid Brigade and in order to prepare the volunteers for the sights they might encounter if Hitler invaded, visited the local slaughterhouse.

We children were persuaded to act as casualties; this necessitated lying realistically collapsed in various locations, some on the beach, in local gardens, even on the floor of the village hall appropriately labelled 'Casualty Clearing Station'.

In one location we were strewn with offal to replicate wounds sustained in battle and to prepare those unharmed to deal with the expected casualties. It was a total failure as nearly all the well-bred ladies who had signed up as VAD's fainted; the only person not affected was the local midwife, who soon had strong cups of tea on offer and restored some semblance of normality.

Following Dunkirk, when the bombing of London started, evacuees covered in lice were, like unwanted parcels, delivered to every household in the village - all they possessed were the clothes they stood up in.

Grandmother South arrived with her parrot and the current Don. Having lived through both the Boer War and World War One, she brought two cabin trunks packed with rice, lentils, sugar, tinned food, candles and matches. A further 30 pieces of luggage included hats for all occasions and a singer sewing machine.

On arrival, regarding the evacuees - two small girls and a toddler - she got to work. The clothes Grandmother South created from old curtains, however, were caftan like and the evacuees cringed, until they discovered that chain stitched seams could be snipped and pulled with the resultant collapse of the garment.

The Jersey based Aunt arrived in England and I went with my mother to meet her at the port of Brixham: how they had communicated regarding her impending arrival I have no idea.

When it became obvious the Germans would invade Jersey she had her car driven over a cliff, closed the house, packed her jewels, commandeered a fishing boat and set sail in company with as many other fishing boats and their families as she could persuade to leave.

I have never forgotten their arrival, some twenty little half decked boats with red sails appeared on the horizon. You could not see the hulls as they were so low in the water due to being crammed to the gunnels with possessions. Unbelievably, as they tied up, the boats were invaded by security police who first smashed anything that might be used for communication, before arresting everyone in case they were German spies. Imagine, you have sailed across the English Channel avoiding U Boats and German patrol vessels, babies and small children crying, older people wondering if they would ever see loved ones again, only to be arrested on arrival. The Aunt did sort out their plight and the families were eventually resettled around Brixham. She also settled in South Devon sending a bag of fish by train to us each week for as the war progressed shortage of food, first experienced in towns, began to occur even in the country.

The war effort required action by all so Rose Hips, a source of vitamin C were collected, also foxglove seeds as a preparation for digitalis. The gardener although over 70 years old, dug an acre paddock by hand and planted potatoes. Encouraged by the Greats we collected blackberries, set night lines, and kept hens and geese. Milk was plentiful, supplied from local farms all of whom kept 'spare' cows hidden from the War Agricultural Committee in remote barns.

Petrol for Undertakers was not rationed and one enterprising family secreted pig carcasses in coffins, enabling transport of their pork to London where it fetched a fortune on the Black Market.

My education was becoming intermittent, a German Governess was taken on in pity, the situation in which she found herself was not ideal. Having failed to get out of England when the war started, she had, rather like Catholic Priests during the Reformation, been forced more or less into hiding, scuttling from friend to friend until denounced, as a possible spy by, I am ashamed to admit, someone in our village. She was arrested while teaching me by three plain clothes men and was removed screaming from our dining-room, sadly never to be seen again although we later heard she had spent the war interned on the Isle of Man.

I joined the cousins at their prep school near Bideford. A large country house 'Morton' belonging to the Stucley family provided a war time base for the school's pupils following evacuation from Seaford.

I was undoubtedly *saved* by the war, life transformed as I became part of an extended family consisting of cousins rather than remaining an only child; I was effortlessly absorbed into this large group of relations, and my situation changed so much: looking back, I think, 'what luck'.

We all settled to a routine, not difficult, for unlike the adult population we had no expectations based on a pre-war existence; to explore we cycled for miles or rode ponies, we sailed, prawned, fished in the Torridge for salmon, and caught rabbits using ferrets. In the holidays we led a pretty free existence provided we kept to the rules laid down by the Hughes Reckitt and Cornell Nannies. The country had not suited the Greats and they had retreated to sit out the remainder of the war in London.

I rode a lot, hacking to local shows, Pony Club Rallies and gymkhanas on a good pony. Dinky came on loan waiting until another family member from Clovelly Court grew into him. He jumped well and due to his expertise, rather than my riding, I began to get spare rides from owners. If I won I was tipped five shillings, a fortune then to a child.

Life continued uneventfully until suddenly and tragically just before my twelfth birthday my father was killed in an accident while out shooting. The Colonial Widow's pension was pitiful so I moved schools once again - no money for expensive fees. West Bank, a girls' school in Bideford, took me in with costs reduced as after tests at interview: I was considered athletic, certainly *not* academic!

I started doing odd jobs in order to pay for my ponies. This was fruitful as all the eligible young, both male and female had been called up and the local saddler was delighted to let me help at weekends and in the holidays. Mr Pridham the saddler and his wife must have been in their seventies; always immaculately turned out: she in a long dark dress, hair plaited on top of her head, he in dark trousers, a shirt with celluloid collar, bow tie, a long white apron, and walrus moustache. They were gracious toward all their customers, he would take time from stitching to discuss the repair required while she managed the till entering every transaction, copper plate writing, in a large account leger. Working there offered an exposure into a bygone time, one when a craftsman was revered for his work.

I started just as any apprentice would have done by sweeping the floor, filling the hods with coke kept in the backyard coal house to feed the circular iron stove, on which the glue pot sat permanently.

Eventually I was allowed, having pulled the stitching threads through a slab of beeswax to thread needles, then to mark the leather, and eventually to stitch.

There was a great deal of work, not only the routine repairs for farm horses and ridden animals but every rediscovered set of driving harness needed some repair. As petrol virtually disappeared anything with wheels that could be horse drawn resurfaced, many, found hidden in barns were dusted off and hammered together: governess carts, traps, and dog carts trundled onto the roads. It was an amazing experience and a privilege to learn from a third generation master saddler; before I left I could choose a suitable hide, cut the leather and sew a bridle, also re-stuff the under panels of a saddle. The tools Mr Pridham gave me have survived and live in a leather attaché case rescued after my father's death, from amongst his possessions before my mother could either give it away or dump it in the dustman's rubbish cart.

I think she became angry in her grief, everything of his was burned or trashed other than photographs. West African memorabilia and 35mm cine films depicting some of their treks were packed away. I discovered these years later in a trunk in the loft at Venn prior to its sale after her death.

One film titled *Subduing Truculent Tribesman*, shows my father striding out wearing ankle boots, knee high socks, shorts, bush shirt and topi carrying a walking stick, behind him trot around 20 coloured soldiers rifles at the ready seemingly pointing directly at his back. The baggage train consists of my mother followed by at least 20 naked men, all with loads on their heads, these varying from her dog in its basket to chairs: a later clip shows the parents sitting in their chairs while the Tribesmen, presumably no longer truculent, perform a dance.

Following my father's death all was not well at home, my mother forced to take in lodgers, the house felt invaded and I begged to go to boarding school. The most successful part of my chequered education was apparently considered to have been the time when Miss Cress was in charge. She had operated under a system known as P.N.E.U. and the organisation had a residential school at Overstone, in Northamptonshire.

Lengthy financial negotiations took place, looking back this must have been very distressful for my recently widowed mother, but eventually I was offered a subsidised place.

Needless to say I arrived in the midst of a year by which time every one had already settled in, ganged up, or were committed to miserable survival having been considered by the pupil hierarchy to be useless. This decision was taken after the new arrivals failed one or more initiation tests set by the sixth form, failure committing the unfortunates to exist in a state of persecution or (perhaps worse) totally ignored. Persecution took the form of horrible tasks: they were 'volunteered' to shovel snow from the inner courtyards in winter, collect the tadpoles from the swimming pool, forced to join the end of the food hand-out queues, to be the last allowed to buy their ration from the sweet cupboard, and to stand furthest from the warmth of the common room fire. School existence can be pretty cruel.

The school was housed in a building that had been a Stately Home set in its own 200 acres of park planted with fabulous, aged, trees; there were three lakes, a private cricket pitch, a chapel and, lurking from the past in his pantry, an aged Butler; a great betting man he kept those of us interested in touch with the racing world outside.

It rapidly became obvious that unless I *survived* the initiation tests I was destined to go it alone. And *survived* was the operative word: why no one was killed I have no idea.

Passing the tests gave you some status also allowed a place only one row back from the huge log fires, the only form of heating, around which we huddled in the winter, Northamptonshire is not the warmest of counties.

Test one: to be able to squeeze under the door leading from the dormitory passage to the washroom block. Lucky for me being very skinny this was no problem but a number of larger girls were destined for an unhappy life.

As in so many houses of that vintage, the Regency period of Architecture, the roof sported a parapet about two feet wide. Test two: climb out of a third story window after lights out and circle the building by walking along the parapet.

Test three: climb, during lunch and remain unseen by duty staff, to the top of a gigantic beech planted too near the windows of the staff common room for comfort, then wave the flag given when you got to the top.

Test four: circle the Cauldron, to achieve this it was necessary to make your way without getting wet, from the shore of the upper lake to an iron platform forming a walkway round a sluice bore hole through which water cascaded downward for some fifty feet to the middle lake. The sluice was known as Devils Cauldron and its walkway a necessity to enable estate workers to clear any debris which might impede water flow which during heavy rain caused considerable flooding in the park.

Luckily I managed to complete all four experiences unscathed, settled in and probably started to learn in sequence for the first time. Until I arrived at Overstone so much had been fragmented: kings started with William the First 1066 to 1087, William the Second 1087 to 1100. What happened between them and the present George? I knew all the British Colonies but the Americas were a closed book other than part of the family were involved with some thing called The River Plate. Where, exactly, was the Far East?

I'd really had a very odd education and Overstone, other than continuity, soon proved to be no exception. In the dining room no English was spoken. If you wished to eat you had to speak in the language of the table to which you were assigned, and conversation was obligatory. Three sentences required at each meal; due to the Family Souris I ate quite well but only at a French table.

We were taken to Stratford to watch Shakespearean productions, visited various castles, abbeys and churches for lectures on architecture and social history. Groups came to play and sing and I actually saw a wine glass shattered due to the reverberation from a single high note.

In the gloom of a vaulted room, lit only by a huge log fire, actors seated out of sight narrated Norse sagas. I can still remember the fear and the feel of the hairs on the back of one's neck standing up when the raconteur spoke in measured, somnolent tones of the deeds of Were Wolves, creatures who could only be killed following dastardly deeds if shot with a silver bullet. The tales from ancient Greece and Rome seemed considerably less frightening, it seemed unlikely that a Minotaur would be met skulking in a corridor having escaped from a Greek island but there were wolves around in the forests of Europe.

We acted plays and sang - or attempted to sing - the works of great composers, I distinctly remember being told I could stand with the chorus during the Messiah but only if I promised only to *move* my lips I was not *make* a sound!

I made friends with a girl who lived locally and on exit week ends, as it was too far to travel home to Devon, often stayed with her; the family hunted with the Pychley and I had some amazing days when the fabled Barker was their huntsman.

Eventually time for the final exams arrived, I had decided to train as a Physiotherapist and had been accepted following interview, by St Thomas' Hospital Physiotherapy School but needed to matriculate rather than achieve just a plain School Certificate.

I did not feel things had gone particularly well until the day of my French oral. Ushered into the library I made my way to a table where a rather bored looking little man was seated. 'Asseyez-vous s'il vous plait Mademoiselle'.

'Certainmont Monsieur, et Mercie'. On hearing the pronunciation he looked up and shot in rapid French 'what can you see from the window'. In my very best French I replied, 'un lac Monsieur'. Hurrah for the Souris family, Yvonne and Yvette had gone fishing in a lake and nearly drowned, I knew the lake bit by heart, then with a flash of brilliance I added, 'Are you a fisherman?' Yes, he was. 'Where do you fish, please tell me?' For the next forty minutes, well over the time allocated, and with him set to continue until eventually interrupted by the next victim knocking loudly on the door, all I had to do was to make appreciative French noises at appropriate places as he recounted his exploits with rod and line. The startlingly high marks gained ensured my place at St Thomas'. I wonder if any one else owes their slot at a prestigious teaching hospital to a family of French mice!

Post War
The war finally ended, I just about to be seventeen and would be able to leave school at the end of the summer. I had time to fill for I could not start training at St Thomas' for three years as at the time they only admitted students aged twenty or over considering those younger insufficiently mature emotionally to embark on a career during which they would meet untreatable disease, appalling deformity, congenital disability, and death.

How to fill in three years usefully? My mother, whom at the outbreak of World War Two could scarcely boil an egg decided I was to be 'finished'. The Edinburgh aunts came up trumps and funded a year at Miss Randall's School for Domestic Economy in Eastbourne. Miss Randall had been at the Scottish equivalent, Atholl Crescent, and while there had met and become a friend of my father's eldest sister. Her school was modelled on the Edinburgh establishment therefore entirely suitable in my Aunt's eyes.

It was a useful transition time, more freedom than school but not total. As we only ate what we cooked we learned to cook well pretty rapidly, we drew chickens, gutted fish, learnt about cuts of meat. We cleaned baths, polished silver, washed and polished glass, ironed with flat irons, goffered frills, were taught to sew by a nun, a pair of embroidered French knickers and a bra both made from parachute silk the result of our toils!

In our final months on some occasions acting as staff, on others as invited guests, we attended especially arranged parties hosted by Rannie, these included lunches, teas, cocktail and dinner parties. It was considered these events served to polish social skills, also cemented the rules of an acceptable code of conduct expected by polite society at such events, we were expected to observe and report behavioural mistakes made by staff and/or guests at a debriefing, all this part of education considered necessary for the time when we ourselves would marry and employ servants. During the course there were also lectures on interviewing and employing staff, the ability to engage a Butler possibly useful to some? A Wet Nurse seemed inappropriate but I suppose you never know!

A fellow student had brought two horses with her, we rode on the Downs and whenever we could, hunted on Saturdays during the winter. There was good tennis at Devonshire Park, the professionals always ready to help improve one's game and we watched International players hoping against hope our group might be noticed by the ravishing Swedes. Good golf courses abounded, thus at the end of a year we were well finished in nearly every respect other than interaction with the opposite sex!

On departure, as the year ended conveniently before Ascot, the change experienced by some students must have seemed Pygmalion-like. They swapped downstairs for upstairs and moved from cleaning baths and loos, and scraping burnt pans to London to be presented; to do *The Season*, continuing onward in the Autumn to Scotland where, absorbed into the Country House set, they moved from house party to house party prior to joining the inevitable marriage queue.

Sponsored by a cousin with a daughter my age and after one or two obligatory dances and curtseying to The Queen, I returned to Devon to race boats: if not skippering then sailing as crew to my guardian. Throughout that summer I also show-jumped for owners who required a jockey, then, in the autumn was invited to go and live with Bill and Desire Ingall on their Exmoor Farm at Withygate for six months to help out while De had a baby.

Bill had become a well known Point to Point rider after leaving the army in which he'd been a career soldier rising to the rank of Major. He was now trying to make a living as a farmer and felt it would be stupid to injure himself schooling youngsters so it fell to me to ride and attempt to school his young point to pointers; an interesting if somewhat painful learning curve and I probably over-ran the number of requisite falls, buying considerably more than the 'seven bits of ground' said to be the number expected before it was considered you could ride the Moor.

When my six months ended I was loath to leave the Moor and with time to fill went to work in Exford for a nag's man - one Frank Mullins - who ran the livery yard. No pay: bed and board only. He was the most amazing stockman, revered by every one who knew him locally as well as those who came to ride or to hunt on Exmoor.

The amount I learned when with him is without price, a stickler for the health and comfort of the horses in his charge no stone was left unturned. I learned to appreciate the sound really good oats should make as you slip them through your fingers, the scent or 'nose' associated with good hay, how to make a straw bed, plait a line to stop the under door draft, and groom. Each horse was inspected by Frank wearing white gloves, any mark and you started again!

He could spot a troubled horse a mile off and would delve into the tack room medicine cupboard, this filled with tins, jars and leaking packages. None labelled but he knew just what was needed, I do not ever remember a vet in the yard.

Watching him feed was an education in itself, each horse an individual, all had a linseed mash once a week, a pinch of salt-petre in their water on Sunday evenings to flush the kidneys. I remember the water buckets: we scrubbed them daily, they were wooden, made of oak, and when full weighed a ton.

After I left I continued to go up to Exford to hunt whenever I could and begged him many times, down the years, to write up his remedies for posterity but he died suddenly, too early, taking his secrets with him.

The girls, there were two of us, started as did the men at 5:30 am, Frank had been in the yard since 5:00 am, six horses were ready for exercise when we arrived, ride one lead two, returning after a six or eight mile round, the next three were waiting, the men did the boxes while we rode exercise. Two lots before breakfast, one after, the horses going hunting were done over before breakfast ready to be tacked up then ridden to the meet, no boxes for travel. On arrival at the meet the owners or visitors would be waiting, you rode to the meet on the horse that would be used as second horse, leading the two first horses.

When you rode home, no matter the time, Frank would be standing on the village bridge listening as the horses came down the road. He could tell if they were even minutely lame or uncomfortable by the sound of their hooves. Back in their boxes they were wisped dry if sweating or rain soaked, groomed if they were dry, nothing was ever washed off.

All the tack and the hunting boots belonging to owners with horses at livery were cleaned every afternoon, the bits were all steel so it took a lot of work to keep them clean, and the hay for chaff was cut by hand. Frank clipped using an archaic device which required a second person to turn a handle on the body of the machine to provide the power for the cutting blades!

I was quite light in those days, an advantage for a second horseman and often had the privilege of riding for a member of the Lloyd family whose association with the Devon and Somerset Staghounds is legendary.

We rarely had a day off, the exception being the day that the yard pig was killed. Frank went about his morning work with silent tears streaming down his face. Horses done the staff were sent to Minehead on the morning bus, and when we returned in the late afternoon there was a new pig in the sty and Mrs Mullins had cooked a chittling tea for everyone.

While working in Exford I rode some of Bill Ingall's green horses rather badly in several point to points but everything is a useful experience. Always looking for a greater challenge Bill bought a farm near Badminton and moved to hunt in the Beaufort country.

It sounds ridiculous today but there was considerable appre-hension, particularly from the Duke regarding the riding abil-ity of those who had entered to compete at the very first Badminton Horse Trials! He did not want accidents, no worries about dressage, who could possible fall off riding circles on a flat surface, and what on earth was a diagonal anyway? As for the show jumping that was something even army officers man-aged. It was the cross country which might cause problems. To overcome this concern, I expect to the horror of the organisers, it was decided that a group of guinea pigs, riding hunters, should 'try out' the course. Bill was invited and telephoned me as he thought it might be fun so off I went. I must confess there were one or two fences, the original coffin for one, that we bypassed, 'never meet them out hunting' it was explained when we confessed, but I can claim that I once rode round Badminton, nearly completing!

Physio School

Suddenly it was time to go to London, the beginning of a very different life. The rules and regulations of the Physiotherapy School were not too much of a shock; it was rather as though the Nanny Strickland era had resurfaced. Punctuality, cleanliness, manners, respect: the latter required that we curtsied to Matron as she passed in the corridor or if she came into a ward where we were working. Why not? Nothing demeaning, rather a mark of respect to bob as she passed; she had risen through the ranks to become titular head of a large, very important teaching hospital.

Medicine, as does each profession, uses a variety of titles within the group: surgeons who cut and sew together prefix their name with Mister; physicians who treat by means other than surgery retain the prefix Doctor.

Orthopaedics is a branch within the vast array of medical specialities and is targeted at treating problems associated with bones, joints ligaments and muscles. Originally treatment tended to rely on surgical intervention only but just before I arrived at St Thomas's a medical extension evolved and Orthopaedic Medicine was born. The founder, James Cyriax orthopaedic physician as opposed to surgeon, subsequently became known throughout the medical world as the Father of Orthopaedic Medicine. He proved many orthopaedic problems could be resolved without the need for surgical intervention. Patients suffering from chronic low back pain were his speciality.

Quite early, during the first year of each new physiotherapy intake, Dr Cyriax hired a hall, provided food, alcohol and a band; a fleet of buses transported the guests, these consisting of a mixed bunch of Medical Students and the new Physiotherapy intake, to the venue. The alcohol was of dubious variety; I have never drunk gin and orange since. The party was given because James had proved Physiotherapy to be of singular importance in the treatment of a variety of orthopaedic cases. It was his earnest wish to ensure that as

James Cyriax, father of Orthopaedic Medicine, with his wife Patsy

many as possible of those he trained, both Medical Students and Physiotherapists, would marry, this would ensure his work was continued nationwide and his 'get togethers' were held with the hope that at least one of the invitees would 'find and marry a permanent partner.' I obliged: more of that later.

For the first eighteen months of the Physiotherapy course we more or less shadowed the medical students, first there was a thorough grounding in anatomy, this included dissecting cadavers, and we were taught histology and physiology, followed by the study of diseases, then general medical and surgical conditions; even observing operations.

When it came to treatment the medical students learned surgical procedures and the use of drugs, chemical medicine while the Physiotherapists were taught machine therapy, massage, and exercises in order to retrain the body to work correctly, this last known as rehabilitation.

Early Physiotherapy training included a compulsory six weeks on the wards. There, enrolled as trainee nurses, we worked under the qualified nursing staff for it was considered essential that we learnt hospital and ward routine prior to eventually starting - under the supervision of a qualified Physiotherapist - hands on work with patients.

My time on the wards was a disaster, assigned to Clayton I could do nothing right. Sister Clayton was a true Nightingale, her ward ran like clockwork. My first crime, having been instructed to change the water in every receptacle holding false teeth, was to get all the teeth mixed up. Then I dropped a tray of instruments just as the senior surgeon began his round reducing any of the patients well enough to helpless laughter. Following this incident I was banished to the sluice and consigned to scrubbing bedpans.

Mercifully my tour of duty was curtailed after arriving one morning scarcely able to put one foot in front of the other, covered in a rash. I was dispatched to casualty and after being diagnosed with measles, I was sent by ambulance to the Fever Hospital in Tooting Beck.

My stay was somewhat enlivened by the fact I was a 'good case' and the entire group of Medical Students studying infectious diseases arrived to view my pink, swollen, torso. amongst them - one whose company I had enjoyed at the Cyriax party - sent a box of Fortnum and Mason chocolates. This was the beginning of a long term, intermittent romance that culminated in my marriage to David Slattery (DS) which took place at the end of our respective final years.

I not only needed, but had agreed to do, casual work to earn some money while at St Thomas' in order to help pay my fees and living expenses as my mother was existing on £500 a year. Mistakenly, on arrival in London, I embarked on an extensive social life rather than settling to the constraints of student living. Cousin John, virtually a brother during the war, was doing National Service with the 10th Hussars and had a London flat. There I cooked and played hostess at evening and weekend do's, drawing on the experience I'd gained during my finishing at Miss Randall's.

The theatre and concerts - the evening always ending at some night club in those days mostly at the '400' - were irresistible during the winter. Ascot, Henley, Wimbledon followed to which I was invited by various young men, and took up rather too much time leaving none for intensive study particularly as even when free of social engagements I either washed up in pubs of an evening or worked as a shop girl if the weekend days were empty.

The Regiment was sent to Germany and stupidly I followed, spending my summer break out there, rather than going home and revising; at the same time I forfeited the show-jumping rides I'd been promised. Along with riding out for Frank Mullins to help get the D & S hunters fit in the summer these would have helped earn much needed money.

Staying with John's sister Liza - by then married to a Captain in the 10th - the summer passed in a delightful social whirl of polo, racing, picnics, and dances: not surprisingly on my return, but to my horror, I failed the first set of compulsory exams. This normally resulted in expulsion.

I sailed through anatomy, but got zero for electricity. Watts, ohms, and volts had never featured high in my education, and why I needed to understand the inner workings of the machine I was manipulating I had no idea particularly as tissue resistance, internal current flow, let alone natural electrical conduction within the body, was in its infancy. I'd learned nothing about electricity at school although my mother had found, the summer before I went up to London, a tutor in the shape of an elderly man wearing a celluloid collar and clip-on bow tie who, arriving by bus, sat down at the dining room table breathing heavily, before sending clouds of tobacco-scented breath over me as he pushed incomprehensible equations under my nose. Unfortunately he appeared to have no real insight into the subject of electricity other than being able to recite, without an explanation of the subtleties, Ohms Law. My knowledge remained zero. Electrical know-how was considered essential, however, and one of the reasons given was that it would enable you to choose the appropriate device when treating a patient, also that if using electrically motivated apparatus you understood the limitations of application, this to ensure not only patient safety, but also your own.

The linkage between externally applied electricity and the body had been glossed over in lectures as I suspect our teachers, all in their late forties or fifties, were even more uninformed than I was, so other than touching on Mr Faraday and his jumping frog's leg we learned nothing. Faraday's research was the principle employed when using a faradic devise to treat injured or weak muscle; provided the electrodes were correctly placed the delivery of an electrical stimulus caused the chosen muscle to contract suddenly and sharply, a very painful procedure for the patient.

St Thomas' also utilised the inventions of one Dr Bauens, who had devised a therapy known as Short Wave; like James Cyriax he was also a member of the Physiotherapy teaching staff, unfortunately the content of his lectures were so far above our heads as to be incomprehensible.

The Physiotherapy Department apparatus also included radiant heat lamps, heat cradles, ultra violet light and concentrated sun light, this last delivered by a devise known as a Chromayer, application burnt the skin! The theory leading to usage of this mediaeval torture device suggested that the creation of sudden acute new pain, in an area where a patient was suffering continual nagging discomfort, would break down established chronic pain patterns! It seemed rather similar to suggesting people with arthritis should be forced to suffer multiple bee stings. I am glad to say both these therapies seem to have been discontinued.

I did not dare tell my mother of my disastrous failure, so much depended on my gaining the Physiotherapy qualification, to me one of the most important being I would no longer be a constant in-road upon her slender means, she might even be able to afford a car when I became able to support myself and retire her only means of transport, a bicycle.

In today's world it may seem incomprehensible to accept that when I trained fees had to be paid up front, students did not get state support, nor could they borrow from the bank, there were no credit cards, the 'nanny' welfare state had not been conceived let alone born.

I was given another chance after a terrifying, lengthy interview, with the principal of the School of Physiotherapy Mrs Vidler, during which she pointed out forcibly the number of people I had let down; these included herself and the Board of St Thomas's Hospital as due to personal circumstances I had, at her request following interview and subsequent selection, been awarded a place with reduced fees, by the Board.

Mrs Vidler followed my career becoming a friend in later life. I visited her just before she died when she told me she had no idea why she had allowed me to stay, but that in hindsight she was very glad she had. So am I.

Marriage

With smart, out of hospital social life curtailed, I began to see more of DS at hospital events and spent some weekends with his family. My mother was horrified when she met him and discovered the family were Catholic, this revelation made worse by her daily lady, a garrulous old dear who pronounced, 'them as is got at by the Popish lot 'as a bun in the oven every year, you mark my words'. When our engagement was announced with the date for the wedding fixed for May worse was to come, 'marry in May, er'll rue the day!'

Pre-wedding our respective mothers both went into meltdown. Mine had always visualised a normal country wedding in our village church, reception in the garden. His, a full Nuptial Mass, reception House of Lords, or if booked probably the Ritz. Both were faced with a mixed marriage at St James, Spanish Place, no flowers, no music, no hymns, and the reception organised by Searcey's, a fashionable London catering firm, whose function rooms were off Park Lane.

The day was saved and organised by my father- in -law to be; having, in World War Two, taken most of the convoys, including the very last, into Malta, during the worst of the U boat attacks, nothing fazed him. A Jesuit Priest, a family connection, was persuaded to take the service; the Catholic Church, still frowning on mixed marriages required that I agree any children of our union would be raised as Catholics. I signed the papers causing my mother to say she would not attend my wedding.

Without her help, amidst the stress of final exams, I chose material at Liberties and three bridesmaids, in that order. The family veil went to the Royal School of Needlework for repair by a great friend, Erica Wilson; due to its frailty and slight yellowing, attributed to age rather than smoke from the blitz, an ivory rather than white material seemed sensible for my dress. Erica was some seamstress and took over: as her wedding present everything was made at the Royal School of Needlework. Later after marrying Vladimir Kagan, now an acclaimed International furniture designer, Erica was responsible for re-introducing needlepoint to the USA.

As the date for the wedding drew near my mother relented and agreed to attend the nuptials; on the day, other than that my father-in-law's chauffeur got lost on the way to the church, and I was unintentionally, rather than fashionably late, we and our respective mothers survived the day.

After a honeymoon in Ireland when, on our first night my new husband fell asleep in the bath as I lay and waited, we only met occasionally as DS was given a resident surgical job at St Thomas's. I remained solo in my flat and got a job at the Fulham General Hospital.

Luck struck once again and I have so much for which to thank Miss McRay, the senior Physiotherapist. The hospital was part general hospital, part old people's home, part workhouse, many of the inmates were recovering from strokes. I was so proud when Miss McRay enquired how much movement I had managed to regain in the hand of a patient I was treating and I was able to demonstrate he could make his first finger and thumb touch. I had anticipated praise but she looked at me pityingly and said 'and can he do up the fly buttons of his trousers?'

That *one comment* turned me from a text book therapist into a practical one; what does the patient need to be able to do? Explain in terms meaningful to their life style: if they have a shoulder problem and golf is their passion they will exercise their shoulder chipping a golf ball while very unlikely to perform a set of prescribed exercises. Following a broken wrist you hope, if the patient is male, he is a gardener, there is nothing like making a fine tilth in the potting shed to mobilise a stiff

Leaving Spanish Place, and stepping into a new life, with my husband, David Slattery.

hand and wrist, if it is a woman ask for a cake or a pie! Familiar tasks are the best re-education on offer because the brain pattern is already there, indelibly imprinted, it usually just needs waking up.

Needless to say my mother's helper was correct in her 'bun' prediction, morning misery confirmed as pregnancy. DS was just about to finish his house job but there was time, before the army beckoned, as he had deferred obligatory National Service to study medicine, for a skiing holiday, off we went with me clutching ant-sick pills. I have often wondered if athletic activities indulged in during pregnancy are imprinted in the foetus. No 1 son Nicholas skied for the Navy, did my struggles with the slopes leave an imprint? I rode until a few days before Penelope was born possibly saddling her with an affinity for horses.

On our return from Switzerland DS joined the Army Medical Corps: his first posting to a base near Greyshott in Surrey was filled with female members of the armed forces which caused me to give up the London flat and despite being heavily pregnant move rapidly down to join him; reports suggesting the duties of the resident MO were social rather than medical!

Nicholas arrived, I hired a nanny and found a job locally, then out of the blue a chance meeting at a cocktail party with an RAMC Colonel, ex St Thomas's Hospital, shaped the next few years of our lives.

2

A Malayan Interlude

An extended visit to the Malaya States followed a request from the Cocktail Colonel: this did not faze me, as members of both my mother's and father's families had supported the British Empire when posted abroad for various reasons, and all had enjoyed their colonial adventures. That I was about to embark on one seemed too good to be true.

There was a brief moment of worry, however, when the buff movement order form arrived. In the 1950s the area was still a war zone: was the posting wife free or not? Luckily the form was stamped, 'accompanied' and I could 'follow' with our, by now 6 month old, son Nicholas.

All army personnel were still shipped by sea half a century ago, so not only a blissful life on arrival to look forward to - a bridesmaid, married to a colonial official living in Penang, had mailed ecstatic reports of life in Malaya - but also a 6 week meander on a cruise ship; first braving the bay of Biscay then on through the Mediterranean, Suez Canal, Red Sea, and Indian Ocean: all at her Majesty's expense.

Our departure was somewhat fraught: my mother-in-law had moved round the world in considerable comfort, always on board luxury liners when flowers were considered essential for departing passengers. I was certainly to board a liner, but she, the *Empire Orwell*, was very much ex-luxury, having been converted to a troop ship. Mother-in-law was driven, unauthorised, onto the dock, arriving with enough flowers to stock the London florist, Constance Spry. The chauffeur dumped these at the foot of a very steep, very narrow gangplank.

We were late and I had wanted to reduce 'good-bye time' to a minimum. I was still on the dockside with a pram and my own things, already struggling with Nicholas, and also his suitcases. Rather than *a case*, as stipulated in our embarkation orders, Nanny, furious at 'her baby being removed' had packed for every eventuality. Ominous ship's noises and activity on the dockside suggested it was time to hurry. Chauffeur Terry grabbed Nicholas and the largest suitcase, I followed dragging the pram, filled with the remaining luggage. As we reached the deck, the cases were unceremoniously thrown out of the pram onto the deck, the pram was turned round and the corporal in charge of boarding sent it shooting downward followed rapidly by Terry, who leapt off the gangplank landing sprawled in the floral display. I remember waving vaguely, before setting off to find my allocated cabin as the ship began to move. Eventually, thankful to discover the correct number on a door somewhere deep in the ship's bowels, I pushed it open to be regarded by three pairs of hostile eyes, a sort of net cage hung from the side of the only unoccupied bunk of four.

The cruise was an experience in itself and I shall never forget the sight of the mushroom-shaped swirl of dirty brown, staining the blue of the Mediterranean, as the Nile waters slid slowly outward.

While the ship was tied up in the port of Suez to be refuelled and disgustingly dirty blocks of ice destined to cool our drinks were craned on board, there was time to visit the sphinx and pyramids.

Tourism had not really hit Egypt and I shall always be thankful to have visited the pyramids before Cairo spread westward for today the sprawling suburbs reach nearly to their base. I saw them standing remote, etched against a setting sun, regal and solitary, in all their glory.

As we left the Canal the ongoing Suez crisis erupted and because of this, for no good reason, the ship was held in Aden. A cousin in the Diplomatic Service materialised, added me quite illegally to his Camel mounted scouting party and I spent an unforgettable three days in the Empty Quarter.

In Colombo I smelt my first Frangipani, beginning a love affair that has never waned. Then the Indian Ocean, sleeping on deck under a canopy of new stars, followed by Singapore and reality, for, as I rapidly discovered on arrival, the army had made one of its classic mistakes: the post was *not* accompanied, the Ghurkha Brigade preferring wifeless officers. This meant there were no quarters available. After two nights in a transit barracks in Singapore we set off by train for KL. On arrival DS was unable to help, departing on an extended jungle mission leaving Nicholas and I 'with friends'. The 'friends' were child-less and Nicholas was crotchety to say the least. Life is often what you make it and DS did find a bungalow in Kuala Lumpur but had forgotten I might need transport.

I decided it was time for action.

Dumping my offspring with another wife, one with maternal instincts which I had not yet developed, I sallied forth. By lunch I had bought a very cheap car: cheap I later discovered because it was an ex-police vehicle, known to terrorists and liable to be shot at.

By teatime I had located the bungalow, Chinese design, therefore cool and with a large garden. Its owners, off to the UK for three months leave the following day, were delighted to meet their new tenant. 'Would I keep on their Chinese couple, he cooked; she cleaned?' 'Of course'. They departed and I moved in. Cookie and Amah had I think, hoped for three months unencumbered by tenants, and they regarded No 1 son with horror. Amah's face said it all: 'me no baby amah mem'. I consulted my Chinese phrase book for the first and last time, 'Find. . . baby. . . amah'. I enunciated slowly.

A slight wail of terror, this Mem might understand their uncomplimentary comments, even work out their mark-up in the shopping account book.

A baby amah, with some English, materialised before break-fast the next day and from then on, until we left Malaya, Ah Yin became my Chinese voice.

A visit to the NAFFI to stock up with stores resulted in my next non-British approach. Nearly everything was tinned, and, lest anyone should the feed the terrorists, all tins were punctured, in the store, immediately following purchase.

The most useful items appeared to be powdered milk and loo paper. I also discovered each family was allowed half a hundredweight of rice a month. The rice was greeted with rapture by Cookie and Amah, this Mem might be OK, but their faces fell when I explained in future I would shop in the local market with Cookie, and as the garden area was very large, we would have hens and grow vegetables. Translation suggested Cookie would *not* garden, so a gardener would be required. The staff seemed to be growing, and soon I realised I would need a job to pay the wages.

A kebun (gardener) was procured, and was happy to come, explaining that the spirit of his grandmother lived in the huge, centrally placed, shade tree. The spirit turned out to be a rather large green snake, of a harmless variety luckily, but fond of young chickens: more of her later.

He became an excellent gardener other than, under strict instructions to water everything daily, he did this sheltering under an umbrella at the height of the monsoon. Neither would he kill any type of pest, and nothing is more irritating than watching a caterpillar with a voracious appetite devour a prized plant while the man you are paying, watches. Scooping up these giant caterpillars I would drive them for several miles then dump them hoping someone else's plants would prove attractive!

On my first market visit, to which I cycled with Cookie, my journey was observed by a group of army wives intent on trying to pretend they were of a superior race by shopping at the NAFFI (entry forbidden to the locals). As we passed I waved: much to their horror.

Supper, including fish and various vegetables, along with two rattan baskets - three scrawny chickens in each - were purchased. As we were about to leave, bird song, cascading from a screened area nearby drew me: cages and cages of song birds. They seemed happy, but crouched, slumped, in a filthy bamboo container was a squirrel, its tail obviously broken. 'Buy him,' I ordered Cookie. Despite remonstration, arm waving and sulks, eventually I won. 'I no eat him,' mouthed Cookie.

'No one is going to eat him' I retorted.

Seen cycling home with a squirrel in a basket was certainly not going to improve my social credibility amongst the wives of the service personnel, and head down I peddled furiously past the NAFFI.

By the time I reached the outskirts of the local hospital I had begun to look around, and in doing so hit a pothole. Unable to balance, bike, squirrel cage and I fell into a heap. Cookie was well ahead by this time, desperate to reach home first and spread the news of my latest madness.

Struggling to my feet I looked up and saw the brightest of blue eyes regarding me through a bearded face. 'You might need help,' said a cheerful voice through the beard. I'd fallen at the feet of Dr. David Molseworth, who, I was to discover later had survived imprisonment in Changi throughout the Japanese occupation. He'd remained when the Japanese left to return to his pre war job as medical director of the Sungai Buluh Leper settlement: the 3,000 inmates making it the largest in the Far East.

'What do you intend to do with your squirrel?' he asked. 'Mend it' I said crossly. 'I am a physiotherapist'.

'Get in touch,' he said handing me a card. 'I need a physiotherapist.'

By the time I reached home the skinny chickens were scratching happily in an enclosure. No sign of any helpers, the Chinese move so quietly you never hear them, but I was pretty certain they had scuttled into their quarters on my return, to avoid the squirrel. How to house him? How to clean him up? How to mend his tail?

It seemed unlikely he would take off, he was in shock and his tail, the main balance mechanism was useless. Choosing the grandly named 'bathroom' - an Ali Baba tub and a saucepan - but totally enclosed, I put him on the floor and rubbed him all over with a wet sponge. Although soggy, beautiful colours became apparent: black back, tufted ears, white side stripe, and chestnut front. I splinted the tail, using matchsticks and sticky tape. This obviously hurt, for still just strong enough, he bit me. This was a good sign, meaning he still had the will to live. Food? Grapes perhaps?

I sloshed out the cage, put a soft towel as a base, and shut him in, grapes and all.

Now he needed an outside cage, the garden was well stocked with trees and bushes, and bamboo came into its own, cut in lengths it was easy to achieve a dome shaped, circular enclosure complete with a small tree.

Ah Yin appeared with a glass of lime - market shopping was paying off. 'Ask Cookie find Kebun, make cage like in zoo'. Luckily Kuala Lumpur had a small zoo built to house a selection of baby animals whose parents had been inadvertently shot by troops when on jungle patrol or eaten by the terrorists. Before night fell the wire enclosure was complete and was, I hoped, squirrel proof.

The following day a much happier squirrel, subsequently christened Jason, moved into his quarters. Taming rapidly, as his tail recovered, he was set free to use house and garden as he wished. Jason was the beginning of a life involving, not just repair of humans, but also of animals.

Avoiding the Cabbage Patch.
Shortly after the rescue of Jason a formal army posting arrived, a three year, accompanied, spell of duty. Unfortunately the accompanied bit meant the army had now recognised my existence.

I had no wish to be incarcerated in the army quarters built on sun baked tin tailings, charmingly referred to as 'The Cabbage Patch'. It was cool where we were although frowned upon, being on the outer edge of the acceptable British residential area which ended about a mile from the scattering of old, well shaded buildings which I found were inhabited by some of the richer members of the Chinese community.

I had often changed my route home to wander through this cool, inviting area. One particular house, apparently empty, had become a favourite. I would stop, even getting out of the car to inhale and enjoy the faint scent from the cluster of frangipani trees leaning out from the large shady garden enclosed behind a bamboo hedge and bordered, at the road edge, by a monsoon drain.

The tenure of the leave bungalow was nearing its end, and I mentioned to Ah Yin in passing, my fears of having to move to the British Base. She looked slightly surprised, 'But Mem. . . all is arranged.'

'What is arranged?' It transpired my favourite house was empty. It belonged to a member of her clan, the Yin Family, and her father had arranged for us to live there. What needed to be done I enquired. 'Nothing', I was told.

'Staff?' I persisted? Her brother was painting the inside and had already built a Jason enclosure. Her father would be the cook, her mother house amah. A sister would become wash amah, and she would remain baby amah. 'Soon there will be another', she said, looking me straight in the eye. Inwardly praying she was wrong, I ignored her.

It transpired the people for whom 'her family' had worked for 20 years were retiring to the UK, and had sold their house, the new owners of which did not want them for they had their own servants. Ah Yin explained there were very nice quarters at the back of her relative's house, and her immediate family knew of them and liked them.

We went to look: a large shady garden, a beautiful old bungalow, tiled floors, taps that worked, and a bathroom in the usual Ali Baba style. The loo an interesting hole in the ground, but equipped with a sort of flush. The family had already put a mongoose in the roof to keep down the rats and snakes.

This last reminded me of the kebun who'd expressed reluctance to move because of his grandmother. She however was as fed up as I with the continual moaning of the resident cook and amah for while I was pleading with him she slid down the tree and made off, via the monsoon drain, in the direction of the new house.

The number of employees was about to increase, I really did need a job. Scrabbling through papers in my handbag I found the card I had been given after precipitating myself at the feet of Dr David Molesworth, (DM) following the squirrel rescue. I must get in touch.

Luck or coincidence? At a reception that very evening, a cheerful voice behind me asked, 'How's the squirrel?' Swinging round, I found I was, once again, being regarded by bright blue eyes shining through a bearded face. 'Improved. I need a job' was my reply.

'Have you got transport?' '

'Yes, but it's an ex-police vehicle, and I keep on being told not to go out of the city.'

'Oh that's easily fixed. We treat terrorists along with the resident leprosy patients, and once I know the registration we'll pass the word round that you work for me. That usually works and ensures the car will not become a target.'

Not daring to ask what might happen if it did not work and the car was a target I set out next day to drive about 20 miles, on a made-road certainly, but through an area of jungle frequented by terrorists, in order to find Sungei Buluh and learn about leprosy.

The reason the British Forces were still in Malaya was because of the terrorists. They were jungle-based groups who had fought for the British against the Japanese, but had not disbanded at the end of the Japanese war deciding to remain as an independent fighting force. Supplied by Communist organisations in neighbouring countries, they were using their British-taught, anti-Jap tactics in an attempt to rid Malaya of the British.

Working with Leprosy

I found Sungai Buluh and drove, as directed, past the entrance to the settlement upward to where DM's house crouched on a hilltop, built high enough to remain cool, the normally soggy air refreshed by a continual breeze. The non-leprous personnel, or clean staff, DM, the English matron Judy Good, and a junior doctor, a Eurasian, lived outside the confines of the 500 acres allocated to the settlement.

Arriving, I parked the car and was both discomforted and startled to hear, as I got out, a long low, definitely very seductive wolf whistle. 'Oh Shit,' I thought. 'What am I doing here? I know nothing about this man.' As I turned furiously to leave I noticed a Mynah Bird sitting on a perch, head on one side as it regarded me and whistled again! Standing my ground I told it, 'You had me fooled.'

'The last girl left before she looked round,' said DM as he

emerged from the house. I felt I had passed test one, but down the years there were to be plenty more.

After a fascinating day I arranged to work three days a week to see if Physiotherapy was useful in the treatment of Leprosy. It transpired that it was. I found myself in the unique position of being the first Physiotherapist attempting to treat the physical problems associated with leprosy; even assisting at operations if no one else was available.

Nothing of help in the text books, but I recognised some of the deformities and movement limitations as being similar to those encountered in the badly burned patient I had worked with at STH and adopted similar therapy regimes.

As time passed the work expanded, I trained an assistant to help treat the everyday physical injuries and conditions found in a normal community of over 3,000 people, rather than working only with those brought on by leprosy.

Like all new experiences it proved a fantastic learning curve, far removed from the constraints of conventional physiotherapy.

Many of the patients had to have a lower limb amputation, they managed with crutches but some lost both legs resulting in total immobility as there were no wheel chairs available, just a primitive wheelbarrow type conveyance if lucky.

To combat immobility I had old-fashioned 'peg legs' made in one of the community workshops. Then, to keep the recipients active and amused, I introduced football. Perhaps we could have contacted the Guinness Book of Records to ask if there were any other totally legless football matches, injury time created because a leg flew off rather than because of ankle or knee damage.

With the terrible loss of limbs caused by injuries from the current Afghan war and the resultant, amazing, modern prosthesis, my efforts seem comparably very primitive. Eventually, because my one-legged father had been well known at Roehampton, my mother persuaded the centre to send crates of discarded legs, and the lepers in the workshops re-fashioned these with great skill and success although to my mild irritation, those lucky enough to have a personal limb especially reconstructed, tended to hire them out to the less fortunate!

The limb shop

Peg Legs

DM was passionate about trying to contain the spread of the disease and resolve the fear of Leprosy within the general populace. The drugs then being used, rendered those with leprosy non infectious and he felt it imperative to try to return the less disfigured to a productive, working existence, outside the leper settlement. Even those who would remain inside needed to work, both for self-esteem and cash. He decided to visit India to watch Mr Brand, a surgeon, who was pioneering tendon transplants for leprosy victims.

The Biblical descriptions of Leprosy are far from accurate, in fact those 'cured' after bathing in sulphur springs were probably suffering from scabies. The disease attacks specific nerves resulting in not only in loss of sensation, but also, in some cases, loss of function in muscles supplied by the affected nerve with the patient losing the ability to control a foot or hand. These deformities are debilitating but loss of sensation is more complicated for without sensation the patient has no idea if they have cut their foot, trodden on a jungle thorn, or are picking up a burning hot saucepan. The wounds or burns usually resulted in complex secondary complications including acute infections, with antibiotics still in their infancy these infections were often the reason for amputation.

Brand had proved it was possible to detach and relocate certain tendons exchanging their original function for that missing thus restoring lost movement; luckily this is possible in both the hand and lower leg, body areas where there are a surfeit of tendons involved in movement, in many instances with more than one executing an identical function.

If ankle control is lost the patient is left with a trailing foot, a situation which makes walking difficult. A patient who is unable to straighten their fingers develops a useless, clawed, hand.

A tendon operation necessitates detaching some, or all of the terminal fibres of the selected tendon from their original site and reattaching them at a new site, one specifically selected to ensure activation of the tendon re- establishes the lost movement.

My job was to mobilise joints and stretch any shortened tissues to ensure mobility in the target area pre-operatively. A tremendous bonus was the fact that, unlike some European patients, who seem to enjoy their infirmities, these patients actually wanted to make their bodies work again. Shown an exercise or stretch routine they worked really hard often getting friends to come and watch while they were being treated in the department so that they could get help on days when I was away.

Assisting in theatre due to lack of trained staff, enabled me to observe first hand, during these tendon transplants, the complex make up of human limbs. The experience has stood me in good stead; living tissue seen in the raw is quite different to anatomical illustrations, however well they are executed, their proportions often giving a false impression of actual size; living veins, arteries, and nerves are so small, minute tendons have the strength of steel cables. What a unique learning curve, watching the operations, able to observe first-hand the care taken to ensure the angle of each tendon was, in order to achieve effective joint function, correct before it was attached at its new site.

With each operation it became increasingly obvious that conformation was closely allied to bio-mechanics, both required consideration not only during operation, but also in rehabilitation as both dictated, to a degree, the final outcome, something I was to remember later when treating Ballet Dancers and of course animals.

The necessity for minute attention to detail is a component of vital importance if, as a therapist one is to achieve efficient, active function. Once again back to the philosophy of ancient Chinese teaching.

Once DM returned from India and began to operate it became possible to restore function in the lower leg and hand, fitting artificial limbs was already under way, then came another lucky break, an enterprising plastic surgeon temporarily committed to National Service and bored out of his brains turned up one day to see if there was anything he could do.

Some leprous patients lose their nasal cartilage resulting in a flattened nose, an easily recognisable deformity, others develop an unusually flat palm, in some the normal bulge at the base

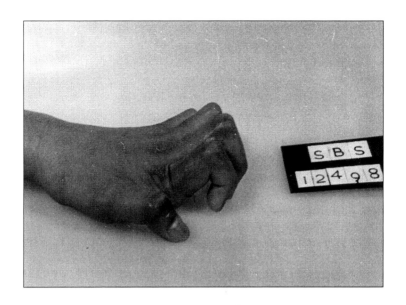

Above: a hand fingers fixed in flexation pre-operation

Below: the hand post-operation

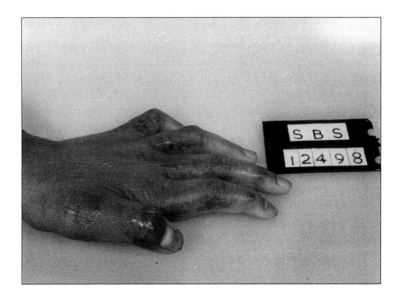

of the thumb disappears completely, such deformities were, amongst the general community, associated with leprosy.

After patients - who were no longer infectious thanks to medication - had left the colony, to return home, their deformities resulted in employment difficulties. The flat nose was obvious but prospective employers always examined the hands of an applicant during a job interview. This was explained to the surgeon, and his response was, 'No problem. Both easy to repair.'

Making moulds (death mask type casts) of patient's faces from Plaster of Paris became the 'in thing'. All who wanted a nose job got a friend to make a mould, then had the greatest fun modelling the shape of nose they wanted!

The opportunity to observe a wide range of differing cultures was a lesson in its self for patients arrived, requesting treatment, from all the countries of the Far East. After an initial medical examination in the hospital block new arrivals were handed over to an internal committee who housed them in a group from their country of origin, because of language this was the first consideration, but religion, still very important to all races, was also considered. Confucius and the Buddha demand differing feast days, Buddhists, forbidden to take any form of life moved voracious caterpillars from their vegetables and re-homed them elsewhere, often with dour results, thinking of my own plants I realised my kebun must be a Buddhist.

From time to time unwelcome guests arrived, the Communist, who were beginning to be severely harassed by the British occupying forces, in particular by the soldiers of the Ghurkha brigade, often dumped one or more of their number, whom they considered had developed leprosy, on the outskirts of the colony. Those dumped crawled to the hospital, arriving ill-nourished and covered in sores. Their fury on discovering the sores were not leprous, and that they were now prisoners of war, was truly terrifying.

As my work became accepted and I became known within the colony I was invited to many celebrations and feast days but the rules were strict. DM was insistent - unlike Albert Schweitzer - that 'clean' (non leprous) staff avoided any possibility of cross contamination. It had been proved that transmission of the disease resulted from close social contact: granny with leprosy looks after the baby while the parents work, end result the baby will probably develop leprosy. So house visiting, socialising, and - for the inmates - accommodating outside visitors was forbidden.

During my time, there was one exception: a Buddhist monk, training in medical acupuncture, came to live in the settlement primarily to observe Western Medicine. He was in his 10th year of training and needed to complete a further five, before being allowed to practice. He considered Western Medicine very crude, its examination procedures faulty because the 'whole' was never considered, only the obvious symptoms explored. In the six months I was privileged to work alongside him I learned the little I know about acupuncture - certainly not enough to practice it - but enough to realise there are no short cuts in an examination procedure and most importantly that the obvious is rarely the prime cause of a problem.

There were amusing incidents unrelated to medicine that I remember, most involving animals. One day, cycling to visit an outlying surgery, I noticed a python busily devouring a goat. The goat had been easily captured as, a milk provider for its owners, it had been tethered behind their house - too near the jungle fringe. The family, alerted by my calls, came and watched, waiting patiently until the last of the goat disappeared, then killed the python, which, following its energetic swallowing efforts, was lying somnolent. They split it lengthways with a Kris and retrieved the goat which, although dead, was still to them a source of food. The snake remains, tied to the back of a bicycle, were dragged off to the Chinese quarter where the money given for the snake carcass would undoubtedly have been sufficient to purchase a replacement goat.

Shortly after this incident, a patient, while grubbing in his vegetable patch, was bitten by a small brown snake. With considerable courage his wife captured the snake in a jar and loading husband, captured snake and herself onto a bicycle arrived at the settlement hospital just as I was about to go home after work. After the man was injected with a general anti venom I was asked to take the captured specimen, and drop it off at the Medical Research Unit in Kuala Lumpur for identification. I

The full staff: clean and leprous. Sungai Buluh.

placed the jar containing the by-now very irritated snake on the front seat. 'Good,' said DM now watching the gyrations. 'It is making plenty of new venom.' Proud to be entrusted with a possibly life-saving mission, I sped off. Driving too fast on jungle tracks is not sensible and I missed a corner, skidded, the jar spun from its resting place and hit the floor and broke. I have never evacuated a car so rapidly, followed luckily by the snake who, moving even faster than I, hit the ground, did a smart left, and shot off into the undergrowth. The bite victim lived despite my failure, and from then on I drove with greater care.

DM was writing a book on the birds of the Malay Peninsular, which necessitated jungle sorties and on many occasions I accompanied him. We visited Dyac villages, the peoples still living in long houses of pre-historic design. If they needed treatment I offered it and in return they introduced me to herbal medicine and taught me jungle lore. An early lesson was, when on jungle paths, to be very careful. They explained the danger, after first trailing a wild pig by following its spore

A native Malayan settlement

they constructed, at a suitable site, a lethal medieval type assault weapon from living bushes, this was then loaded with a bamboo spear designed to kill the pig on its journey home. The need to always read the angle of bushes in front of one, to avoid these hazards was emphasised.

I had seen some interesting injuries amongst the troops following jungle sorties and realised the Pig traps undoubtedly caused problems. The forehead of a wild Asian pig and the nether regions of a man are roughly the same height off the ground and when raw recruits found something that actually resembled a path, many experienced a sudden searing pain in their under-carriage as they sprang a pig trap.

The only draw back on these trips was the unwanted invasion of one's boots. Differing leech families could be seen hungrily approaching from every direction through surrounding vegetation. It was not possible to *feel* them, but their swollen bodies, forming anklets, viewed on removal of jungle boots created a feeling of revulsion I never quite got used to.

Compensation was afforded by seeing monitor lizards, four foot tall, wandering about, bathing in streams, generally mind-ing their own business. Hornbills flitted through the tree canopy, untroubled by our presence, their numbers beginning to recover, for during the Japanese occupation they had been a food source for the jungle dwelling partisan.

On one of these sorties I was lucky to see a bird thought to be extinct, a Frog Mouth, there it was squatting over its single egg balanced on a plate of mud and spit.

Horse Repair Begins

Living off base there was no allowance for servants as enjoyed by those living in military quarters, but shortly after beginning to work for DM I realised I was earning enough to pay the household wages. I could also afford to keep a horse, and it was over six years since I had ridden regularly. Having had a pony rather than a pram as a child I had been fortunate to be able to continue riding and competing through my childhood, in my teens and early twenties moving steadily upward through the varied levels of show jumping on horses of ever increasingly size and quality, even falling off at point to points until hospital training, marriage and pregnancy had got in the way.

There was no recreational riding in Malaya as in the UK, just polo and racing. I felt a visit to the Turf Club was a must. Tentative enquiry revealed, due to lack of facilities (no grazing or turn out) it was impossible to retain lame horses. The official policy of the Club was to insist on euthanasia, rather than sell a horse when its racing career ended and have it end as a half-starved commercial animal attached to a bullock cart.

I learned that if I became a paid up member of the Turf Club I was welcome to buy a damaged Thoroughbred for its slaughter costs, although the animal would remain the property of the Club. Lame behind 'Silver Reeds' became mine for the fore-seeable future. I can remember as though it were yesterday my badgering one Jim Marsh, the Turf Club vet, and his turning in exasperation, 'You mend the F'ing humans. Why don't you try your physio on the F'ing horses?' Despite the hour - 7.00 am - sweat was already making his white shirt cling to his back as he strode off. A Frangipani flower fell at my feet: a lucky omen. Crushing the petals and inhaling the fragrance, I thought, why

Jim Marsh. The first vet in the world to accept Animal Physiotherapy was useful.

not? Of course word got around. 'Jim has said give broken horses Physio! He must be mad!' Then as Silver Reeds improved owners sidled up with their lame animal, 'Can you help?' My stable increased in size!

Telephone communication with England did not really exist, or, if you could connect, due to the time difference, it was a middle of the night job. Letters could take up to six weeks as only Diplomatic Bags moved by air. After some pleading an OHMS letter to my long-suffering mother was dispatched, and a book on horse anatomy and grooming tools duly arrived.

Silver Reeds had his own racing tack and I scrounged, begged, or borrowed the rest of the kit necessary. Shoeing was no problem: Cavalry Regiments still existed, and the King's Dragoon Guards who were on duty in the Malay States travelled not only with a farrier, but also a saddler - both disguised as troopers.

None of the syce (grooms) had ever brushed their horses, just thrown buckets of water over them and scraped off the sweat, using anything handy, usually part of a coconut shell and despite my efforts they continued. Thus newly acquired brushes and combs disappeared, purloined for domestic use: the wife's hair, and scrubbing floors. I was furious, if they refused to groom as directed, using brushes, they could groom with their hands. Once initial resentment had been overcome the syce flaunted their results with pride. The animals in their charge developed beautiful coats, their muscles rippled, the horses loved the attention and to my astonishment, in many cases, lame horses not only improved but, after a few sessions became sound. Thus began the *re-introduction* of massage for horses, apparently ignored for centuries. Research documents its use when Xenophon wrote his treatise on Horsemanship in the 4th Century BC. However, after this the practice appears to have been either discontinued or not to have been worthy of note.

Introduction of hand grooming was certainly not on a par with other life changing discoveries, antibiotics for example, but like so many experiments its use did suggest that simple, unplanned actions, often spawn amazingly useful results. I now had sound horses, polo or racing which should I choose? The Selangor Turf Club managed the polo and controlled amateur as well as professional racing, the other centres were in Penang, Ipoh, and Singapore. The Sultan of Pahang kept his main racing string in Kuala Lumpur but held, at his Estancia on the East Coast, polo tournaments and race meeting when he felt like it.

I decided racing would suit me better than polo and as it turned out this was a sensible choice for the Rio Rajah Hanut Singh, sent as Ambassador from Pakistan, brought with him two high goal teams. To watch they were poetry in motion, the riders seeming to melt into and become a part of their pony.

As soon as Silver Reeds was sound I had to learn to ride on the flat, not quite the same as show jumping, hunting or riding in a point to point. All amateurs were required to pass a starting test before being allowed to ride in a race. It is not easy to stay with your horse as it accelerates from standing motionless to galloping at 40 mph.

The test day duly arrived and ten of us lined up. Luckily I stayed put as four unlucky riders went straight out the back door as the tape was released. A sudden buzz as Silver Reeds, completely restored to pre-lameness showed her ability and powered forward. I felt I was flying: I had never been so fast before.

When I realised, as predicted by Ah Yin that child No 2 was on the way it seemed sensible to carry on with life as normal, after all that was what the Malays and Chinese did. Toward the end of the eighth month of my pregnancy, riding a finish I lost a race I had hoped to win. I had banked on the fact that, for the first time, I had not needed extra lead to make the weight required. My riding weight then was, amazingly as I look at my current rotund figure, seven stone. Early on in my training career, I'd realised dead weight on a horse's back is a considerable hindrance to optimum performance.

Nevertheless, I duly produced Penelope - daughter No I - at the army base hospital, managing to escape after a short stay during which both she and I were garlanded with floral ley made by the Ghurkha patients. The note on mine said: 'glad girl come safe, better luck next time, boy best'.

Back to work, with Ah Yin joyfully now an established Baby Amah, requests to work on lame horses came and went, each a new learning curve. Anatomy book to hand I prodded, poked and watched. So many horses appeared stiff for several days following a race. Why?

My horses, massaged, seemed to recover a little quicker but one trainer never seemed to have stiffness problems at all. Why? One day, watching his post-race wash down, I noticed his horses dropped their heads to suck, from the ground, the sweat soiled water that had just been scraped off their bodies.

Nothing ventured, nothing gained, I stuck a finger into a puddle that had not yet evaporated, smelt, and tasted. It was salty: interesting!

I had never heard of electrolytes. Knowledge then, in the late 1950s, was miniscule and not until considerably later, in the 1980s following research prompted by the deaths of several horses in the Endurance discipline, were Electrolytes recognised as important dietary requirements. In hind-sight the horses I had watched knew instinctively they needed to restore their natural electrolytic balance and must have been

Silver Reeds comes second due to the rider being eight months pregnant

reabsorbing those lost in their sweat by drinking the soiled water. Mentioning this in a letter home I learned from my mother that offering the scraped, wash-off water to his horses, should they have sweated profusely, had been used by my father. Often when living abroad they found themselves in areas where water was scarce and he'd conserved as much as possible when his horses were washed down by having the syce scrape the excess into a bucket against future need, never dreaming he was collecting electrolytes. Then, quite by chance, he had found the horses eager to drink the liquid.

I relaxed my 'no wash off rule', because, remembering the routine learned from Frank Mullins, I had made the syce rub the horses dry if they had sweated profusely, now, it became wash down, scrape into a bucket, offer to the horse. They nearly all drank, then, when dry they were massaged. The results appeared to be reduced post-race stiffness, quicker post-race recovery, and less injuries. Luck again, by chance stumbling over an effective aid, one not to be identified or proven until some 30 years later.

These sort of experiences, backed by information gleaned from peoples still living predominately naturally, has enforced a belief it is sensible to enable animals to choose their own dietary supplements always supposing these are available; for example some dogs eat blackberries, horses, if allowed, will often pick selectively from hedge rows, eat earth, chew bark or wood.

I have on many occasions, particularly if an animal is out of sorts rather than ill, tested their mineral balance using hair analysis: this usually demonstrates any lack or imbalance of body minerals. The UK does not seem to have mineral rich rocks as are found in some countries. In South Africa all feral species living in the Karoo are known to visit, usually twice a year, a rocky out-crop where they lick the rocks, obviously replenishing their mineral store. North America lists the predominate or lack of minerals in every state thus if you buy hay from an area deficient in selenium it should be added to the diet.

The Move

The leave tenancy ended, time for the move. Kitchen equipment was provided by Cookie II, Ah Yin's father, I had some linen, a few pictures, the inevitable books, but no furniture. A few weeks previously the officers had been soundly beaten by the sergeant's mess in the annual tennis tournament, victory attributed to the cannon-ball type serve delivered by the quarter master sergeant, who, until I treated, had been sidelined with a nagging tennis elbow injury. Pay back time.

An army lorry arrived under cover of darkness, and duly unloaded a full set of household goods, 'Officers for the use of.' The unloaders partook of the beer I had acquired from the NAFFI and left as unobtrusively as they had arrived. It seemed pointless to agonise about the need for a set of fire irons complete with their hanging pedestal. Why, I wondered briefly, had valuable cargo space been wasted: not only in the packing of fire irons but also in the transporting of bamboo and rattan furniture firstly shipping these items to the UK and then returning them to their country of origin.

Ah Yin fell on the fire irons with delight. 'Keep by door,' she announced. 'Bad man come: bang, bang.' Vaguely hoping this would never happen of course it did, and awakening one night, alone but for the children, I saw a bamboo pole with a hook hanging off the end, trawling through the slatted blinds. This was the accepted method of handbag theft. I slid out of bed, moved noiselessly, found and grabbed the poker, and 'bang, bang'. A subdued curse and scuffling suggested departure. I hoped if there were a next time it would be as easy. DS was often away, either on night duty at the hospital or out on jungle patrol and I did not expect the servants to be on duty 24 hours a day. To employ a night watchman, as the American expats did, seemed excessive, so discussion with Ah Yin suggested a dog was the answer.

A departing General wanted a home for his Dachshund bitch. She arrived in a staff car: red, long haired and very fat. Several whiskeys later I enquired her name. 'BB' he mumbled. Very French I felt; the General was known to be partial to any woman who was easy on the eye. Eventually the General, his driver supporting him to his car, departed sniffing loudly into a large handkerchief. BB cased the joint, clambered onto the most comfortable chair and fell asleep. Her fatness was resolved a few weeks later when she gave birth to Buster. Although probably of 'pie dog' lineage (the term used to describe semi feral local dogs) he retained his mother's shape, other than growing slightly longer in the leg.

As is so often the case when the British are moved abroad they attempt, on arrival, to establish their preferred English way of living. A newly arrived wife, missing her customary dog shows, decided there must be a Malayan Kennel Club. Approached to become a member I protested loudly, explaining it was not my scene, I already had plenty to occupy me, but I was over ruled, 'You must register BB. How did you spell her name? Does she have papers?'

In some desperation I traced the General to Hong Kong, in between telephone cracklings, periods of silence and static, I asked 'had she papers'. His retort suggested not. 'How was her name spelt, like a Honey Bee, perhaps?' Noises off suggested I had got it wrong and eventually I made out, between his guffaws: 'It stands for Bloody Bitch, you stupid woman!' The day was saved and Kennel Club membership skilfully avoided. There were to be no registration papers for a dog named Bloody Bitch.

BB and Buster became useful in their designated guard dog role, for the noise they made, barking in unison, rather than their actual ferocity, achieved a satisfactory deterrent to any unwelcome visitor.

The Otter Rescue

The Chinese market still drew me, particularly at festival times, pre Christmas after consultation with my other half, a goose seemed the answer. We would probably be celebrating Christmas a deux, for, due to our respective jobs we were not really socially acceptable; cocktail party conversation went something like this, senior wife to me: 'And what does your husband do dear?' 'Actually he is a TB specialist,' the, 'Working with the Ghurkha' bit usually trailing into thin air, as, lest I be contaminated the questioner moved off; or, 'How do you keep yourself amused living so far away from HQ?', 'Actually I have a job.' 'How fascinating, what have you found?' 'Er, I work at the Leper Colony, I am their Physiotherapist', immediate space around one, lest leprosy jump from person to person.

Cookie II did not mind my accompanying him to the market, in fact I think it may have given him elevated status to be seen in the company of his Mem explaining the use of various fruits and vegetables, medicinal and otherwise, giggling politely as she tried to master Chinese names. By now, because of working amongst the varied races living at Sungai Buluh, I could examine a patient in both Malay and Chinese but questions such as, 'can you feel this finger' did not have much culinary value.

On the pre Christmas visit we wandered happily through the vegetable area and onward toward the poultry, supermarket signs were neither invented nor required, you just followed scent or sound.

In the poultry section geese of all sizes, firmly anchored by rattan leg straps squawked and screeched at each other. Poking and prodding, in order to save face was required, no one just bought, you actually secretly chose, then moved on, certain that as you passed the stall a second time, the price would have dropped by several Malay dollars.

Sometimes it required a third passing before cookie was satisfied that the price, while fair for his Mem ensured a reasonable cut for him as well. The chosen goose, with leg tether firmly wrapped around its body, to avoid flight, was then handed over. I have to admit it had taken time to get used to taking live poultry home, rather than the neatly plucked and trussed equivalent found in England.

As we were leaving I realised we were not taking the usual route past the aphrodisiac animal area. This suggested there was something I was not meant to see. 'Mem stay, she look longer' I told cookie 'You go home'. Christmas was still a week away, I knew the goose would be behind the staff quarters when I got home grazing happily, putting on weight. We did not have a fridge, these of course now standard, along with air conditioning, then killing and eating on the same day was the Chinese method, we stuck to this and never got sick as many of the families, trying to live in an English life mode, seemed to do.

Cookie departed reluctantly and I retraced my steps, then heard a thin whistle, an otter, surely not, but it was. A young otter cub was caged in a metal container, probably from the construction, the trap that had ensnared it. Bleeding from the mouth and with a front leg obviously badly damaged, both conditions probably caused by frantic efforts to escape, its large luminous eyes pleaded. The price was exorbitant, eventually with an acceptable compromise reached, he and the cage were mine. Not easy to take home on a bike, never mind.

I often wonder if some unseen presence watches over me, for in times of real crisis help seems to appear if by magic. This time it was in the shape of Tommy Barr whom, despite the fact her husband was the Senior Air Attaché, did not conform to diplomatic principles. She weighed up the situation in an instant 'how lucky I have a car and driver outside,' into the boot went the cage, 'I have to get my bike home', the luckless driver, a rather overweight Malay, was, to his consternation, given the bike.

Tommy's Malay was impeccable, none of the wives of the senior Malay officials, whom she, as part of her husband's remit had to entertain, spoke English. I only got the gist of what she said to the driver, but it was effective, and he peddled sadly off. Staff pennant flying, she took the wheel and we were home in no time. I opened the boot and regarded my newest madness, even though he is a baby he will bite I reasoned.

I had some otter experience, Henry Williamson, author of *Tarka the Otter* had been a close family friend, we had otter watched on the rivers Taw and Torridge, through him I had met Gavin Maxwell when on a visit south with one of his charges. At the time he, Gavin, had just started working with otters in Scotland, subsequently writing of his experiences in *Ring of Bright Water*.

Under instructions, Ah Yin brought the baby bath putting it in the Jason enclosure and the kebun filled it with water. We lifted out the cage, carried it to and placed it by the bath. As I gazed I said, 'Food, I ought to have bought fish.' Tommy to the rescue again, her presence in the market that morning was because she had needed to buy fish for a dinner party, she had plenty in the car. We examined the cage, discovered the trick of opening the front, agreed it would be sensible to put some fish in the bath and retreat for half an hour or so, then open the cage. I hoped the base of the enclosure would hold.

'He will need something resembling a Holt' said Tommy, as we refreshed our selves with lime juice. 'Drain pipe?' I queried. 'Why not?'. The kebun, not exactly eager, was dispatched to a nearby building site dump and told to acquire a broken bit of drain. This was duly installed in the enclosure near the roots of the central tree, the otter seemed less frantic, I opened the front of the cage, despite the injured leg with one smooth, seal like movement he was in the bath devouring Tommy's dinner party. It took three days before he ceased to bolt and hide in his drain each time anyone or anything approached his enclosure, other, I noticed, than if BB were in the vicinity. As she approached he mewed loudly, pushing against the enclosure base, obviously trying to reach her. She was still feeding her puppy, worth a try? I let her into the enclosure, after sniffing the cub she licked its head and lay down allowing him to suckle.

From then on she did more of the taming than I, licking the leg wound, cleaning him, feeding him her milk. I was severely bitten several times in these early stages as I tried to sterilize the wound with an antiseptic spray-on of Gentian violet.

Despite all attempts the leg laceration remained persistently obstinate, until eventually a patient, one with who I could communicate in a mix of languages and from whom I was gleaning herbal knowledge, professed surprise that I had not used honey. Pure honey was available from wild mountain bees, but they tended to become agitated when honey collection was attempted; fortunately a group of Ghurkha's, hospitalised for their TB treatment had, to alleviate their boredom, recently captured a swarm, they provided some honey.

The treatment was miraculous, not only did Ot - his given name - become a honey addict, begging rather than biting when I dressed his leg, but the change in the condition of the wound had to be seen to be believed. Another remedy proved by circumstance, to be of use, and one I have used so many times, on a variety of wounds ever since.

As he became tame Ot would roll onto his back in his bath, cupping a proffered hand between his clawless front paws, an expression of pure delight on his face as one rubbed his tummy.

He eventually joined the two dogs, free by day, but confined to his enclosure at night lest he stray and be recaptured. He loved car rides, surveying all, lying back on the bed made by the tonneau canopy of the recently acquired drop head MG. His greatest joy was evident when he was taken to a rubber plantation owned by friends, bordered on one side by a tributary of the Kulang River. I feared lest the first time when free near a river he would disappear and I might lose him but he stayed with the dogs splashing in the shallows and gambolling with the children in deeper pools.

All went well for about eighteen months until his surrogate mother BB, came into season. He was by now a mature male and became very hard to handle; eventually the servants lined up, either he went or they would. He had apparently bitten cookie on his ankles several times, this was something quite new, and I was concerned lest he turned on the children.

Permission for his release, following negotiations initiated by DM, was eventually obtained from a Dyac headman up country. The area, a remote upland selected as it was sacred to the local community and therefore avoided by the superstitious Chinese. Ot had no fear of people and I was concerned lest he be caught once again and ended up as a powdered aphrodisiac.

I freed him on the bank of a sizeable river, at first he was uncertain, no dogs, no children, what should he do, nice pool, try for a fish, to my joy he caught one, then unbelievably, a whistle, head raised he answered, a swirl and a female slid, with that wonderful, sinuous grace peculiar to otters, into the pool to join him.

A Journey

The Selangor Turf Club was informed that the Sultan of Pahang wished a race meeting to be arranged at his Istana (palace) to celebrate his birthday. While couched as a request, the term 'demanded' would be more appropriate. At the time he was the Senior Sultan of the country and his territory, about the size of Wales, extended over the middle and southern segments of the East Coast, bordered to the east by the China Sea and to the west by a central mountain range. Other than an area where the costal hills - discovered to be 90% pure iron ore - were being mined and from which he obtained his not inconsiderable wealth, his lands were in the main primary jungle dotted inland by a few settlements, with clusters of fishing communities scattered along the coast.

The Istana lay on the coast and was a nightmare to get to as there was a mountain range to cross and five rivers to be navigated. There were no roads or bridges and the Sultan - for reasons of his own - preferred to retain a situation ensuring complete privacy. This was rumoured to be due to his entertaining troops of dancing girls, a trait frowned upon by his senior wife who - having presented him several fine sons - went off to live solo, but comfortably, in Singapore.

Besides working four days a week at the Leper Colony I was also training his flat horses in Kuala Lumpur. This may sound a ridiculous work load but although the actual race meetings were held in the afternoon the horses were trained and

The river where Ot was released.

exercised at 5:00 am before it got hot and again in the late evening, so it was easy to fit everything in.

The race meeting the Sultan demanded would require at least five races with a minimum of six horses in each. There was only one thing to do and after consultation with the Turf Club officials those owners wishing to partake all agreed the sensible route was to request an appointment with Frankie Festing, the General currently in charge of the British occupying troops. I knew the General liked the Sultan and anyway orders were to fraternise whenever practicable to try to soften the irritation resultant from the continued occupation by the British of the Malay Peninsula.

Fortunately a childhood friend Johnny Cornell was his ADC, and he duly liaised. The army rose to the challenge, and agreed to commandeer some tank landing craft, take the horses down the west coast, through the straits of Singapore and land them on the nearest beach to the Istana. They would supply all personnel to run the meeting, these ferried in by helicopter. The 'exercise', apparently, could be disguised as a jungle training activity and I suspect it had a code name but was far too busy wondering how I could cross the country fast enough to arrive ahead of the horses to give that much thought. Hitching a lift in a helicopter was out: I did ask but the troops were to make a jungle sortie on their way over to justify the use of Taxpayers' money and there was 'no room at the Inn'.

As luck would have it, shortly after the horses set sail, a message arrived from George Saloshin, the controller of the Sultan's household. George was a European of unknown origin who managed both the legitimate and slightly dubious sides of the Sultan's life. 'HH has a car in KL, it has been repaired, please drive it over.' This was too easy: a Daimler arrived, petrol in the tank, on the back seat six full cans for topping up rested on a line of tin boxes, each marked, in both English and Rajah Malay: State Papers. HH Sultan of Pahang.

There were no number plates on the car, just *HH Pahang*.

I packed racing gear, spare tack, water, then as an afterthought dress, shoes and a hat - you never know - and set off feeling distinctly Royal.

The first 100 miles were slick with the first river crossed on a flat pontoon type barge. The second, third and fourth rivers behind me, I put my foot down to speed along: no response, other than a rather sad cough. Pumping the accelerator the car wheezed to the next river, thankfully the last.

The ferry was not only full, but had left and was half-way across a very wide expanse of heaving floodwater, the result of one of the unpredictable mountain storms. Looking back and seeing the number plate the ferry operator reversed direction, rushing back with such speed that it crashed into the landing ramp. A number of passengers, several bundles, and crates of chicken fell into the churning waters. The shrieks as ejected persons and debris were retrieved, changed to yells and stone-throwing as crocodiles rose silently from the murk and ravaged a crate of luckless chickens. I am certain they were not worth the sum I paid in compensation.

When order was restored the, by now very reluctant car, was manhandled onto the ferry and we set off. I prayed for every minute of the 10 minute crossing, the weight of the car not only had us partially under water, but with each current swirl, the fragile structure threatened to capsize. As we made it to the opposite side two waiting crocodiles slid off the bank and submerged.

Phut, phut, the car crawled off, at the first mild slope, although still making an, 'I am trying to move' noise it halted. No mobile phones in those days, no sign of life. I had a mountain to get over and 15 miles of hairpin bends to negotiate. Somewhere in the depths of my brain I remembered hearing, sometimes reverse gear works. It did. Going up a mountain backwards takes time but once over the top I was able to coast gloriously, if somewhat dangerously, down hill. Phut, phut, the last few miles were covered at snail's pace.

George was waiting, leaping up and down: not in an anxious, 'are you all right mode', rather in an extremely frenzied one. 'What took so long?' he bellowed rushing for the tin boxes. 'My bacon will be ruined.'

Unwittingly, in a country where the pig and all its by-products are not only unclean, but it is unlawful to handle or transport them, I had been ferrying sides of bacon in boxes supposedly filled with State Papers.

It was lucky I had both dress and hat in my bag, for, after the third race had finished a scheduled two hour interval turned out not, as might be supposed, to be a rest period for horses, jockeys, assisting personnel and stewards, but to allow time for a garden party.

The Sultan withdrew, every one who could, changed rapidly, behind rattan screens, into clothes acceptable for such an event; full regimentals despite the heat for the men, and dresses for the women.

Tables, chairs, refreshments and potted plants appeared born by staff appropriately clothed in the livery of Pahang. As if in a play, the scene was changed from racecourse to garden, a throne like chair held centre stage, shaded by the obligatory yellow umbrella, yellow in Malaya signifying both luck and happiness despite being shunned in Indonesia as an omen signifying bad luck!

His Highness reappeared escorted to the throne by body-guards armed with ceremonial Keris (Malay dagger); when seated, he clapped his hands. Unlike the Queen, who moves along the line of an assembled company, the handclap was the signal for the guests to file past him: a deep bow by the males, and as near a court curtsey as was possible, from the females.

Homage paid, he rose and moved amongst the guests; although fluent in English, perversely he usually only spoke Rajah Malay on social occasions, a language confined to those of Royal Blood, the 'upper crust'. With remarkably few able to converse with him he once again withdrew; the garden was immediately revamped as a racecourse and the final three races were run.

Despite the no alcohol culture, there appeared to be a number of sore heads the following morning as the day had concluded with a free for all meal. Malayan food is an acquired taste, definitely requiring added liquid refreshment.

Animal Guests.

A Slow Loris - another market rescue - turned out not to be slow at all. Loosed into the squirrel enclosure it shinned up the central tree, burst through the cage top, then, bounding from branch to branch of the adjacent trees, disappeared, never to be seen again. Luckily the children had not seen it, but I had been captivated by its beautiful eyes: large, for night vision requirements, and by its soft coat and endearing expression. Tamed I'd imagined we would have a cuddly, yet animated, teddy bear.

During the Emergency there were more casualties from friendly fire than those caused by the enemy, particularly as the British contingent included a number of raw National Service Recruits from the inner cities of the UK to whom the jungle was not exactly a home from home. Most were terrified, loosing off rounds indiscriminately at the slightest noise. One of their unintentional victims happened to be a female tiger. By chance, a member of the patrol, Trooper H, happened to be the son of the Lion Tamer from Bertram Mills Circus; and upon examining the carcass he realised the tigress had recently given birth. Everyone was immediately deployed to search for what turned out to be twin cubs. When they were found the patrol, thankfully turning itself into a rescue party, rather than killing mission, high-tailed it out of the jungle.

Needless to say the twins were brought to our garden. I seemed to have acquired a reputation for animal rescue. Fast-talking ensured the appropriate patrol member was seconded to accompany them as nursemaid. They were about the size of month old Alsatian pups, eyes still tightly shut and, on arrival, wailing with hunger. I took orders from Trooper H: milk, bottles, teats makeshift or otherwise, required. It is amazing what a helpful Quartermaster can produce.

Goat's milk is a wonderful replacement for mother's milk in the young of all species, so, as the cubs needed to be bottle fed at four-hourly intervals several goats were procured as a milk source on the hoof. The cubs thrived, but as their eyes opened and they began to play it became obvious our garden was becoming too small, and as their gentle, cat-like patting began to result in fairly substantial lacerations, it was decided they must be relocated. At a convenient nearby Army Camp a cage was constructed on an area of grass under a large shady tree outside the sergeant's mess, not too far from the cook-house, they and Trooper H moved happily.

Their presence created considerable interest and visitors were numerous, the cubs usually behaving like prima donnas and Trooper H, released from jungle warfare, was in his element, playing with, caring for, his two fast growing charges.

On one never to be forgotten day I was bidden to take the wife of a visiting General to see them. They were well grown, each the size of a Deerhound. Demanding entrance to their enclosure the visitor, announcing that she had handled cubs in Africa and that the twins would treat her with respect, claimed she would indicate, by replication of tiger sounds that she was the boss and would demand her space. Troopers do not say 'no' to the wives of Generals and reluctantly he unlocked and opened the cage door.

Moving in with assurance, the lady squatted and began to make low, growl-type sounds; used to visitors, both cubs had been lying happily stretched out in a patch of shade. Perhaps, though, African and Malayan tigers do not speak quite the same language because after listening, then tensing through their bodies, they rose to their feet and began to advance stealthily: the accompanying aura suggesting they were in an, 'I am going to get you' frame of mind. Observing what was happening Trooper H. made a run for the cookhouse shouting 'give me some meat'.

Unless the said lady was totally unobservant, the thought 'this is not going to plan' must have penetrated her brain, but unfortunately not fast enough. As they advanced she did stand up and began to back away; both cubs leapt as one, luckily landing short, but the claws of their outstretched front pads caught her dress ripping the fine fabric to shreds. There she was, stripped more or less naked, in front of an admiring audience leaning on the veranda rail of the sergeant's mess; no one, thank heavens, had the temerity to wolf whistle. The cub's attention was diverted as a large lump of meat, accurately bowled by Trooper H. landed almost under their noses. A red faced sergeant proffered a towel and the lady withdrew.

Shortly after this incident, arrangements were made for the cubs to be sent up country, to be cared for prior to release back into the wild; their destination a recently designated conservation area, the Templer Park.

The Tour Ends

The final Communist Cells were rapidly being mopped up and departure for the British was on the horizon, not just for the Troops but for the Administration Officials including the Governor. Malay was preparing for self-rule and the cessation of the law-enforcing British presence, an administrative force that had been intermittently present since the 18th Century.

DM set off for Malawi, his post at the Leper Settlement filled by Dr Reddy, an Indian doctor who, having also trained under Brand, would be able to carry on the tendon transplant work, pioneered by DM in Malaya. Financial aid, previously provided by the Foreign Office, was slashed and my job ended. This was sad, but was tempered by the fact that I felt the teams trained could carry on building limbs, preparing pre-operative cases for tendon transplants and help post-operative cases regain mobility, for after four years of teaching a stable infrastructure was in place which could be managed by those taught, many of whom would never leave the settlement. It proved to be the case, Christmas cards, even letters, occasionally arrive, with news from inmates who were children 50 years ago.

As we packed to leave, there was a sudden, short stay of execution; DS, his spell of National Service ending, was asked to move to and run a large Tuberculosis hospital, while the Medical Director went on nine month's leave. The hospital built in 1952 bore the name of Lady Templer, a lady devoted to helping the less privileged, she left a legacy of care world wide, having worked tirelessly for the peoples of every country to which her husband had been posted.

The extra months meant we would be in the country when the British handed over control to the Malays: Merdeka, their longed-for freedom had arrived.

After Merdeka many things seemed to change, organisations that had worked like clockwork faltered, Malay and Chinese members demanded separate bars at the clubs, service became slack everywhere. I wondered if I was noticing changes because unwittingly we had been forced into in a differing social life, previously DS had been attached to the Ghurkha rather than to UK Troops while I had worked with a mix of races other than just Europeans and our social lives had enabled us to integrate freely, mixing without apparent difficulty or constraint with all races, accepting differing customs, communicating in varied languages, now, suddenly we were 'whites'.

Realisation dawned, the order of life in Malaya was about to change dramatically, under British control the varied races had co-existed within a structured, colonial regime, however the Chinese did not respect the Malays. Many of the Chinese were inow third generation immigrants, and these families began to seek control. The Malays, generally, were laid back - despite some rumbling if things did not go quite as they wished - and they had mostly left the British to run their country. A local comment summed the situation well: 'A Chinese will climb the tree to harvest a ripe coconut, but a Malay will sit under the tree and wait for the coconut to fall.'

Mixed within multiple emigrants were Tamil workers, fleeing poverty in India and employed as labourers, their contribution providing the essential work force required in the rubber plantations, tin and iron ore mines. They also planted and tended the newest income source, huge plantations of oil palms. These peoples were despised by both the Malays and the Chinese, with no one seeming to appreciate the fact that mining tin and iron ore, harvesting rubber and palm oil would, once British funding ceased, become very necessary sources of income for the country.

Shortly before Merdeka, at the conclusion of DA's army career, we had moved to the Lady Templer Hospital complex. Cookie, Amah and Ah Yin had agreed to come and remain with us until we left, after which they had decided to buy a coffee shop in the Chinese quarter and retire. There was one request, Cookie's mother, recently widowed, needed to be cared for. Could she join them? As the servants' quarters at the Medical Director's bungalow were very spacious this was no problem and she duly arrived, accompanied by her coffin, a beautiful ornately carved wooden structure, lined with silk, comfortably padded and in which she slept! The Chinese coffins were works of art, and examining some when visiting the Chinese quarter I noticed a sign, which proclaimed boldly: 'COFFINS, CHRISTIANS INSIDE'.

In our new temporary abode, for the first time since arriving in Malaya, we had a European bathroom and air conditioning in the bedrooms. We found we hated the latter and threw open all windows and doors in order to enjoy the temperature and humidity to which we had become accustomed. Compared to our previous Chinese-designed home the house and garden assigned to the Medical Director, built European style, was air-less, the heat made worse because when the hospital complex had been built all the shade trees had been felled.

The main hospital block sited above the staff quarters, over looked a Chinese Graveyard: not exactly inspiring for patients, but a source of pleasure to the local children. The fair head of hair, belonging to Nick was often visible, marking him out amongst a group of black haired Chinese children all of whom had left their play area in the hospital grounds in order to glean sweets by joining a funeral procession. He taught his Chinese contemporaries English Nursery rhymes, and they responded with Chinese.

A nest of Cobra had to be dispatched after Nick complained bitterly about the 'Nake' that came in through the open widow when he was resting. It was a while before I discovered this was true and found that the snakes had been installed to deter investigation of the thick scrub at the far end of the hospital property, where rice had been left for collection by Communist Guerrillas, one of whom was related to the stores superintendent, a large round affable Chinese. When tackled about the snakes, for all difficulties seemed to be dealt with by him, he explained now the emergency was over, the Cobra colony could be removed as there was no longer need for caches of rice. He became a good friend and we often ate with him learning about and experiencing superb Chinese food usually visiting various chop shops owned by his relatives in the Chinese quarter, all of whom had sensibly benefited from his position at the hospital.

The Lady Templer, the first of its kind in the Far East, had been designed for the treatment of tuberculosis and included facilities for the surgical removal of diseased lung tissue. Operative removal, a relatively recent procedure, was replacing the previous Sanatorium approach of bed rest and time. Patients, when anaesthetized, were put into baths of ice and frozen almost solid in order to slow down their general metabolism before the surgeon opened the chest in order to remove diseased lung tissue

For me the move provided yet another new and interesting learning curve; I was the only physiotherapist available and the patients all needed respiratory therapy. As students, while on the chest unit, we'd had to learn to breathe using one lobe of one lung to prove to patients this was possible. We also 'tipped' patients, positioning them on their front on an inclined couch, head and face downhill, then beat their backs. This brutal approach forcing them to cough mucus from their lungs; it had not been my favourite occupation when training but it did mean I knew a little about lungs.

Nothing had prepared me for removing dressings, discovering an incision wound had not healed and that I was looking into the chest cavity watching a bit of lung doing its best to keep the patient alive. Those who wanted to survive were

Lady Templer Hospital

amazingly resilient many arriving with a Haemoglobin level so low it should not have been compatible with the ability to continue to stay alive.

Shortly after DS had taken the reins, under an International agreement called 'The Colombo Plan' nurses from Australia arrived to teach the Chinese nurses who staffed the hospital. This was not a great success as the Chinese girls had never heard of shifts or time off: they looked after their allotted patients and when they needed a rest or meal, the patient's relatives, who camped in the hospital grounds, moved in and took over.

The Ghurkha soldiers who developed TB had, before DS was posted to run the army unit, been sent back to Nepal infectious and pensionless, deemed no longer fit to fight for the British. The Lady Templer Hospital was not supposed to include these unfortunates but DS managed to change this enabling Ghurkha soldiers with TB to be admitted for treatment. The scheme was pretty successful other than that the army insisted all operable cases, rather than be dealt with on the spot, were sent back to the UK; reminiscent of purchasing rattan furniture in the Far East, sending it to the UK to be logged by a quarter master before returning it to be used in the Far East.

Letters saying 'thank you' from those sent to the UK arrived, many containing photographs of the writer standing beside a sentry outside Buckingham Palace, with captions reading 'me outside the Queen's House'. Of those I spoke to when they returned to convalesce it became obvious that their main source of amazement while in the UK had been the size of the cow's udders.

An offshoot TB unit, used to house some of the worst cases in order to improve their general health pre-operatively and to rehabilitate others post-operatively, had been built at a hill station in an upland area, the Cameron Highlands. The duties of the Medical Director included visiting the unit and one day we set off in an open Sunbeam Talbot, Ah Yin and the children packed in the back.

I had no idea how cold it would be! At 1,930 meters we needed blankets on the beds and a log fire in the evening to keep warm. The children hated it, they spent the entire trip undressing, then getting cold, something never before experienced, crying and fighting as they were re-clothed.

For the first time in our entire association Ah Yin was useless, wrapped in a blanket, still shivering and turning the rather odd colour associated with cold or sick Chinese, she wept silently: the food was wrong, the staff were dirty Malays. For the first time I had to look after the children, then it dawned, it will be cold like this in England! There would be no Ah Yin, shock horror!

I was very tempted when, shortly after returning, both DS and I were approached by the Tunku Abdul Rahman and invited to remain in Malaya working for the fledgling medical service. He was very honest explaining that neither salaries nor facilities could not match those we had previously enjoyed, all costs were being reduced to a level affordable for the new administration. With a young family to raise and educate we felt sadly, tempting though the invitation was, that we must decline.

Even today memories associated with the chilly trip are the flowers; the hill station had been named after the Cameron who discovered the plateau in 1885, bungalows and rest houses were built in the early 1900s and the area established as a rest station: a place to get away from the eternal heat and humidity of the plains. Over the years all manner of flowering shrubs, many imported, had been planted and due to height, rainfall and virgin rich soil those that survived grew in profusion. I shall never forget the Fuchsias, their massive bushes dripping with blooms, these affording nectar for swarms of vibrant humming birds.

Departure
November, the month of departure arrived all too soon. The farewell parties began, we packed and the heavy luggage was collected for its sea voyage back to the UK. We were to fly, departing from Singapore in a transport propeller aircraft, resembling those that now bring the casualties and coffins back from Afghanistan

International telephone communication was still erratic, no internet, so no means of letting the family in the UK know that, at last, after three date changes, we were actually *en route*. To add to the joys of life a cable arrived from my father-in-law the day before we were to entrain for Singapore, which read, 'We are about to leave for Australia, house and staff at your disposal, Terry will meet you. Bring pearls for mummy's Christmas present. Temporary nanny hired' It was signed 'Matthew'.

Translated this indicated the parents-in-law were off to Australia - he had just been appointed Chairman of BOAC - at the time a loss-making corporation, and told to make it viable.

House at our disposal sounded good, theirs was a lovely country property set just outside the village of Beare Green in Surrey. I wondered what the 'staff' would turn out to be, my mother-in-law, not easy to work for, hired and fired with amazing rapidity. Terry, the chauffeur who had helped me depart, had obviously survived, it would be nice to be met. Temporary nanny! Bless papa-in-law.

Singapore, as we would only be there on a Sunday did not hold out much promise for the purchase of pearls. I contacted George who had come over from Pahang to say goodbye and had added to my carry on, a gold cigarette case, a present for his brother. It seemed reasonable to say as I accepted this, 'I need one last favour I need to buy some pearls'.

'The jeweller of His Highness. You must go to him. I will arrange.' I wrote down the address.

We entrained for the overnight trip to Singapore. Unable to find anyone prepared, at the transit barracks, to look after the children, let alone the shot gun DS insisted on taking back to England, we piled, gun and all into a taxi. The driver queried the address as well he might, for as we drove deeper and deeper into the slums of Singapore it became obvious that the premises of the jeweller was not located in a part of the city normally frequented by the European community.

Disgorging us outside a small, boarded-up shop front, the driver refused to wait. After several conservative raps on the door with no result, DS, never good in a crisis, lost it, and started ed kicking the wood. The door opened, but only a crack, it was obvious George had made contact, and a little Chinese, seeming almost in tears admitted us, then, on seeing the gun made a deep moaning noise. A second door opened and we were ushered, through a narrow passage, into a small dingy room. I have never before, or since, seen so many beautiful pearls, case after case of necklaces, earrings, brooches, and bracelets. Loose pearls filled boxes strewn over the floor lying mixed with sapphires, emeralds, and rubies.

Our host, rushed to unlock a case, then threw rope after rope of pearls at us. 'Choose,' he pleaded. 'Choose quick, please!' As we debated, the children, fascinated by the shining stones, began scrabbling amongst the boxes on the floor and the little man's pleading became even more fervent.

We chose a double rope for mother- in- law, a single for my mother, then, as it was nearly Christmas, three ropes of lesser pearls to be given as presents; a pair of single pearl ear rings for myself. When I asked 'How much do we owe', he looked astonished. 'No, no! His Highness, he no pay. Nor friends.' He added rather sadly, 'Please go now, go quick.' He may have been feeling he had got off lightly and was obviously hoping we would not scoop up the odd precious gem stone to add to our loot. 'Taxi please.' I felt I had to see this through, as though purloining goods, due to friendship with the Sultan, was a daily occurrence. I would sort it out with George later.

'Wait please. Wait.' He disappeared, then, reappearing ushered us out of the back of the building and into a waiting rickshaw.

I wondered how to clear customs. Obviously I could wear one necklace but not five. All DS was fussed about was his gun and the fact that although no longer a serving officer he had been put in charge of the troops returning on our plane.

It was to be a lengthy trip with no food on board. The plane would hop across the world and at each stop every one would disembark and eat: Singapore to Calcutta, then Karachi, Ankara, Brindisi, onward to the UK military air field at Stansted. I had decided to take milk powder for the children; why, I simply cannot remember, but a sudden brainwave occurred: the pearls could travel in the tin, after all in the early days of trading precious Chinese porcelain was packed in pepper corns as it journeyed west. The pearls could nestle hidden in milk powder.

All went smoothly until after we left Karachi when an engine failed. We landed in the middle of nowhere and everyone was evacuated before being taken to a concrete structure sited in a small oasis, a large notice proclaimed the building to be, 'Miniwaller's Hotel'.

It was, hot, dusty and the bed coverings appeared much used! This in part, as I subsequently discovered, was because they were aired, laid out on a square patch of dry earth over which camel trains walked as they arrived from the desert laden with goods. It took three days for a replacement engine to arrive. When we arrived in Ankara it was the middle of the night and bitterly cold and we were fed in a shed under the watchful eyes of heavily armed Turks. Italy next, warm with oranges on the trees in Brindisi: an overnight stop in a sort of hotel-come-boarding house while another bit of the aeroplane was repaired. Most of the troops went AWOL and got rather drunk, rounding them up was difficult and we missed our 'over Europe' slot, eventually landing in an England drenched in cold November rain.

Terry was waiting, alongside my mother longing for her grandchildren. Ah Yin had obviously prepped Nicholas before we left for when introduced she received a bow and the customary Chinese greeting, in Cantonese, 'Honoured grandmother' from him, this followed by a beaming smile and unfortunate conversational attempt from Penelope, 'You new Amah? No like your colour.' That finished her, and she climbed into her car agreeing to wait until we had recovered from the journey before attempting any further grandmotherly overtures.

The 'staff' turned out to be an extremely fat girl hired to look after two horses belonging to my sister-in-law and a very recent Austrian import recruited as a cook who spoke no English. Between them they had cleared the house of all food. There was nothing to eat, and no sign of a nanny.

As I stood and wondered where I should start the telephone rang: would DS return to the Air Base immediately to collect his gun. Resignedly Terry got the car out of the garage and drove him away.

I handed the children over to the Austrian and told her in fairly forceful German to find something and feed them before cornering the horse girl and demanding to know why there was no food. It transpired that, yes, Lady Slattery had left a list and money, she had shopped but they had eaten everything because we had not arrived when she had been told we would. There was no money left, and no, she knew nothing about any 'nanny'.

3

Home Again

We tried to resume normal life, my mother came and went, her initial visits not a success although subsequently she became the children's favourite person. We attempted to become organised, the in-laws returned bearing gifts given at the varied functions they had attended. Re-wrapped by the following Christmas these were doled out as presents: mine a rather nice silver compact still had *'Presented to Lady Slattery on her visit to Australia'* card attached. As the Christmas before we left England I had unwrapped a dust pan and brush, admittedly from Harrods, the compact was, I felt, an improvement even though not especially chosen.

The children refusing to play in the cold wet garden, rampaged through the house. 'What happened to the nanny?' demanded Mathew after several days of frustration. I explained I had no idea, she had not appeared.

He exploded, secretaries telephoned and that evening a sort of Mary Poppins figure arrived clutching a large carpet bag, apparently her only luggage. Escorted to her room, she showed no interest in meeting the children, stating she would meet them the next day after breakfast, this to be served to her, in her room on a tray at 8:30, two soft boiled eggs. Exhausted I put the children to bed hoping things might improve.

No such luck, my father-in-law was woken very early next morning by loud noises from *his* bathroom; investigating he found the newly arrived nanny in the tub surrounded, apparently, by all the children's bath toys. Told to vacate the bath immediately, she told him she was a lost seal and refused which caused him to dial 999 and she was eventually removed in a strait jacket. Investigation revealed she had recently been discharged from an asylum. I have no idea if the secretary who had engaged her survived.

It was time we moved. We had been away long enough to have become an independent unit and choosing either grandparent's home as our base would create difficulties: there was still an armed neutrality and if either establishment was selected it would undoubtedly cause resentment in the non-chosen camp. The answer seemed to be to rent a cottage.

The one offered and to which we moved, was on an estate in Kent; originally built for a gamekeeper. It was bitterly cold for the walls were only one brick thick, and cost a fortune to heat.

The Malayan contract had ended and the Army had discharged him, so an unemployed DS started to look for a job. Suitable medical ones were non-existent but eventually he was offered a post as Medical Officer to the Gas Board. 'Where will we live?' I enquired.

'Sheffield.'

I was rather hazy even about *middle* England, and knew *nothing* of Yorkshire, so telephoned a cousin who had always appeared intimately acquainted with every part of the British Isles. 'Tell me about Sheffield.'

His reply did not inspire confidence, 'All I know is that if your luck is in, you go through it very fast on an express train.'

DS had been awarded an MBE for his work in Malaya and accompanied by his parents we set off for the Investiture. I had thought I might be pregnant but realised all was not well when I visited the loo at Buckingham Palace! What a place to start a miscarriage. I survived the ceremony only to be dumped in a nursing home to be tidied up afterwards. I recovered, my mother agreed to house the children and after moving them to Devon I drove north to start house hunting.

Still the epicentre of the Steel Industry and often described as 'Hell surrounded by seven hills' the city of Sheffield and its surrounds were not immediately inspiring but then I found the Lady Bower Inn. Nestling below the hills of the Peak District, adjacent to the 'in winter, impassable' Snake Pass, the Inn, an old 16th Century building crouched at the edge of the man-made Lady Bower lake surrounded by beautiful country. Not a speck of industrial pollution visible.

Roger, the third generation landlord, was happy to offer a double room and board. Over time friendship and trust developed between us and after learning the difference between a mineral water and a half-pint glass of beer, I was allowed to help behind the bar. There was a near riot when, proudly serving for the first time I had got this wrong.

The house search did not go well, we had very little money and large expensive houses, built to house Steel Barons, seemed the only ones available: there was nothing more modest, for the area was one of long term settlement, the locals were born, lived and died in their cottages, a family member taking over the tenancy following a death.

I was very happy exploring the area and met up with the Barlow hounds, the pack owned and run by two sisters who owned a snuff business, Elsie and Anne Wilson, who, despite sharing a house, communicated only by exchanging written notes!

After a month or so, of what can only be described as idle indulgence, my mother began making, 'you have responsibilities in the shape of two children' noises. I stepped up the house search, found and bought for £1,000 a dilapidated house in a nine-acre market garden created on the site of an old farm. The yard was untouched, comprising a useful barn and pigsties.

The house, a typical Victorian Villa, stood surrounded by glassless greenhouses and an acre of rhubarb. Sadly the property was not in the Peak District but on the east of the city in a village near the home of Dame Edith Sitwell: an area where every horizon boasted one or more slag heaps. The village school was a three minute walk from the gate.

I had expected my mother to be pleased. We had somewhere to live and the children could be removed. Like my cousin she had not been particularly enthused about Sheffield, and unfortunately *The Times* published a leader on pollution informing the world that the annual industrial fall-out in the Sheffield area was calculated as being one ton to the acre. This, she stated, was not acceptable for her grandchildren who by now, after two months in her care and that of a 'brought out of retirement nanny' could speak, dress and behave as English children should.

As usual under a slight parental cloud we moved in, I bought a double bed base, old metal spring variety, from a rag and bone man, splashed out on a new mattress and begged spare furniture from all and sundry. As we unpacked long crated wedding gifts we discovered fifteen cooking trays; however there is a use for everything, and tin trays make excellent toboggans. We were in a land guaranteed winter snow!

We civilised the house, cleaned out the cellars then began to attack the broken green houses and salvage anything useful. Their central beds were planted with some of the most beautiful in-curling Chrysanthemums I had ever seen: in full flower at Christmas a bunch made a wonderful gift.

I had hoped the horse repair work, begun in Malaya, might be accepted but despite a racing community associated with Doncaster no one was really interested. While trying to sell the idea to various trainers I met Eddie M. who kept his string in the centre of Doncaster racecourse, often using anything empty, including his dining room, to house a horse if he ran out of boxes. It was not unusual, if riding work, to have to extract your mount either through the front door or persuade it to duck down in order to squeeze under the low lintel of a pig sty.

Eddie did send several 'past their sell by date' animals to me in the hope I could put them together, but they were all quirky and after being bolted with, rubbed up against a wall as one tried to scratch me off, also kicked and bitten, I reluctantly decided on self-preservation and parted company with both the trainer and his horses. This was just as well as the child count rose to four, Simon or Sam arrived to be closely followed by a second daughter christened Jennifer but now known universally as Rabbit.

Before they arrived, and as the older two became more proficient, I had got sick of running with their ponies and decided I needed four legs to carry me so I borrowed a trailer and set off for a mixed sale at Doncaster. Buying a horse because it has a nice head is neither the most sensible nor most scientific reason to purchase, but the moment I saw Sebastian's head I knew I wanted him. A rich chestnut, white blaze, hogged mane, his confirmation that of a genuine old fashioned Irish cob, he stood around 15 hands with a leg, ending in a white sock, at each corner. I never had a moment's regret: he was an admirable lead rein escort, carried me through two pregnancies hunting with the Barlow, Grove and Rufford, High Peak, Meynell, and the Furness Blood Hounds. What he did not go over he went through, on one occasion hunting in Devon with the Torrington Farmers the field was baulked by a bank topped by a visually impenetrable hedge, the shout from behind - for hounds were in full cry - was, 'Do 'e go fust Mary and make an ole, an us 'll foller thee!' Uphill he refused to go faster than at trot but made up ground both downhill and on the flat.

Animals accumulated: chicken, sheep, goats, cats, dogs, pet mice and of course ponies, acquired from Mansfield market, the venue of a monthly horse and pony auction, the likes of which have all but disappeared today other than possibly Appleby Fair.

The majority of the vendors were genuine Romany gypsies and I was lucky, for when it became known I repaired people and animals I was often invited to visit a camp to do just that; long dog injuries were a completely new field. Acceptance over time was a privilege, and it was possible when working to gain snippets of information concerning age-old methods of animal husbandry including herbal remedies, nothing written just knowledge handed down. It's amazing what a cabbage poultice can do for a filled leg!

On one occasion, the pony purchased - having behaved like an angel at the sale - turned, within a few hours of arrival in our yard, into a monster. Back she went to the next sale, with

Sebastian. Confidential cob.

hogged mane, pulled tail and white blaze dyed black she looked different. I persuaded a pint-sized, red haired boy, to show her off, and with him on her back she presented as a classy animal. Amazingly she was bought by the original vendor and I made five pounds on the deal. It was not until many years later, when he trained a horse for me in Lambourn and we were reminiscing, that I realised the boy I had paid to ride her at the sale was, in all probability, Brian Smart.

The summer holidays were spent at my childhood home, with my mother, in North Devon; the journey from Sheffield was tedious: a long wheel based Land Rover packed with dogs, mice, currently rescued bird or animal and four children pulled a trailer with two ponies *and* Sebastian all squashed in; unfortunately as he journeyed, leaning against the side of the trailer, over the years a slight bulge developed making lifting, lowering or securing the ramp very difficult.

Animals accumulated

Devon was local shows and gymkhanas, sea, sailing, prawning, swimming and surfing. It usually started to rain the day we arrived but this made no real difference. The house was expandable, plenty of drying space, the nursery exactly as it had been in my childhood: books, toys and games all stacked away in the toy cupboards waiting to be loved and used again. There were of course disasters when something very special got broken, one such object an Ostrich Egg, brought back from Africa by my parents, it had survived my childhood, but succumbed to the poor catching of the two youngest.

Life in North Devon could be unconventional and on occasions different, for my mother had a number of eccentric friends. One of these collected stressed Zoo animals and if she ran out of space moved them to friends to be housed. On one occasion there was a reluctant Llama in the garage, why it spent a great deal of time lying down was of concern until one day there it was suckling a baby. On another, a seal requiring hourly hosing was dumped. Eventually the son of the Zoo lady bought her an empty farm converting it into a mini Whipsnade. The stressed animals sent to Devon from other larger Zoos, were, to all intents free ranging. Visiting the Zoo was meant to be child-pleasurable entertainment, and perhaps I should have remembered my own experience at Edinburgh Zoo but it was not until years afterwards I discovered the children had dreaded these visits. The animals were supposed to be in a rehabilitation programme, because of this their behaviour was neither curtailed nor controlled, a feature particularly exploited by the young chimps, who, rampaging freely, leapt onto the young visitors tearing clothes and pulling hair.

Sadly the Zoo had to be closed following endless complaints from locals who did not appreciate waking up to discover that varied escaped specimens, ranging from snakes to monkeys, had taken refuge in their gardens.

Summer 'musts' included the Donkey Derby held at Westward Ho! and a visit to the annual Fair in Barnstaple, spoils from the latter often goldfish, necessitating careful conveyance during the long drive home.

Back in the North there were plenty of other children of similar ages around and I fell into the normal motherly routine of entertaining. We held miniature pony trials, birthday fireworks, and Christmas parties. Not too many disasters other than taking five to see Father Christmas and discovering I only had four when I unloaded at home: speeding back into Sheffield I found my brain making up excuses to explain her possible demise, but there was no need to explain anything - there she was still sitting at the feet of Father Christmas gazing upward.

The children's meet of the Barlow Hounds was usually held at Oakes Park, an old Steel Baron's property at the time well on the outskirts of Sheffield. The house had been inherited from a great aunt by Tom and Hilary Bagshaw, still alive when they were summoned to look after her she inconveniently departed life a few days before they would have escaped death duties.

The house was huge and decaying but Tom and Hilly existed valiantly while trying to recreate the life-style of the early 1900s which they felt the house deserved. Their highland dance evenings were fun but not really much of a success because the 'needle' of the hand-wound gramophone, would leap from the record as the drawing floor began to heave in response to our reeling efforts.

There were no modern kitchens in the house and cooking was done on an enormous coke-fired range. Once, there was a never to be forgotten evening when a *Cordon Bleu* friend was visiting. I do not remember the reason for the celebration but the food had been unwisely prepared in the old copper pans twenty four hours before the party. When heated, because the copper had caused the food to ferment, it had become tryfid-like exploding from the pans and creeping stealthily over the entire ground floor.

I'd had, for some time, a mild niggle of apprehension when I actually remembered the existence of my Edinburgh-based aunts and this increased when the Bagshaws arrived to care for their's. Mine, my father's spinster sisters, were also getting older, hand knitted socks arrived for everyone at Christmas and we kept in touch by letter. To them, the telephone was for emergencies only as they considered it an extravagance.

Although I did write and send photographs I knew in my heart I should visit.

Suddenly one died to be followed, a few days later, by the other, and consumed by guilt I travelled north for their funerals. On leaving the graveyard I was taken aside by a very elderly man who informed me he was in charge of their affairs. 'Will you be wanting me to continue?' he enquired. He was their Agent, a Mr Mushett: it transpired I had inherited their house and several properties in the Royal Mile. Obviously I needed to stay on in Edinburgh and sort things out.

The properties turned out to be a number of very derelict tenements, most with demolition orders pending. Those habitable appeared to be housing past employees of the family, and when I visited with the agent they fell upon me asking for repairs ranging from new roofs to new ceilings, and from new baths to inside loos.

There seemed to be endless problems. I'd never heard of *feu duties* - the Scots equivalent of English ground rent - which in England is normally paid in pounds sterling but there were several in Edinburgh for which annual payment was a live cock and hen, apparently no one had thought to change this by substituting a monetary value. For years the agent had solemnly and annually purchased a cock and a hen delivering them to the descendant of the original benefactor, in one case this had been happening since the mid 1700s; down the years it must have cost a small fortune!

The rents were pitiful and I realised why the telephone had not been used by the Aunts.

DS came up and we sorted the house finding silver squirreled away in knitting bags, household accounts from the turn of the century, endless books filled with nameless photographs. Several elderly bodies, claiming to have 'looked out for the Miss Millers as if they had been their own' appeared daily, each leaving with something that they 'had loaned' and quite a lot they probably had not. We burnt the rubbish and the removers arrived to pack, collect and store the pictures, furniture and other items we decided to keep. It was a pity we did not insure the paintings as when they were eventually delivered, and after two years of storage, those by the Scottish portrait painter Rayburn had been 'replaced'. Similar but not identical ancestors stared out from their gilded frames.

Eventually the lawyers took over. I hoped the sale of the house would at least cover the repairs and tenant appeasement costs. All went well, and it even looked as though there just might be a bit left, until a frantic call from the solicitor: the people who had bought the main house were digging foundations for an extension and had dug up bones, both animals and human. There might need to be a murder enquiry, and the police had been notified. Travelling once again to Edinburgh I met and explained to all parties concerned that both my father and his brother had been medical students; my father also going on to study veterinary medicine. As a child I'd been told how they had bought specimens to help their studies, they had probably buried them in the garden. No, I did not think a mass murder grave had been discovered. Eventually, particularly as none of the individual bones matched up, this explanation was accepted.

I cannot remember what prompted me to invest in a pedigree Shetland mare but Riora arrived, followed by Heather Honey, to become known as Fussy. Of all the differing pony breeds Shetlands are undoubtedly one of the most exasperating yet at the same time one of the most entertaining.

One thing inevitably leads to another, and when the two eldest children out grew them, child 3, Sam, announced he was never going to ride, settling for Guinea Pigs. By then I had bought Bramble, and while pedigree Shetlands are predominantly black, she was a lovely silver grey. Child 4, Rabbit, was keen to ride at a show, Bramble was pulled out of the field, bathed, and off we went to Lincoln County. To my horror when her mane was un-platted (native breeds are shown with their manes free) a number of dead lice needed to be brushed out. Yet to my astonishment we were placed second in the lead rein class by Mrs Gosling a notable pony judge, probably the only Shetland ever to be so honoured!

After this Rabbit lost interest and so Bramble joined the other two mares, all three were pedigree so it seemed reasonable to breed and fortunately the stud at Chatsworth was amenable to visiting mares. I was invited to see their stallion and met Debo

Devonshire, the meeting resulted in a long and lasting friendship.

Anyone who has bred a foal knows the feeling of excitement as the day draws near, anxious visits to the paddock usually on seemingly the wettest or coldest night of the year, then a bundle on the ground beside the peacefully grazing mare. In the case of a Shetland, one creeps, on hands and knees, then, torch directed to the rear end, the burning question: what has arrived, Hector or Hermione? Sadly probably a Hector, Hermione could have joined the brood mare band.

We did keep our first foal - a colt of course - and he was named Oirag, Gaelic for Cloud Berry. Amazingly he was quite successful, even winning his class at the Royal Show.

The two elder children progressed onto larger ponies. This was a good area as there were plenty of local hunter trials, shows and gymkhanas to keep them occupied. Sam showed his guinea pigs and Rabbit just came along because she had to; if unlucky she was put on a pony to compete in the lead rein gymkhana classes. There was never spare money for clothes and the children made do with other people's out grown or discarded riding gear. To my consternation a Black Jacket, rather than a Tweed, appeared in the show ring: there was no way I could afford these. I was mortified on one occasion when a friend, Jean Hope, arrived at a small show with her daughter correctly clad. Enquiry revealed she had cut up her husband's dinner jacket!

The market garden that went with the house had not really been profitable despite my harvesting the rhubarb. To take the crop necessitated pulling each stem individually, cutting off the leaf and then making bundles of the sticks each of which had to weigh fifteen pounds. These then had to be transported to a local factory. Mine, when gathered, filled the back of the long wheel based Land Rover. I drove proudly to town, but imagine the deflation when, on arrival, I found the factory yard filled with enormous lorries from Lincolnshire, each with trailers attached, transporting literally hundreds of tons of Rhubarb. End of that money making hope!

With four children and too many unprofitable animals life was continually becoming more expensive. School fees were

Investing in Shetland Ponies. Why?

Above: Bramble inspects Oirag - Cloud Berry - as a foal.

Below: Cloud Berry wins.

on the horizon yet all available physiotherapy jobs were full time. None of my schemes for income boosting - Market gardening, breeding ponies, delivering milk, working in a specialist rose nursery - had really taken off. Incidentally never buy 'bumper bundles' of roses usually advertised cheaply in the New Year: in my experience they consist of grafted briars that have not taken, with stems cut down to two or three inches to disguise this - you can end up with a jungle of viciously thorned bushes that will never flower!

Just when money was urgently needed, a lucky break. I had kept in touch with Mrs Vidler, head of the Physiotherapy School at St Thomas's, and out of the blue she telephoned to say the principal of The Lady Mabel College of Physical Education at Wentworth Woodhouse, Elma F Casson, needed a Physiotherapist and she had offered my name. The appointee would be required to treat student injuries, and also lecture to the aspiring PE teachers as the Government had decided to close a number of specialist schools and relocate some pupils within general schools. This meant the PE teachers, who seemed to look after general health, needed to be taught the basic physical limitations associated with some of the medical and physical conditions they might encounter in their pupils.

'Any idea of the sort of conditions they might meet?' I enquired wondering frantically where I had last seen any of our Medical Books. 'Oh ask your husband,' then as an afterthought, 'You *are* still married to that Doctor?'

'Yes'.

'He's in industry isn't he? He must know about special needs. Just remember to teach them it is stupid to allow an epileptic to climb to the top of a rope in the gym: that sort of thing.' With that she rang off.

The job was ideal, the College was only about a half hour drive from home and I could arrange my hours to fit in with the children's lives. The periods of attendance for study were similar to those of a University so not only would I be free during the holidays but would also be paid. Tell me what other job gives you about sixteen weeks paid leave in a year!

The great thing about any new job is that you usually gain invaluable experience. I had been athletic rather than academic at school, and had a reasonably wide exposure to most sports having attempted to play tennis, hockey, lacrosse, cricket and squash, enjoyed gym particularly vaulting, and had also fenced, played golf, and been involved in track athletics. This background experience was useful when I joined the Wentworth Woodhouse team, participation and previous exposure coupled to an interest in muscles usually enabling me to relate many of the student injuries to faulty technique.

The linkage of poor technique to muscle injuries was a radically new concept in the world of PE and led to extensive discussion with other members of staff. We reviewed the exercise routines, making changes to ensure training programmes were appropriate for differing sports.

The staff were able, as their own understanding of anatomy improved, to appreciate the vastly differing ranges of movement present in each individual and also to accept that some physical problems, were unavoidable when related to conformation and range of available joint movement. Even, in some cases to poor balance perception.

When treating students it became increasingly obvious that for successful outcome it was essential to constantly relate function, good or bad, both to body conformation and the development of individual muscles. This learning curve was not only helpful at the time but was invaluable later when treating ballet dancers not to mention animals.

Wentworth Woodhouse had been the seat of the Earls Fitzwilliam and the famous equestrian portrait of Whistlejacket, an anatomical masterpiece by Stubbs, hung in the Great Hall. The painting, originally commissioned to include George III riding the horse, had either never been finished, or Stubbs had just not bothered to add the King. Able to study the portrait, noting the anatomical excellence and portrayal of muscle, life-like in execution, I suddenly realised how foolish I had been not to have linked, as I was now doing with human athletes, conformation, muscle development and function when mending racehorses in Malaya.

I was going to start working with horses again. I was certain I would, but 'when' I was not so sure. This certainty was then further endorsed when a new breed of horse entered my life.

The Chatsworth Estates added the Haflinger to their woodland enterprises. Their Head Forrester had been having difficulty retrieving felled trees from the high scarps. It was before the invention of agricultural tracked vehicles, and nothing could climb over the slippery shale to pull the trunks down to the saw mills. On holiday in Austria he had seen some Haflingers at work and realised they would be ideal so several mares and a colt were imported. The Austrian Breed Society requested a British branch be formed as they wished to retain breed standards world-wide. After visiting the Folenhoff in Austria where I was privileged to be trained by Herr Schweisgut, then director of the Austrian Haflinger Society, I was invited to become the UK Breed Inspector.

Herr Schweisgut was an exemplary teacher, nothing involving conformation or movement escaped his eagle eye, I learned so much under his tutelage and at last began to realise how to begin to put together some of the many pieces of the jigsaw puzzle of knowledge I had amassed while working with horses and ponies over the years.

Life Changes

Life became complicated with the end of my marriage to DS, necessitating temporary relocation to Devon where my mother nobly housed the remnants of mine and the children's lives, which included furniture, dogs, and horses. Then, as when marrying a Catholic first time round, I announced I was to marry a divorcee, I once again incurred her displeasure.

Philip Bromiley, NPB, was a Director of British Steel and the role of Director's wife was, I found, irksome. I was not cut out for trying to upstage other wives at overseas forays held in the guise of conferences, but which seemed, to my inherent Scottish frugality, a complete waste of money in an industry teetering on the brink of financial collapse.

Not only were we based in London - so no animals - but there were endless very lengthy dinners, these a nightmare particularly when obligatory manners (family training and Miss Randall) demanded that out of politeness you make conversation with the man seated to your right only to discover he is intent on talking across you, to the man on your left. To relieve the boredom and to pass the time I began to amuse myself by likening my dining companions to Beatrice Potter animals but had to abandon that ploy when found I was about to address the spitting image of Pigling Bland, seated on my left, as Pigley Wigley.

Management of the Welsh division was obviously promotion for NPB; accommodation, similar to Grace and Favour quarters went with the job and we set off for Mathern Palace. Sited on the north bank of the Bristol Channel, just below the mouth of the navigable River Wye, not far from Chepstow Castle, it was an amazing structure. Built in the Middle Ages as a fortified Palace for a Welsh Bishop the walls were several feet thick and sported a watch tower from which, research suggested, a beacon had lured treasure ships returning from the Indies to their death on adjacent shoals, their salvaged cargoes ensuring increased wealth for the incumbent, possibly even for the Church. The Chapel at neighbouring St Pierre has both roof and pews fashioned from the timbers of such wrecks.

Local investigation exposed a number of interesting pieces of information. I have no idea if the clergy of the time were meant to be celibate but a quote from a Will suggested they probably enjoyed life to the full, the text on the old parchment document stating: 'I bequeath to my serving wench, who has oft warmed my bed, a gold piece, my palfrey and my fur mantle.'

A breath-taking discovery, in an old wood chest, was a set of Easter Vestments, painstakingly and beautifully hand embroidered with spring flowers, birds and insects; crumbling documentation suggested they had been embroidered by a nun in France and sent to Wales to be worn, at Easter, by her brother during his ecclesiastical stewardship at Mathern. Examined by the Royal School of Needlework the dating of the threads confirmed the work as executed in the mid 1700s.

Mathern had stables so when we moved I was able to collect the horses from Devon. The space also meant Rabbit could have a dog, a promise made at the time of the divorce and not yet fulfilled. My younger son reminded me of this as we were packing up the London flat with Rabbit due home from school in two days: she was expecting a puppy to be waiting.

The flat was in Knightsbridge so I fled to the pet department at Harrods. In a cage sat a red Daschund puppy, after enquiring his price I sat down feeling weak and wrote a cheque. A taxi was willing to take us back to Winstay Gardens, I marched into the flat and set my purchase on the floor, 'There' I said 'Puppy procured'. My younger son looked, 'Only you mother, only you, could buy shop soiled goods from Harrods'. 'What DO you mean?' 'Look at his tail.' I looked: his tail had a bend in the middle; it still wagged but never grew straight!

We settled in, hunted with the white hounds of the Curre. The Broom family lived practically next door. I mended the odd horse for them, rode some youngsters - falling off a lot - thick enough not to realise I was only put up on things shunned by other members of staff.

The Mathern period passed without too much incident, other than one memorable disaster when we had filled the house with guests for the Welsh Grand National - a race, to be won many years later by Carvills Hill after I had 'mended' him under the watchful eye of Martin Pipe.

On this occasion there had been a lengthy dinner the previous evening and I woke with a thick head, scarcely able to comprehend the information I suddenly heard tacked onto the eight o'clock news: all racing cancelled. A glance outside showed deep snow. Lunch for twenty was already in the box, at the racecourse, the staff having been told that after breakfast they would not be needed.

Luckily most guests slept in, and a cold lunch of sorts was assembled, before the electricity - never good at Mathern - shut down, and there was not even Telly to keep guests amused. Around mid-day loud banging on the front door heralded an arrival. Wondering who on earth it could be I slid the back the bolts and, opening the door, enabled two snow covered figures to stamp in. Horror of horrors, unexpected and unannounced, the head of British Steel, Monty Finneston had turned up with his wife. They had been guests at a party given by one of the local steel mills, when snow had closed the Severn bridge: they were trapped in Wales. Monty had decided Mathern was far more comfortable than a hotel, and he knew it was always staffed and that his rooms were meant, not only to be available but ready for him whenever he chose to arrive, night or day. A type of Lord Sugar he was not amused to find the house full.

Shortly after this the Welsh division of British Steel began to lose serious money, first a million a week resulting in savage economies, these in turn leading to strikes when the losses escalated to a million a day ending that job as far as NPB was concerned. He was not sacked but rusticated by being sent to North America: the posting, necessitating continual travel, required he be unaccompanied.

I packed Mathern, returned the horses to Devon, homed The Emperor Maximillian, bent tail and all, in the Bolton's, and flew to Canada as it seemed sensible to at least be in the same continent as NPB. I was not qualified to work in the USA, this came later, but I could work in Canada. Doctor Don Fraser, who knew James Cyriax was interested in Orthopaedic Medicine and he needed a Physiotherapist trained by Cyriax so I set off to join his practice based in St Catherine's, Ontario, south of the Great Lakes.

Arriving in November might be described as a numbing experience, I had never encountered such cold. Leaving a rented two room condo each morning, unable to afford indoor parking, I negotiated the ice rink called the car park, turned the car on, heater at full and slid back to the comparative warm of the foyer to thaw out and wait while the car shed its overnight accumulation of ice.

NPB made the odd sortie north insisting we ski, I was terrified, the worst descent one particular run called meet thy maker with moguls six to eight feet high and no way down other than negotiating them, rather different from the kind slopes of Switzerland.

Fortunately when we visited Québec my French was good enough to enable us to eat, we admired the ice sculptures and wondered what on earth had driven Wolf to scale the heights.

Working for Fraser expanded my knowledge in the musculo-skeletal field, I had a wealth of new physical injuries to treat, there were those sustained by skiers, ice hockey players, workers who rode the logs as they travelled by water from forest to mill, workers from the local paper mill.

There were unusual cases, one patient had been hospitalised following a near fatal accident sustained when he had ridden out to inspect cut timber in an area of forest several miles from a mill. The logs, huge trees, are laid one on top of another in piles to dry after being cut. The forester, had climbed up a pile to inspect those at the top, then, as he scrambled down, the pile started to roll and he was left hanging head down trapped by his lower legs. Several hours later, after his horse had returned rider-less a search party set out. When I was asked to see him he had been in hospital for about a month and was about to go home in a wheel chair. It was arranged I would treat him at home; he was a night-mare, nothing was right, no that was impossible, no, why should he bother, his life was over. The only thing he was interested in were his horses, visiting them seemed therapeutic, one day while pushing him to the stables and while he went on moaning I lost patience, 'ok today you are getting on a horse', stunned silence. Fortunately there were two strong men in the yard heaving trees around as though they were spillikins, I explained I needed help, I wanted 'the patient' lifted onto a horse. In answer to a startled query, 'NO, no need for a saddle, just lift him on'. Horses are amazing, the one we chose sniffed him as he sat in the wheel chair then stood like a rock as he was manhandled aboard.

It was obvious he was not going to fall off for without thinking he sat up straight, in balance, suddenly he said, 'His back is warm, I can feel it through my trousers'. There was no point in telling him everyone thought sensation had returned to his legs, but it had taken familiar contact for him to appreciate this. 'I should walk him round the yard before he gets bored', I suggested, then 'Time to get off', he commented after a couple of circuits. As we stood, ready to help him dismount, he threw his leg over the withers without thinking and slid off, luckily caught by the helpers on landing as his knees did give way. I ceased to need to go and treat him as from that day on he rode for increasing periods recovering full use of both legs in about six weeks.

Having been denied contact with horses in St Catherine's suddenly I had access to a stable-full offering an ability to explore the locality on horseback riding out in the company of a forester who turned out to be a David Attenborough type character, both a naturalist and conservation expert.

The locality was completely unspoilt, the forests had a scenic beauty of their own, there was water everywhere, tumbling streams leading to endless small lakes. The precision with which Beavers gnaw to fell a chosen tree needs to be seen to be appreciated as do their dams. In the spring there were new birds, new flowers, a wealth of fantastic experiences all the result of unconventional therapy.

Karen Strong, an International, long distance, competition cyclist sought help from Fraser. Fortunately my identifying the reason for a chronic knee problem enabled a cure, but only because, remembering Wentworth Woodhouse, I watched her technique while she rode her bike. My part in her recovery cheered up the winter for me because the Canadian cycling team, of which she was an important member, made training forays to Florida to escape the winter cold, I was delighted to be invited to accompany them to the warmth; to begin with, despite Karen's enthusiasm, the young men were a little unsure, the term 'massage' probably associated with erotic relaxation in a suitable establishment, certainly not given by a woman their mother's age, wearing a white coat. They soon began to realise massage helped tired muscles, and despite some resistance from Fraser, I spent a number of long week-ends with the team at their training area near Orlando in Florida learning a great deal about competitive cycling.

As the Canadian weather began to suggest spring was on the way we flew off for the final session; everyone had seemed rather excited in the departure lounge and it was whispered there was surprise in the offing. Never in my wildest dreams could I have predicted the surprise, in the hold was a bike for me so that, it was explained, 'I could ride with them and really experience the buzz of a long distance racing cyclist!'

By now their short rides were 50 miles, on previous trips I had travelled in their wake, relaxing comfortably in the open back of the support vehicle, plucking and savouring the odd orange from boughs overhanging the training roads along which we drove.

Nothing to be done, I had cycled in London as a student but that was years ago, I just hoped I might survive. Lady Luck came to the rescue, as the bikes were unloaded from the aircraft's hold one fell off the luggage wagon, before this was appreciated it was run over and crushed by the driver of huge refuelling truck. In magnanimous tones, while hiding my relief, I was able to say to the distraught owner/rider, 'Please, please borrow mine'.

Work Overseas

By the time NPB was recalled to the UK and 'retired' my children had either embarked upon a career or were at boarding school. We bought a small flat on the river in Fulham, just room in a postage sized garden for the Harrods purchase, The Emperor Maximillian who had enjoyed his stay in The Bolton's while we were away.

Bored out of my mind with nothing to do, a return to work was appealing. I went to see James Cyriax (Jimmy) at his rooms in Harley Street, luckily he needed a Physiotherapist. He was growing older and had decided he wanted to promote his brand of Orthopaedic Medicine Internationally; this idea, when I joined his team, had recently been fuelled by the fact he had successfully treated a wealthy lady from North America. A director of Kodak, she offered to fund a trip, even set up a Cyriax Foundation in North America.

It was obvious a teaching group to run overseas courses was needed. Jimmy decided Bernard Watkin who worked with him could hold the fort in London for short periods, while he, Jimmy, would travel to deliver the theory lectures, accompanying physiotherapists, probably three, would teach his manipulation and massage techniques; there would be an option, in the lecture package, for one of the therapists to remain for several weeks to continue educating and working with those interested. Having recently done this in Canada I was selected as a teaching member of the team with the added responsibility of overseeing the practical aspects of the courses, this included ensuring he turned up on time.

He was tiresome to travel with, demanding English bacon for breakfast wherever we landed up; refusing to get up, or even consider his tight schedule until he had downed a bacon based repast, suitably prepared and served English style, delivered to him in bed. This caused so many hassles that in the end his bacon travelled with me, in my brief case.

In tandem with the bacon problems was the fact that green was the only colour he would tolerate, underwear, suits, shirts, ties, shoes, socks, when we arrived if he was given a Hotel room with no green in the décor, he sat on his suitcase and sulked until a green room was found.

The early trips were successful, then as the word spread requests for courses escalated and I was lucky enough to be dispatched to lecture to, and work with, Physiotherapists all over the world.

The fact that work has taken me to so many countries to treat humans and latterly both humans and their animals has enabled an insight into the real lives of many peoples rather than one of merely looking in from the outside, as tends to occur, if visiting as a tourist.

The work although fascinating can be lonely, for wives never seem to display quite the same level of friendship after you have worked on their husband and they realise, as treatment often necessitates their having had to strip off, you must have seen 'their man' in his under pants. Why, I wonder, are these often faded, frayed, even full of holes!

America
In the USA, somewhat ridiculously, examined by those I was teaching, I took and passed their relevant exams enabling me to add, RPT Registered Physical Therapist, (USA), to my qualifications, fortunately this also cut the costs of insurance.

Working in California while instigating a programme for back cases at the Peninsular Hospital, I met an outstanding Neurosurgeon, Jerry Javer, who allowed me to watch him operate on back cases.

The low back is constructed from five bones balanced one upon another held firmly in place by tiny local muscles. In some instances acute back and/or leg pain necessitates operative intervention to remove the cause of the pain, usually a damaged disc. Following any form of back injury, operative or not the bones become unstable due to muscle weakness. Without local stability larger muscles are unable to function efficiently leading, in many instances, to post-operative failure.

At open operation it was possible to actually view the deep muscles. Case after case presented with a similar pattern, the multifidi the deepest and most important layer had more or less vanished.

This muscle deterioration is now accepted as an associated feature of low back disease, then it had not been recognised, but as we studied, observing cases post-operatively, we began realise the full significance of the muscle loss. Jerry gradually became certain, just like Jimmy, that no treatment or operation could be wholly successful until the muscles within the damaged area were targeted and strengthened; this necessitated choosing appropriate exercises. The difficulty was to identify which exercise or activity influenced these minute, supporting muscles.

Eventually a group of students at Stamford University, where Jerry taught at the Medical Faculty, were persuaded to have needles inserted into the muscles of their low backs. During activity the electronic data supplied would enable the firing pattern of all muscles to be recorded.

The exercises and activities chosen were drawn from those suggested in the many books on The Back; we tried back extensions, leg lifts, abdominal exercises, in fact put the volunteers through the entire gambit of procedures considered to strengthen the low back. No matter what the students did no real activity was recorded in the important, deep muscles.

Watching one victim who appeared to be standing still, other than he was lifting one foot slightly off the floor, while keeping the leg stiff, then doing the same with the other, I wandered over to ask what he was doing. Glancing at his recorder I saw, to my amazement, the little muscles were working furiously. 'Please' he begged, 'please I need to go to the bathroom'.

The simple activity, his hopping, stiff legged, from foot to foot, the result of his bathroom need, demonstrated active contractions in the vital, tiny, supporting muscles of the area, known today as the body core! Most of the time the core muscles work in a static manner, that is they tense or lock, so maintaining stability of the bone column comprising the low back, but to build, they must become active.

From this experiment it became obvious that the simple activity, today called the hip hike, was the key to successfully strengthen the vitally important, tiny muscles, of the low back. It is so simple, stiffen knee and ankle, then lift a foot just off the floor, only one inch is enough, put it down and lift the other foot, just six times each side, the activity does not need time out of a busy life to 'do exercises'. A reasonable formulae seems to be, lift each foot six times, on the hour, every hour, for six weeks.

Germany

Ebehart and Ilse Just were the Cyriax course hosts, he a physician, she a Physiotherapist, when I arrived Ebehart said he felt he must tell me he had been a member of Nazi youth fighting, as a dedicated member of Hitler's army, in the war. If I did not wish to work with him he would quite understand. I suggested there seemed no point in raking up the past, the war was over, England and Germany were in a state of mutual co-operation, the three of us had a common goal, to improve the quality of life for our patients.

Working in a different country can always be a massive learning curve if you are sufficiently open minded. The Just's had built a beautiful clinic at the foot of a mountain range, overlooking a lake, the atmosphere so peaceful patients relaxed visibly on arrival.

They had incorporated a number of new, somewhat revolutionary, treatment ideas and had instigated a differing, rather than conventional approach, toward therapy far more akin to that associated with Chinese philosophy, treat the whole, not just the symptoms. One of their aims was to reduce patient stress so counselling was included. They also insisted patients must accept they must make an effort, taking responsibility for problems associated with their health. At the initial consultation it was emphasised that unless a patient was prepared to co-operate they could not be treated successfully, therapy alone was not the answer.

Accustomed to the attitude all problems were someone else's fault this was very refreshing. We arranged an interesting work schedule combining their new approach with the Cyriax methods of examination and treatment. It was an extremely successful approach and one I have retained, although I am the first to admit it is a shock to some to realise they need to make an effort if they want to recover. With animals explaining to owners is particularly difficult, particularly when obese dogs or horses turn up.

I know plain speaking can lose clients but not always: a memorable case was when eventually, in exasperation I said, 'This horse is a lump of lard, how can I tell you what is the matter. Take it away. If you like I will send a suggested diet and exercise regime with my report, and no, how can I charge you, I have done nothing'. Give the owners their due they obviously did as suggested and 18 months a letter arrive saying, 'We did what you said and the lump of lard won his first novice event yesterday. Thanks for your help'.

As the three of us got to know each other, I asked Ebehart, one evening over supper, to tell me about life under Hitler, why had he joined the Nazis? He explained that he had been the son of an impoverished blacksmith, a chance meeting with a friend, already recruited led him to join the Hitler youth. 'You have no idea,' he said. 'We had nothing. They gave us shoes; shoes that fitted, your own sleeping bag when camping, you did not have to share, at home we were three in a bed, there was food, three meals a day, there was organised sport, games, swimming, skiing, playing soldiers, always something new to look forward to.' He fought for Germany because it was, he believed, a way of thanking Hitler for what he saw as unbelievable generosity. He ending his war in France, as the Germans retreated, and he was taken prisoner. While awaiting, when the war ended, repatriation to Germany, he had been taken to visit a concentration camp. Then, while talking to me, he broke down. 'Mary I promise: we had no idea such places existed.'

I could believe this, I have no knowledge of what happens in Somerset let alone all that might be taking place locally. Are people growing cannabis in their greenhouses? Are there paedophiles in our local village? Are there husbands who beat their wives, and mistreat their children?

Returning to Germany Ebehart had visited Belsen to discover if the French camp might be a one-off. Horrified by what he saw he determined to train as a doctor and dedicate his life to helping the sick and injured. It had taken him 12 years to qualify as he had needed to work throughout his training to pay his fees.

While I was working with them I explained I felt physiotherapy could be appropriate for animals. Ilse, who had her own horse, only rode Dressage but learning I rode she invited me to ride a Grand Prix horse for the first time. It was quite an experience; although enjoyable I was not over enthusiastic, probably due to the fact I felt I was certainly not in charge.

The Justs were a kind and generous couple and to enable me have 'a little holiday' doing something they assumed I would enjoy, also because they understood everyone who rode in England hunted, they arranged I should do just that. I knew Hitler had stopped foxhunting but that a form of hunting, presumably drag, had continued

Without much thought and as I hate walking and have always considered the best way to explore new country is from the back of a horse, I agreed to 'join the hunt' particularly as I felt it would be interesting to see if the German Forests were as magical as the Canadian.

Anticipating a pleasant day with drag hounds, I set off, in borrowed clothes, to meet my mount. The experience proved to be rather different from that envisaged. We drove to a clearing in the forest and joined a group of around 40 people already mounted; one was having a foxes brush attached to the back of their coat collar. It was explained this rider, the trail setter or quarry, would be given a 30 second start and that the person who caught them and retrieved the brush had the honour of being the next quarry, they so hoped it would be me.

My horse began to leap about alarmingly as soon as the trail setter departed, half rearing, neighing, kicking out at anything near it, fighting for its head, seeming to have little in the way of manners, then, when the field set off, in response to 'gone away' blown on an English hunting horn, no brakes either. I do not ever remember being so frightened. There must have been nice wide glades in the forest, pleasant and safe to ride along, but this was obviously not the object of the chase - it was more like a bending race at full gallop. The trees seemed horribly close as they hurtled past, there was no question of choosing a line to ride, and any attempt at steering would surely court disaster. 'What should I do?' I yelled at my nearest companion in my best German. 'Lie flat and pray,' was her reply. Luckily the brush was retrieved before I was killed and as the followers regrouped and the wearer of the brush rode up, my horse immediately calmed down and nickered. 'We had so hoped you would win,' said the brush bearer. 'That is why we put you on my mare's baby: they have never been parted.'

Sweden

The Forestry industry in Sweden expressed an interest in the Cyriax approach for back problems. The work days lost to the industry, secondary to back problems, were considered excessive when compared to figures shown for other industrial work. A research centre The Rygginstitutet (Ryggin back) had been built by the forestry industry at Sundsvall in the north of the country. All employees complaining of back problems were sent there for examination and treatment. The patients were a mixed bunch, some worked in the Forest using chain saws and axes, others drove tree felling machinery, some came from the paper mills and of course there were office workers. All were resident, they were paid their normal salary but in return were expected to agree to co-operate, no matter what they were asked to do.

Assessment was not confined to patients alone, everything involved in their working environment was investigated, the work places were examined, the way they felled trees, used the chain saws or axes, drove vehicles through the forest. The office workers had chair to desk height assessed and the manner of telephone use was examined. Holding the receiver between shoulder and ear was not allowed, nothing was left to chance, and every feature of the work environment was evaluated in order to avoid a possible work-related injury.

At Rygg all patients received counselling on pain control and were taught back mechanics. They exercised in the gym, and worked in the pool. Tracks enabled orienteering through the country surrounding the complex.

To my great joy besides giving Physiotherapy in house the organisation also required staff members to personally experience the varied work environment of the patients; Mona Wåhlin the senior therapist and director considered being alongside, performing the same tasks, enabled one to analyse movement patterns and identify potential causes for injury. This broad approach has been invaluable, always consider the life style of a patient, not just their conformation and how they move, so another feature to be added when examining really an extension of the Wentworth Woodhouse protocol.

After my initial visit I was invited to return, on a consultancy basis, several times a year. I was delighted, I had fallen in love with the area for the institute was built on the edge of the forest in northern Sweden and nothing is more beautiful than a forest in each of its varied seasons. In Sweden the start of each of the four seasons is celebrated on a set date, when huge fires are built, then, when lit, people dance around them throughout the night in an almost pagan ritual, offering a welcome to the new beginning. My first was for the arrival of spring: the snow melt. We danced all night and to my astonishment, there, the next morning, peeping through the snow, were the first spring flowers.

There are unique scents from the pines in summer, the fungi in autumn are astonishing, weaving multi-coloured patterns to carpet the ground. In winter for me, moving silently on cross country skis over the snow to join and work with the foresters was a privilege. Those men were all unbelievably appreciative of the natural order of the forest in all seasons, they revered their place of work disturbing as little as possible as they felled the trees. They carefully watched the birds: had they nested in a marked tree? If so that tree must be left until the fledglings had flown. They knew the flowers: the best places for lingum berries (Swedish whortleberries) and looked for the presence of elk, recognising and leaving undisturbed their areas of fodder moss.

Coffee is a standard refreshment world-wide and a fire, kindled from birch bark, will, in seconds heat water for the beverage. This gives it a unique taste, for the brew, very black, is drunk out of mugs also carved from birch. In the extreme cold, china would absorb the coffee heat immediately: who wants cold coffee at -10 degrees or lower. Plastic, another mug alternative, becomes dangerously brittle, but with wood there is no danger of breakage.

After several near mishaps I learned to fell a tree correctly, cutting, with a chain-saw, the correct angle of the first wedge to ensure the exact fall line required. It was interesting to learn how much depends, for safety, on foot placement, this was reflected in the ground preparation, time and care were taken to ensure the tree feller cleared the area around the chosen tree efficiently to enable not only space for a correct stance to avoid back injury, but also to ensure under foot security, first while cutting the wedge, then when moving in order to cut through the trunk, for the line of cut needs to be at the correct angle to ensure the tree falls cleanly. This was a lesson in its self and I have, over the years, treated a number of tree surgeons with hand injuries, often loss of balance resultant in frightful wounds including single or multiple finger severance. Discussion suggests nowhere, other than in Sweden, do they seem to be so precise in pre-felling ground preparation.

Returning on a regular basis to monitor progress it was fascinating to see the rapid improvement in many patients after we included the hip hike exercise but there was still too many back cases amongst members of the work force who were using machines rather than felling using chain saws or axes. These men drove huge machines felling paths through the forest to enable access for other members of the work force.

Volvo, who were interested in back related driving discomfort, were re-investigating the Gate Theory. Research by Professors Melzac and Wall in 1965 strongly suggested that cyclical vibration, occurring over a period of time, in an identical, uninterrupted manner, temporarily disturbed the normal rapid and efficient communication between muscles and the brain by blocking transmission of messages at a known gate, or synapse, existing between the nerves in the body and the spinal cord. Mona Wåhlin, the senior Physiotherapist at Rhygginsttitute was able to access the work and although it took time and I suspect many people considered she was barking mad. Armed with information from Volvo she had the tree felling machines tested and the results demonstrated that, as they crept forward, felling tree after tree, a continuous cyclical resonance was created. Careful documentation indicated that the vehicle drivers appeared to damage their backs after leaving their cabs, often appearing momentarily disorientated, unsteady, tripping for no reason as they walked away over the rough ground.

It was proposed that the drivers be made to stop once an hour, get out of their machines cabs and loosen up on the ground for two or three minutes before starting again. Coincidence? I have no idea, but the incidence of back-related problems previously identified in the machine drivers, dropped by 75% when this time break was instigated.

The study was published, but unfortunately only in Swedish and German. While those two countries took note and acted accordingly, particularly in Germany, where the rest areas contain activity apparatus and are installed on all autobahn, I am doubtful if the work was ever considered elsewhere.

Alaska

Don Fraser telephoned Jimmy from Canada: could I join him in Alaska. He'd been summoned to deal with an unusual number of severe neck problems affecting USAF pilots based in Anchorage. It was essential they were able to fly in order to monitor activity in the north eastern area of Soviet Russia as America was suspicious of invasion via the Bering Straits.

On arrival our plane continued to circle the airport, rather than landing on an apparently deserted runway, closer inspection showed a swarm of small planes below us, all jostling to land it was these that were keeping us airborne. Our pilot explained landing was delayed due to excessive local traffic. It mattered not to me, our height and clarity of outside air allowed time to absorb, as if seen through a bird's eye, the amazing snow clad landscape below.

After about fifteen minutes we began our decent and looking out I saw we appeared to be making our way through an even bigger swarm of small private planes than those I had originally viewed, crackling over the intercom, as we prepared to land, suggested our pilot had had enough and was exercising authority. To my astonishment as we landed I saw a bunch of large dogs leaving a small aeroplane down an obviously purpose built ramp.

When we eventually cleared customs and left the terminal I wondered if we had arrived at a Northern Crufts, there were groups of seriously large dogs of a breed I did not immediately recognise, piles of what appeared to be harness, and masses of sleds, but why, what on earth was happening?

It transpired sled dog teams from all over the Northern Hemisphere were arriving to race from Anchorage to Nome. The race, the Iditarod, is a virtual re-enactment of the original journey made in 1925 when vital supplies of vaccine were required in Nome to combat a serious diphtheria outbreak, the life-saving serum needed to be transported from Anchorage across an unforgiving 1,150 miles of road less terrain. Flying was in its infancy, the weather apparently atrocious, and while the first part of the journey was possible by train dog teams were the only method of transport able to cover the last 674 miles. The life-giving delivery was organised as a relay, each team ran 100 miles before handing the phials over to the next team, the safe arrival of the vaccine averted an epidemic that would have killed many Eskimo children. It was a fascinating story, I wondered if time would allow me to see the start or watch a training session. The race, considered to be the most exacting in the world, is now run annually in March following the first re-enactment which took place in 1973.

Upward of 50 teams are usually entered, the mushers or drivers, each with a team of 10 dogs take between 10 and 17 days to travel the distance between Anchorage and Nome, crossing 1,150 miles of the ice bound, intervening wilderness.

I started work next day in the Catholic Hospital, the pilots all presented with very similar symptoms and this, remembering attention to work place detail in Sweden, led me to request I be allowed to look at their aircraft seats, the cause became obvious. The aeroplane was a new design, unfortunately the pilots had to turn their heads, angling them upward and to one side, in order to read a particular instrument, discussion revealed this requirement coincided with exact moment when the G force acceleration at take-off forced their heads back into the head rest; treatment was easy and I suppose the USAF moved the instrument, we never heard.

As I walked the corridors it was impossible not to notice the old sepia prints hanging on the walls all depicted small groups of nuns, clad in conventional habit and wimple but shod in thick leather boots, of a type that used to be called butcher boots, some seemed to have added an odd looking fur over-garment, others a rug, all were dragging loaded sleds across an apparently frozen snow clad wilderness.

Enquiry revealed that reports of the injuries sustained by early trappers had reached their mission in Canada, these amazing women had set out and walked, in the middle 1800s, over 600 miles from the Canadian border to Anchorage and set up a hospice to offer treatment, their pioneering unit has remained functional ever since.

As a working day ended, I was approached by a nun, 'Did she need help?' , 'No, but one of the sled dogs had sprained a shoulder jumping out of its private plane, the team belonged to her brother,' she wondered if physiotherapy might help, they had taken an X-ray, it was negative.

It was -40° F outside, I felt a white coat and ski anorak would be inadequate to withstand the cold if the dog needed to be treated on its tether. Luckily it could come to me, no one in the department seemed phased by the arrival of a large, slightly bemused but definitely irritable Husky, severely lame in front.

Although at that time still not officially treating animals the use of Physiotherapy had seemed a rational idea to some forward thinking vets I had approached. Greyhounds and coursing dogs were prone to injuries and I had 'sat in' on Paddy Sweeny, a legendary vet in the greyhound world. He had been kind enough to allow me to work on some dogs for him and these had included a number of coursing greyhounds and lurchers all prone to shoulder injuries.

The Husky moved as I had noticed my Sweeny dogs did after injuring an elbow. After explaining what I needed to try to do, I described how the dog needed to be positioned and held, it also seemed prudent to ask if his muzzle could be bandaged.

When this had been achieved I stood in front of him and grasped the lame limb just behind the elbow joint; pulling the leg gently forward, I was both thankful and gratified to feel, at the very end of the movement a subtle clunk. The noise the dog made was not exactly a polite 'thank you' but he did put the foot to the ground and walked, rather than limped away. It seemed sensible to check him the following day when, much less aggressive, he tolerated some deep massage, possibly because he no longer seemed to be in pain as when we had first met on the previous day

As a 'thank you' I was offered a once in a lifetime experience, 'would I like to drive a dog team?' What answer could there be but 'Oh! YES please'. The sensation of power, the silent rush through freezing air, the feeling of total isolation as the sled, drawn by ten dogs, hurtled, seemingly effortlessly over snow and ice was truly amazing.

I felt I had gone back in time momentarily able to appreciate the feelings experienced by those early trappers, an adrenaline rush, excitement, nothing out there but you and your dogs.

The Bernard Period
Spells in London, between overseas trips, increased a working relationship with Bernard Watkin particularly after looking at our respective 'horror scopes' in a dumped magazine in the staff room, we discovered we had been born on the same day of the same year: he an hour older than I.

As senior Physiotherapist one of my tasks was to open up 32 Harley Street, first checking the consulting rooms, then inspecting the building to see the cleaners had left everything spotless, double check Jimmy's list and sterilise, by boiling, all his gear, also pre-sharpen the needles as he refused to use any modern, autoclaved, throw away equipment. I also had to get out all the notes for that day, arrange Bernard's list and allocate patients attending for follow up treatment to those of the Physiotherapy staff best suited to deal with them.

On a never to be forgotten Monday I arrived, luckily well early and had nearly finished my preliminary work when the phone rang. Normally we only started to take calls when the secretary came in at 8:30 am but something made me answer. 'Dr Cyriax rooms'.

'Mary, this is Patsy [Jimmy's wife] he was trimming a tree yesterday and he sawed off the branch he was sitting on. He's broken a leg, has a broken nose and concussion. He's in hospital. I'm sure you can manage.' With that the phone went dead.

Where was Bernard? I telephoned Jenny, his wife, 'Oh dear,' she said. 'I was just going to let you know he's still in France. He went out to visit his father for the weekend and missed his plane.' Marvellous. Both saw a patient every half hour, and many of the lists had waited weeks for an appointment. What now? Luckily I knew the number of the house in France: timewise it was an hour earlier out there. His voice suggested I had woken him. 'B I do not mind how, but get back *please!*' Of course he did, borrowing a private plane he arrived, suave and unruffled, by mid day. Everyone worked late and he got through the two lists.

The following day Jimmy, having discharged himself from hospital, arrived dressed in a sort of toga, his face looking rather as though he had done several rounds in a boxing ring. Taking up residence behind his desk and lying back like a Roman Emperor, broken leg propped on a chaise longue, he demanded to see his patients.

We had a difficult few months while he healed; overseas trips had to be cancelled, then to cap it all the lease of 32 came up for renewal and the proposed rent rise was horrific. Almost overnight Jimmy moved his consulting rooms from Harley Street to his home in Regents Park; then, despite having turned the house upside down he had to scale down the extent of the practice: there was just not enough room for more than one doctor and one Physio.

62 Wimpole Street had a medical suite available and Bernard took this, asking me if I would join him. He explained he only wanted to work three days a week, particularly as in the

summer this would enable him commute to France where he could keep an eye on his ageing father.

The new arrangement suited me down to the ground, NPB had found a property near Lambourn. It was quite obvious he was not going to get a new job; even if titled as a Senior Director, to have been off loaded by British Steel hardly looks good on a CV and he decided country retirement was in order. The place he found was, as all Estate Agents so charmingly describe derelict properties, in need of modernisation, but it had 5 acres of paddock, some pig sties and stables. There was good riding over the Berkshire Downs which were on the doorstep. It was also near Lambourn, The Valley of the Racehorse.

Friends lived locally, many of them commuting to London, so that was obviously feasible for me. Naming the property rather unimaginatively, Five Acres, we started reconstruction. This kept NPB amused when I was in London working. After the house was habitable he made contact with Shrivenham, a large Army base literally a few miles from Five Acres and became a member of the mess, and when he indicated he was looking for something to occupy his time they put him in touch with SAFFA. The organisation was desperate for ex-army volunteers and he took on an executive role enjoying the contact with soldiers once again. I had no need to feel guilty as this kept him both happy and busy until eventually his activities were curtailed by Alzheimer's and Dementia of a severity that necessitated a care home.

When we moved, through mutual friends I met Rosie Lomax, the first woman to be granted a Jockey Club Licence, who was training from a property called Downs House. One day, while discussing racing, she asked had I ever treated horses, and I explained about my work in Malaya.

Rosie disclosed she was having an awful season, injury after injury, all of them apparently muscle related: could physiotherapy help?

Physiotherapy is not, as many people suppose, confined to the use of electrical machines. It also involves rehabilitation, which equates to re-training damaged or weak muscles following injury in order to restore both muscle strength and efficient, economic function.

Coincidently, Penelope, my eldest daughter, had just returned from working with dressage horses in Australia when Rosie approached me and agreed to see if anything else could be done to improve damaged muscle other than just using massage as I had done in Malaya. Rosie sent three 'broken race horses' to see if we could help them recover.

Flat racehorses need no basic training other than learning to balance when galloping and to carry a jockey or, if running in National Hunt races they must add jumping fences at speed when galloping.

Penelope and I discussed methods of targeting muscles and she decided to try working the horses in long reins incorporating some basic movement routines utilised during the early preparation of horses in the Classical schools of equitation, rather than riding them.

While I have no idea if the past masters of Classical Education appreciated that each individual training activity targets specific muscle groups this is certainly the case. Even if they did not appreciate this subtlety obviously they realised their structured training routines were effective because horses so worked became better balanced, stronger and generally more athletic.

The skill, if using the Classical approach, is to identify the weak muscles or muscle groups then ensure they have to work, this necessitating selection of an appropriate activity. It is useless to put a horse through several varied exercises, in a manner similar to the popular human gym circuit, and hope it works. Unfortunately horses are able to perform by changing muscle recruitment in order to comply with trainer/rider command. Following even a minor muscle problem they will continue to work as requested but can only do so by moving in an uneconomic manner, eventually this tends to result in very tiresome secondary problems leading to poor performance, usually the *cri de coeur* from trainer or rider. Rosie's horses had adopted an incorrect way of going following muscle damage with resultant poor performance.

The instigation of appropriate exercises, accompanied by massage, did improve Rosie's cripples but thinking back her yard had been one of the first to be hit by 'the virus'; her horses had all been sick; none of us understood, even considered there could be muscular side effects following viral infections, or that these could continue to affect muscle function leading to poor performance even after apparent recovery.

The 'virus' plagues the horse world, and sadly there is still no explanation nor reason for a sudden unpredicted invasion of an apparently healthy group of horses. Recently investigation of the transmission of disease from animal to man and man to animal, Zoonotic transference, has become of interest and it is now an accepted fact that this can occur. It is possible, though as yet unproven, that if a human carrying a virus coughs near a horse that horse might well, after inhaling infected air, start coughing. Discussing this recently I was interested to hear first-hand, of problems experienced by a farm that reared calves. They had been plagued by salmonella, not until they tested all employees did they isolate the cause, one worker, although showing no signs, tested positive indicating they were a carrier.

While treating a patient, himself an owner, and discussing racing I explained I had used Physiotherapy for muscle injuries when I was training my own and other horses in Malaya, also mentioning my recent attempts at trying to 'mend' injured horses for Rosie Lomax. I was interested to learn that in the valuable bloodstock industry, despite the fact there were numerous injuries, no one appeared to be doing anything positive; the common approach for most injuries seemed to be box rest, or if a tendon was involved, firing the legs then turning the horse away for a year: the latter method often representing the end of a career for a flat horse.

Before leaving he suggested if there were results to prove appropriate therapy given following injury led to improved recovery he felt the bloodstock world might be interested. Therapy would be a preferable alternative to euthanasia, which, in many instances was all that could be offered to despairing owners who did not relish the expense of having to keep an unsound horse. Another point made was the fact there were rumblings from various animal protection organisations who considered racing cruel. These were of great concern to the racing industry and any form of help enabling an injured horse to return to a useful career, not necessarily to racing, would be welcomed. These were encouraging comments.

My next patient gave me cause to wonder if one's future really is pre-ordained. She informed me she was off to take a weekend course after which she would become a Horse Physiotherapist. I found I was unusually irritated: but it *did* seem unreasonable. I, after all, had undertaken long, arduous and expensive training before being allowed to treat humans and enabling, after qualifying, to suffix my name with MCSP, Member Chartered Society of Physiotherapists. I certainly felt, despite numerous successes with horses I had treated and trained, that I had no right, as yet, to call myself a Horse Physiotherapist.

I made an instant decision. I had been messing around for too long, and action was required. Who would help? Was there no one to whom I could turn who was treating horses?

Bernard was a great browser, wandering through markets and bookshops, not necessarily buying, usually just looking. I had told him of my irritation; that I was certain someone must be treating horses. A day or two later he dropped a book on my desk with the title: *Horses' Injuries, Common Sense Therapy for Horses* by Charles L. Strong. MVO MCSP. Riveted I stared at the suffix letters, MCSP clearly printed, the author was a Member of the Chartered Society of Physiotherapists.

Keen to track him down I telephoned the membership secretary of the CSP, Chartered Society of Physiotherapists, who was distinctly frosty; the reason I later discovered, was because in 1980, Charles was the only physiotherapist to have been accorded any sort of honour, first made an MVO, then Knighted, not in recognition of his human work, but because he had invented a muscle machine that worked on horses! I did not dare to explain it was for his horse, rather than human expertise that I needed to find him.

Charles had rooms in Upper Wimpole Street and agreed to a meeting. A square well built man, although due to his age slightly stooped, he listened patiently as I explained I wanted to work with horses. His response was not auspicious, 'Go away and learn anatomy.' Then he continued, 'I have no time to teach idiots. Believe you me there are plenty of you out there. You all think it's easy - no one realises you stand in shit, take shit, you get kicked and bitten. And the vets - how they can call themselves veterinary surgeons I do not know - half of them know nothing when it comes to discussing or understanding muscles.'

I stood my ground and proffered some background information, veterinary childhood, riding experience, horse involvement in Malaya. He pounced on the fact my father had been a vet, asking, 'What was his name?' I gave it. 'Did he work in racing for Holliday at one time?' 'Er, yes.'

'Oh I met him, played a bit of polo, despite only one leg, nice chap, sensible.' Then, 'I am going to see some ponies next week. You can come along if you like.'

Association with Charles was rather a two edged sword: the Chartered Society disliked him, because not only was he treating animals (he had invented a muscle stimulator superior to the faradic battery used for human patients) but he had cornered the Royals, both human and animal, through Lord Louis Mountbatten.

The Veterinary profession hated him. He never asked permission before treating animals indicating he worked in response to Royal Command. At the time I was unaware of the Veterinary Act, this states that, no person other than a qualified veterinary surgeon may see, diagnose, or treat any animal. There is an exemption, allowing treatment of animals by a suitably qualified person, but only if the vet in charge of the case has given permission.

Following the earlier claim made by a patient, 'I will be a Physiotherapist after a weekend course,' I had immediately reported back to the Chartered Society, informing them that there were persons titling themselves Physiotherapists and working as such with no recognised training. This took time to sink in, the immediate reaction of the CSP Council being no one would do such a thing. A reasonable supposition, for in the 1980s you took people at their word, and trusted them. People simply did not behave badly or cheat.

I also requested a meeting with the Council of the College of Veterinary Surgeons explaining I wished to propose that appropriate Physiotherapy techniques could be administered to animals with veterinary agreement, always provided those treatments were given by a member of the Chartered Society of Physiotherapists. Wheels grind slowly, but eventually the organisation agreed to discuss the proposition and called a meeting requesting that the Council of the Chartered Society send a representative other than just myself. The CSP appointed Penelope Robinson; she understood negotiating, and ACPAT, the Association of Chartered Physiotherapists in Animal Therapy, a clinical interest group associated with and regulated by the CSP has much to thank her for, as by the time we met the members of Veterinary Council, she had formulated my somewhat haphazard ideas into a factual proposal.

The group of assembled vets were elderly, clearly not very impressed by the proposal; their attitude quite reasonably being, leave it to nature, given time animals got better, that was the way the profession had always worked, leave things as they were, enough troubles with new fangled ideas as it was.

One was obviously Irish and luckily into racing, I managed to mention, when asked to relate my reasons for considering Physiotherapy might be of use to treat horses, the Selangor Turf Club. 'Ever meet Jim Marsh?' the Irishman enquired. 'Yes, he allowed me to work under him.' It did not seem appropriate to say it was because of Jim we were all sitting round a Victorian table in a depressingly cold room, the walls decorated with portraits of past members of the Veterinary profession, who, bewigged in many cases, glared down from their canvass, nor to point out if Jim had not said, 'You mend f**** humans, mend the f**** horses,' I would never have considered using physiotherapy to treat my race horse's injuries.

The meeting was getting nowhere. The Irishman, probably needing to ring his bookie, suggested he talk to Jim Marsh, they would both be racing at the Curragh the following week, and he would report back. This was agreed and the Council members, stating they would call another meeting, thankfully withdrew.

4

Downs House Created & Becoming a Recognised Animal Physiotherapist

uoyed up with hope following the initial meeting I realised Five Acres lacked space and facilities. Calls from trainers in Lambourn were on the increase, Rosie had had a winner and been generous in her comments. When I learned she had decided to retire from training and put Downs House on the market I realised the property was ideal, a 20 box yard, tack rooms, a huge storage barn, turn out paddocks.

On closer inspection it appeared the house was really two, a very old back and Georgian front, far larger than we needed, the roof doubtful, central heating archaic, the rotting wood frames of the sash windows were undoubtedly letting in more air than they kept out, but the stables were in reasonable order. I decided to buy the place.

Included with the property at no extra cost were Mokey, an aged donkey, 'useful for looking after stroppy colts', explained Rosie. Sam Cat, was stated 'to live in the yard to keep down the mice'. The yard bit really was a fallacy as he moved into the house within 24 hours of our arrival. Finally Roy - the maintenance man - an invaluable asset.

It was a pity that the veterinary profession had not yet come to a decision in favour of Animal Physiotherapy (how could I know this would take another 3 years?) also, just as I paid the deposit on Downs House the financial crisis of the early eighties hit, and the interest on the bank loan I needed, originally quoted at 3½%, rose to 21½%. Added to that no one went to the auction of Five Acres and it became a second country property to maintain. I had counted on a profitable sale, and there was also the cost of the London flat. No chance of retirement from London! To survive and avoid bankruptcy I must continue to earn and try to prove Physiotherapy for injured horses was a viable option for owners as a replacement for box rest or death. To achieve effective results I realised I would require rehabilitation aids: an arena, a walker, and a swimming pool.

Martin Collins had begun experimenting with all-weather surfaces, nothing venture nothing gain, I approached him. In one of the paddocks a dressage sized arena area was railed round, the base boarded on all four sides with sleepers to retain the new surface, the top of the paddock was scooped off to make it flat and Martin filled the area with a prototype all-weather surface.

The Claydon horse walker had just been designed, the horses able walk loose in individual padded sections rather than as on the American style Hot Walker where horses walk one behind the other with no dividing panels between them attached by ropes hanging from the outer rim of a circular, revolving frame, resembling a rotating clothes drier although far larger. Viewing one of these before deciding Claydon or Hot Walker I had been to a local racing yard, and seen seven horses walking happily round the large circle of a Hot Walker, then with no warning, obviously spooked by something, they took off at full gallop, a truly frightening sight. The Hot Walker I was watching had a centrally placed on/off mechanism, the head lad, risking his life, had to dive between horses to reach the controls. After this experience that exerciser did not appeal, the Claydon seemed the sensible choice and there was a space just outside the main yard gates for the small, four pen model. No money for a floor, shaving from the boxes were barrowed out and gradually, although not ideal, they bedded down providing a safe surface.

Swimming pool next, the first salesman arrived in a huge BMW; 'No thank you' before he even reached for his pigskin brief case. 'Why', 'because your car suggests you are making very large profits, I cannot afford to keep you in the manner to which you have obviously become accustomed'. Departure of a discomforted sales man. Eventually a pool was built, the final design influenced by Ray Hutchinson MRCVS, who had built the first straight pool in the UK at Epsom. For rehabilitation he recommended a straight pool, with under water jets to increase resistance and generously shared his considerable knowledge, suggesting length, width, depth, filtration and heating.

A wash box doubled as a drying box and until funds allowed the purchase of a commercially produced solarium, infra-red and ultra violet pig lights were hung from a wooden frame, very home made but effective.

My father had always had a sand roll constructed in all the big racing yards where he had worked for he considered the best way to help horses with back discomfort was to allow them to roll, this enabling them to self-adjust any minor intra vertebral misalignment. Another plus associated with a sand roll is that horses need to be properly groomed (massaged!) to get the sand out of their coats after rolling. The area needs to be sufficiently large to avoid a horse getting cast and with this in mind four boxes 24 feet square, filled with sand to a depth of around three feet completed the immediate extras. The complex was open for business - if it ever came.

Tiresomely just as everything was completed and a few boxes were filled with resident cases, the hurricane of 1987 arrived and while the roof of the 16th Century barn lifted as I watched, the oak pegs held it together and it lowered its self-downward, returning as a complete structure to settle back at its original site; not so the roof of the sand boxes. The entire roof, 48 feet long by 24 feet wide, sailed upward and then twirling like a propeller as it dropped landwards systematically scythed all the post and rails we had just put up in the paddocks behind the yard, chopping them into match-wood. Fragmenting as it fell it spat out all the metal pins holding the individual roof sheets together, it took hours with a borrowed metal detector to find these pins. Repairs began, sadly Acts of God are not covered by insurance!

Manuela Koch De Gooreynd (Manou) joined as a part time secretary, splitting her time between us and her cousin, Johnny Ciechanowski (Chicken) who was training, in Lambourn, for Sheikh Maktoum al Maktoum.

Rosie nobly spread the word amongst the trainers that Downs House was now a rehabilitation yard, and we held an alcohol-laced open day, for the local vets. I needed veterinary co-operation as there was no way I was going to ignore the veterinary act; this meant every case required veterinary referral prior to admission. Following their yard tour and probably deciding we were unlikely to do much good but equally unlikely to do any harm the local vets agreed to allow horses under their care to either be given physiotherapy in their own yard or to become a temporary resident at Downs House.

Timing has to be attributed to luck, Garry Pickford master farrier and equine podiatrist had opened a forge in Lambourn at approximately the same time as we opened Downs House. It rapidly became obvious his skills were required, no foot no horse. Peter Baker had been shoeing our own horses but graciously admitted Garry had skills to which he did not aspire.

Following veterinary permission there was another major hurdle to overcome, racing yards are run by head lads, the horses are theirs, their word is law; steeped in successful traditional methods they were understandably suspicious of electrical muscle stimulation, magnetic fields and massage.

Head Lads
Lambourn, known as the Valley of the Race Horse, housed several notable trainers when Downs House opened, amongst them Fred Winter, National Hunt, with head lad Brian Delaney; Peter Walwyn, Flat, with head lad Ron Thomas; Nicky Henderson emerging in the Nation Hunt field with head lad Corky Browne; and not far from Lambourn, at West Ilsley, was the legendary Flat trainer Major Hern, who relied on Geordie Campbell.

I had to gain the respect of these head lads: I was a woman and racing was male oriented. Rosie had been the first woman to be granted a licence, and yes, she'd had some winners but she'd had to sell up. There was no doubt that opposition from the head lads, renowned figures, would be formidable if ordered to allow a horse to leave their yard and move into the care of an unknown. And not just an unknown but a woman, to be given therapy: something they had never heard of and did not considered necessary. They felt the need for therapy reflected lack of care on their part, and after all trainers are human, nothing is worse than a silent or grumpy head lad whose mood can affect the entire yard. On the plus side I *had* trained horses and ridden races - admittedly in Malaya, but I would be able to talk in racing parlance. Before sallying forth I recalled just how important ward routine had been at St Thomas's. I assumed - correctly - that this would apply in a racing yard.

Major Hern had bought one of the first magnetic rugs, so cumbersome it required its own loose box to house both rug and electrics. When installed no one really knew its use let alone how to work it, I was asked by his vet to go to the yard to see if I could explain the possible benefits. An appointment was arranged, on a date suitable for Geordie, with the provision that I was to arrive after evening stables. Following discussing the pros and cons of the magnetic rug there was a successful outcome and I was invited to meet his wife Margaret. Over a cup of tea we talked racing, and his hand shake, when I left, suggested an on-going, mutually beneficial, relationship.

Ron Thomas was next. Peter Walwyn sent in a flat colt chronically lame behind when Ron was away taking one of his Welsh mares to be served. Welsh ponies, of which he owned several were a passion. The Governor (trainer) and flat horses in the yard came first, with Welsh ponies a very close second, breeding canaries and gladioli featured as a relaxation. Within hours of returning with his mare he arrived to see if his colt was being cared for correctly: the yard and staff passed the inspection test.

John Francome, principal jockey to Fred Winter, was always open to new ideas, he persuaded Brian Delaney to allow me into that yard. It took time but eventually we worked together successfully. Brian's sense of touch was amazing, when tendon scanning became available, despite the fact that the horses he suggested should be experimentally scanned were still in training, not even lame, every horse he proposed showed a minute core lesion.

Nicky Henderson and Corky, when eventually they moved to Seven Barrows, were at the beginning of their highly successful National Hunt training partnership and very receptive to therapy. Penelope began to work some horses in long reins in their schooling arena and ride out ex-casualties, not resorting to dressage schooling but riding them, when on the gallops, in a manner which prevented them from moving incorrectly and forced them to balance rather than resorting to the popular methods, either just working them on the bit or in a bungee rein to try to alleviate a problem. There is a very fine line between teaching a horse to move economically for its particular discipline and completely changing its way of going when there is always a danger of ending up ruining previous pre-injury performance ability.

The first successful resident patient came from Toby Balding, who sent in 'a leg' for treatment. Fortunately his vet Clive Hamlin, who subsequently became of the greatest help during our time at Downs House, was enthusiastic as was Toby's wife Caro.

Chicken sent a very rotund, very expensive, colt with a mind of its own. He needed a new ploy to try to get him fit as the colt refused to walk from the yard to the gallops, this walk an essential part of a training routine. Apparently he worked perfectly well and quite happily when he arrived at the gallops, but only if conveyed there in a box.

Might a change of scene and routine help he enquired? I had no idea, long reins was a new experience but on day two he said NO very firmly. It was decided to try the pool, swimming head collar fitted, he stood looking round while his legs were bandaged, some curiosity, but no fuss. Elated we led him to the

Above: Geordie, head lad to Major Hern accepts me. Nashwan had just won the Derby!

Below :The Yard at Downs House on a very wet day.

shute, into the water he walked, no problem, amazing, what was all the fuss about I wondered, arrogantly thinking, if correctly handled, etc, etc. . . then he stepped off the bottom of the ramp and, out of his depth, making no attempt at trying to swim, he sank until only his nose, eyes and ears were above water; luckily he floated just like a hippopotamus.

The horses were swum wearing a special padded head collar with a rope attached to each side, these ropes held by the swimming team who walked, one on each side of the pool, level with the head of the horse. I do not know who shouted first, 'Pull him out, *pull* him *out!*'. The team tugged and along he floated, down the entire length of the pool, until, on reaching the exit ramp and feeling the ground, he walked up the ramp, shook and stood there virtually smiling. As every one present began to recover, and I realised I had not just drowned half a million pounds worth of horse, we decided, despite some trepidation, to try again. Repeat performance, he never did get to a racecourse.

It was fortunate when Penelope and I created the Rehabilitation Unit at Downs House that the number of owners in racing were expanding, many of whom did not have facilities to rest injured horses at home and were seeking a positive approach toward recovery from injury. They were reluctant to pay their trainers for months of box rest, which, pre Downs House had been the norm, thus it was as a result of owner pressure rather than trainer choice that the boxes began to fill enabling us to utilise the facilities we offered. One of the associated problems was that trainers did not want empty boxes. Although most residential fees were well below those charged if the horse was in training an empty box was an empty box. Charging horses coming to swim perhaps two or three times a week was easy, we billed the trainers and the swimming charge was added, just like gallop fees, to the owner's bills, but for a trainer to lose full fees, for sometimes up to six weeks, was another matter. I felt the horses must be resident because in order to be successful the number of treatments would vary daily, dependant on progress. There seemed no way to solve the problem and persuade trainers to let us deal with injuries in-house until Manou had a brilliant idea, she suggested we bill the trainers rather than the owners. She pointed out this would enable the trainers, who like us needed to make a living, to decide how to adjust their bills in order to help cover the cost of an empty box whilst the horse was out of the yard.

As racing expanded there was a similar escalation in the number of pleasure horses. Many of these new riders found due to the increase of traffic that hacking along roads to reach and ride over open country was becoming difficult, even dangerous, thus competition became the favoured alternative to pleasure riding. The riding club was born providing a social environment for people of like mind to meet and compete. Interest in Three Day Eventing expanded particularly when the discipline became the chosen preference for The Princess Royal and her husband Captain Mark Phillips. Civilians moved into disciplines that had previously been predominately monopolised by the armed forces particularly the Cavalry with, at one time, only serving members allowed to compete internationally.

As interest in equestrian competition sparked world-wide attention even the Japanese became interested in both sport horses and racing. Eric du Vander a Swedish three day event rider, now coach to the Kiwis, was appointed to train the Japanese event riders. When in his yard seeing to his horses I watched their early efforts. They fell off, remounted and fell off again, their balance perception seemingly non-existent but for tenacity they deserved medals, eventually making sufficient progress to qualify for and able to send a representative to the Sydney Olympics.

Peter Walwyn was selected as the racing expert most likely to be able to teach the representative, sent from Japan, to learn about flat racing. The fact the man could not ride was to Peter ridiculous. 'Got to learn,' he said. 'Simply got to learn.' I do not know how well the early riding lessons went but I can only imagine they were not a success as one day when treating a horse in my yard a message was relayed from the office by secretary Sue, 'Mary come at once, the Jap has fallen off and is lying on the ground making Japanese noises.' By the time I got there the assistant, Patrick McEwan, had got him up and was

Half a million pounds worth of colt walks unscathed from the pool.

feeding him hot sugared tea; Peter had deserted and taken the string up onto the gallops. His teaching must have been an ultimate success as Japan is now a force to be reckoned with in the TB industry.

Before leaving the country the Jap gave a series of thank you meals. It took Ron Thomas some time to get over the fact he had to take off his shoes before entering the house and then squat on the floor to eat uncooked food with chop sticks. Generous filling of the thimble-sized glasses with sake undoubtedly added an unforgettable glow to the evening: I know this was my experience. The presentation of a ceremonial scarf was a problem - in Tibet you exchange these - but I had nothing but a copy of *Equine Injury and Therapy* to offer in return.

Suddenly the demands of the horse owning public were changing and horses being asked to perform tasks requiring considerably more athletic prowess than that required if just being hacked around. Inevitably, without sufficient pre-training to build muscle efficiency in order to combat the physical strain of these new requirements, there was an increase of injuries, these not confined to the horses alone but also to their riders, the number of horse and human patients expanded gratifyingly.

I can still remember a sense of relief when, arriving from London one evening and on walking down to the yard I was met by Penelope who said, 'The yard is full, mother'.

Jockey Repair and the Flying Physios

Already treating human injuries in London, many of whom were competing athletes, it seemed sensible to open a small clinic at Downs House. There was plenty of space as one of the rooms on the ground floor leading off the main hall was ideal; the hall itself was large, and comfortable enough to enable patients to sit while waiting. There was only one slight drawback: Sam Cat. After he'd decided he was a house cat rather than a stable cat the hall became his favourite place: one to which he returned after any successful hunt, often to regurgitate his prey. He seemed the have an uncanny knack of choosing VIP people when performing this unpleasant act and most, unlike the Princess Royal who shooed him out making certain he had picked up his offering, were neither practical nor amused. He became well known in the locality and I was away when the household was informed he'd been killed and his body was lying in the road. 'Mother will kill *us* if he's not properly buried.' When the body had been scraped up and placed in a sack the family and stable staff set to. It had been very dry and the grave digging was, I understand, arduous but eventually all was finished and the last turf patted down. As the burial party turned to go into the house for a much needed cup of coffee a large black cat emerged from the bushes, and sitting down Sam Cat began to wash his whisker's. To this day no one has any idea of the name of the cat who was buried.

A steady flow of jockeys began to arrive after Richard Fox (Foxy) had turned up following a seriously damaging fall in India where he went, at the end of the European Flat season, to race ride for the winter. Luckily treatment was successful but he was still apprehensive about riding until persuaded that as a part of his rehabilitation, he needed to ride and he agreed to sit on Penelope's point-to-point horse.

Following several sessions in the school where both he and the horse became bored he rode off out of the yard, and up onto the Downs. All went well and they hacked along happily until, at the exact spot from where he knew he was expected to gallop the old horse took off; surviving this Foxy decided his racing career was not, as he had feared, over. Subsequently his stories, recounted in the Lambourn pubs, resulted in a stream of both the injured and the curious coming to see the eccentric woman at Downs House who cured people by sending them out on a horse.

This was not quite true, but following injury patients often find exercises difficult where as familiar task are easy and most day-to-day tasks can be utilised as exercises.

The late Major Hern was more or less unable to move after he broke his neck: certainly not able sit up despite extensive phys-iotherapy given in a gym environment. One day, recalling the Canadian experience, I had his saddle put onto a stable wood-en saddle horse, two men lifted him on, and he sat up without thinking. His hands were of little use and when I handed him a bridle and suggested he take it to bits his valet suggested I leave the room: his language could only be described as colourful. Two bridles later he could hold a pen and sign his name.

As the number of Jockeys needing treatment increased my younger daughter, Rabbit, agreed to come and help with the work load. A qualified masseur and holding a Degree in Sports Science and Sports Therapy - thus better qualified than I - Rabbit had been one of the first to have attended a three year Degree Course in Sports Science. She became an invaluable third member of our team: Penelope in the yard, Rabbit coping with human injuries, and myself shuttling between London and Lambourn.

It was an era of change with everyone involved in sport sub-jected to ever more demanding training routines in the pursuit of an increased level of excellence and teams began to employ their own therapists. What about the jockeys? They certainly needed help: what other sport demands optimum performance 7 days a week, 363 days a year with the possibility of up to seven races a day?

Recent statistics, and these will not have radically altered since the 1980s, suggest a Nation Hunt jockey expects to experience a fall at least once in every 15 rides, sustaining a bad fall with severe injuries once in every 350 rides.

Lesser injuries range from bumps and bruises which do not prevent riding but therapy helps remove discomfort and is definitely needed if they have been unlucky enough to break a bone, or dislocate a shoulder.

The Jockey Club Medical officer Dr Michael Allen agreed it might be an idea to offer therapy in the weighing room, this an area sacrosanct to the jockeys and their valets. Within the complex there was already a sauna, a canteen, and a medical room staffed by doctors and nurses containing couches and all the equipment necessary to deal with injuries from minor to complex.

Backed by help from John Francome and Peter Scudamore, both involved in The Professional Jockeys' Association, and after lengthy negotiations, including personal Jockey Club clearance and agreement from the officials of courses approached, the necessary specialist passes enabled Rabbit or myself to attend - with no form of remuneration - a few selected race meetings as an experiment.

To these meetings we lugged our own portable couch and everything we felt we might need in order to offer appropriate therapy. We were usually allocated a space in a sort of in house laundrette, where mud stained breeches whirred round in the rows of machines.

Michael Allen retired and Dr Michael Turner, his eventual replacement, proved incredibly supportive. The experiment was an astounding success and the 'Flying Physio' service was born, now sadly renamed 'The Injured Jockeys' Health and Welfare Scheme': what a mouthful!

In the early days Rabbit not only attended the race courses to treat the jockeys but also undertook all the administrative and liaison work necessary to run the scheme. She consulted with the Jockey Club Medical Officer, the varied Racing Authorities, and the Jockeys Association in order to ensure an exemplary level of professional care could be offered, at no cost, to the jockeys.

Eventually the scheme was accepted, due in part to pressure applied by the late Lord Oaksey at the time Chairman of the Injured Jockeys Association. A set level of daily attendance payment, albeit well below that charged for private Physiotherapy treatments (with nothing toward travel costs) was negotiated with the race courses

The scheme has continued to expand with nearly every race meeting covered, and a residential rehabilitation unit for injured jockeys, Oaksey House, in Lambourn was completed just before Lord Oaksey died. A second centre the Jack Berry house is planned in the north.

Bob Street, riding for Avery Whitfield won a good race at York on a horse called Numismatist. Bob was kind enough to tell the racing press, when interviewed after winning, that both he and the horse had been treated at Downs House. This was newsworthy - a first - and the BBC arrived to film the yard. Why they sent world renowned footballer John Fashanu to be the interviewer I have no idea. No Claire Balding back then.

John arrived in a chauffeur driven car. Beautifully dressed he had brought seven extra suits explaining that to maintain his public image he needed to change several times during a filming. As we walked down to the yard he explained, rather endearingly, that he was feeling nervous as he had never been near a horse in his life!

He managed really rather well, and luckily there were not too many mistakes requiring a scene to be reshot: horses do not pose well for long, and John forgot about changing! Noticing he limped I enquired why, and it turned out he had an ongoing foot injury. He found this frustrating for he was at the height of his football career, and no conventional treatment seemed to help. He'd had so many steroid injections that the skin had lost its colour leaving a large pink area on a normally black foot. Arrogantly I offered treatment and after three sessions he was pain free. I shall always remember him as a charming, very caring person despite the adverse publicity to which he was subjected sometime later. There must be an internal grape vine amongst the sporting elite for the next unusual patient was Randy Smith aiming for the title of Mr Universe 1996. Having massaged horses certainly helped!

John Fashanu, sent
to interview me by
the BBC

Randy Smith, injured
pre- Mr Universe
competition 1996

When Manou left for family reasons Sue Langfrey replaced her, coping not only with the increasing yard paperwork, the accounts and my diary but also deciphering my hand written notes, turning them into drafts acceptable to the publishers, Blackwells. The raison d'etre for writing Equine Injury and Therapy was to explain, in lay terms, the effects of varied therapeutic modalities, it was the first of several tomes written in the hope that the horse fraternity would appreciate that injury need not always mean the end of a useful life. I had originally approached Mr Allen of J. A. Allen the famous equestrian book shop to see if he would publish but he turned me down. Subsequently we met many times becoming firm friends, and in a letter to me, penned shortly before he died, he said had he had turned down many Authors but of these I was one of the few he regretted.

Learning

As the boxes filled I realised I needed to learn more, we were being reasonably successful but that was not good enough, I have always worked on the principal that if you think you can hang up your L Plates it is time to retire. There was no spare money to go to Veterinary conferences, they are very expensive, Veterinary delegates have their fees paid by their practice, not only was I self-employed but also heavily in debt to the Bank.

Out of the blue I won a £50:00 Premium Bond. Betting is not my forte, I wish it were but I had been involved in a horse belonging to the formidable Jenny Pitman, treating him in her yard. Shortly after the Premium Bond win, I learned the horse had an entry in a very small, possibly a prep race prior to bigger things if it remained sound. Despite coming from the Pitman stable, the odds were very attractive, probably as the horse had been off the course for some time.

The sum I collected after the horse won, enabled me to fly to Canada to attend, in Calgary during the famous stampede, the first conference ever to be held on Equine Rehabilitation, with enough left to allow Penelope to go to Portugal, visit Villa Franka, and learn the Portuguese methods of Classical preparation, working horses from the ground to prepare their muscles for ridden activities.

The Chief Rider of the Portuguese School, Rodriguez, considered it was essential to prepare the muscles of the horse without the encumbrance of a rider. 'Do this and you will build an indestructible athlete,' was his philosophy.

Over the years Penelope has devised a series of very successful programmes, enabling countless 'write offs' to return to full, pre-injury performance levels after having been worked from the ground, in long reins.

The Jenny Pitman connection ended abruptly when, rather than have me go to her yard, she actually sent a horse to us. It was lame in front and arrived with the forthright comment: 'I can't get him sound. I've sent him to see if you're as good as you think you are.' A week later, surprisingly, following treatment using a Low Level Laser, the horse was sound and I left a message on her answer phone. No response.

When I went into the yard to unlock at 6:30 am, on the morning following my telephone call to Jenny, I was horror struck to see the main gates off their hinges and the stable, where her horse should have been, empty. When Shergar was stolen I knew exactly how their connections must have felt when they discovered he was missing.

Communication was still in the Dark Ages, a time people now scarcely remember; a time before the mobile phone, computers, and email! What to do? Dial 999? About to rush back to the house I heard the unmistakable sound of an approaching horse box which stopped and through the open gate I watched Jenny climb out. 'Though I'd try him on the gallops,' she said. 'Seems sound- I'll collect him tomorrow.'

I was too angry to think of being diplomatic. 'You can f******* take him now. Who the f****** do you think you are, breaking into my yard leaving it open, taking your b***** horse without so much as a by your leave. It was in my care and you are trespassing. Get out, and go home!' To give Jenny her due she calmly left, taking the horse with her. I swore that was the last time I would have anything to do with her yard.

The yard at Downs House continued to attract patients, and as the number of staff increased, we built a hostel rather than using rented accommodation. Penelope trained a head girl which relieved her of a number of duties leaving time to work the horses in the school, to hunt with the Berks and Bucks Drag Hounds, and to train and ride her own horse in point to points.

Many people, including a number of vets, were sceptical of my approach toward animal therapy and vociferous in their condemnation. I was reported to both the Chartered Society and the Royal College of Veterinary Surgeons, and accused of violating the Veterinary Act. Fortunately on every occasion meticulous note-keeping and the fact I had recorded written referrals from the practices in question meant all investigations found in my favour. However these incidents not only rankled but were very time consuming.

Give up or go on?
Publicity, both good and bad, resulted in media scrutiny and I was invited, by a professional organisation, to lecture and present my findings. With the lecture date widely advertised I prepared a mass of slides and set off for Newmarket - the venue chosen.

In my wildest dreams, never could I have imagined the organisers would choose, of all places, the Sale Ring at Tattersalls!

Marvellous seating, the place was full to overflowing, and there I was on the auctioneer's rostrum, slide projector and screen in situ. Suddenly the happy sun decided after several days of gloom to give its all, and beamed down dazzlingly through the unshaded glass roof. Result: a slide-less lecture.

I had no idea that a member of the audience was Martin Pipe who was embarking upon a training career:, one which subsequently resulted in 15 years unchallenged as National Hunt Champion Trainer.

Undeniably in the 1980s Animal Physiotherapy was a new concept, but even following numerous lectures - often including veterinary input and backed by slides to illustrate case studies, given both to the veterinary profession and riding public - scepticism continued and on several occasions I was heckled from the floor and accused of violating the veterinary act. Other lay therapists hated me and I realised I was taking bread out of their mouths as the horses we treated recovered and did not seem to require continual ongoing maintenance help. Some disbelief was associated with the fact that there were no 'double blind trials' to prove the effects of electrical therapy even in the human field, let alone the animal, and such trials, for the purists, are the only way to provide irrefutable proof: their lack gives reason for acceptable doubt.

In many ways I was probably my own worst enemy refusing to believe it was possible for a horses to have several vertebrae out of place and remain functional. Even if there were a vertebrae out of place surely it was impossible to manipulate the back of a standing, fully conscious horse: I refused to even try.

I spent hours dissecting horse's backs at the local kennels trying to prove I was wrong; watching the ferocity required by the kennel man, wielding an axe, in order to sever the vertebral column reinforced my 'not possible 'view.

I have nothing against manipulators I have worked with some who were brilliant: the late Anthony Pewsey for one, Ronnie Longford for another - both highly professional, neither claiming to achieve miracles. Anthony nearly always sedated the horses he worked on, often they came on to Downs House following adjustment and we rebuilt muscles to ensure stability. Ronnie and I gave several joint talks and he always said to an audience: 'I can make a horse better, Mary can tell you why.' I was able to explain that with selective use of pressure it was possible to influence nerves and relieve pain so reducing muscle spasm, this last usually ensuring a natural realignment. I had learned this while with Cyriax as I had been involved in a double blind, human manipulative research programme. The experimental work demonstrated if there is disruption in alignment of opposing surfaces, provided this is not disease related, anatomical surfaces will, given the chance relocate correctly.

Despite success in 75% of cases we worked on since Downs House had been established I had never considered even moderate success would have a roller coaster effect, but I got tired of trying to prove a point. It would have been so easy to say, 'Stuff the lot of them, we have proved in carefully selected cases that Physiotherapy works: forget box rest, use controlled activity, rebuild the muscles, and stop nit picking.'

I could have changed my work load concentrating on London, where I thoroughly enjoyed treating a wealth of varied patients. I could reduce my hours, live a normal life (whatever a normal life is) rather than flogging up to town late every Monday evening, working three ten hour days to pay the Bank and the bills, then on the evening of the third, travel back down the motorway to Lambourn to begin a four day stint at Downs House.

In London, Bernard and I had the account for the Royal Ballet and Monica Mason, then one of the principal dancers, had been lecturing at a conference. When meeting her over lunch I was appalled to discover that therapy for ballet dancers in the UK was a bit hit and miss. I had watched dancers training in Denmark with Vera Volkova a personal friend and director of the Danish ballet. Therapy there, if required, was over-seen by Dr Eivind Thomasen whose approach and techniques were all based around the importance of improved muscle function, and leading on from this to movement re-education.

I had worked out for myself that muscles are very informative: this is not written down in text books! It seemed logical to assume if a muscle or group were not working correctly a joint would be compromised. If you knew your anatomy this would lead you to nerve that supplied the muscles; also important was to appreciate that a nerve root services an area of skin. If the skin is not 100% responsive the nerve must be compromised and you are dealing with a nerve associated problem - rather more serious than just a muscle deterioration.

To have had these ideas confirmed by Dr Thomasen was another useful piece to add to my jig saw of collected facts. All Ballet dancers knew of his skills and were eager to see him if Bernard and I were unable to effect lasting repair. He eventually agreed to visit on regular basis and see cases in our rooms. We both learned a great deal and his visits were a huge success

Merle Park, prima ballerina to the company, pain free shortly after seeing Bernard, ensured that a steady flow of dancers began to arrive at Wimpole Street. The chance meeting with Monica expanded the practice from athletic and general to becoming recognised as specialist in the Ballet world. Marguerite Porter had been selected by Madam Dame Ninette De Valois to follow her, to learn and adopt Madam's, own personal interpretation in Swan Lake, of the dying swan. Tuition was exacting, requiring hours of work mostly, *en pointe*, but with quivering rather than straight knees, she needed constant help to contain, let alone remove the pain, and to enable her to perform. Marguerite was also dancing with Rudolf Nureyev as her partner and he could be exacting, almost cruel, seeming to miss lifts, or not give adequate support, and tiny near misses do not help muscles.

On occasions ballet demands required me to sit in the school studios in Talgarth Road watching experimentation as modern ideas began to replace the age old Classical approach. If a dancer failed to perform a movement sequence the choreographer would often turn and say, usually with considerable irritation, 'What is the matter, are they injured?' As modern choreography began to replace Classical it was often difficult to explain to someone like Kenneth MacMillan that a human, trained for years in Classical movements sequences only might be incapable of adapting to the new relaxed, often somewhat contorted movements required.

The Ballet led to theatre after some members of the Company moved and joined the Lloyd Webber organisation to perform in Cats. Of all his productions Starlight Express produced the largest number of casualties.

Bernard had canoed to Olympic level, and his conections led to us treating international athletes. There was a mass of orthopaedic referrals mostly chronic back cases. We also drew patients from an amazing GP Mannie Herbert. Of White Russian origin his patient list included many displaced Europeans, most of whom had worked for the British during the second world war: some were ex-spies, others had been under-cover agents, there were couriers, and mistresses of high ranking Germans, a truly fascinating bunch. Mannie also attracted eccentrics and explorers: Aspinall, Thessiger, Fiennes, and Freyer Stark amongst them. Such a wide range of personalities, each sharing, during treatment, fascinating personal reminiscences gave an added spice to each day. Then due to

Downs House jockeys, event riders, polo players came, recovered and sent their friends. We still managed to cope by working flat-out and there were always amusing incidents: a girl with a bad neck asked, as she joined me for treatment, 'Is Bernard always as rude as that?' 'Why, what did he say?' 'How many fellas do you sleep with?' she said furiously. 'I am afraid he often swallows words. You have a bad neck, I think he may have meant pillows.'

Ran Feinnes, off on an expedition to the pole, and due to be filmed, had booked an appointment for back treatment. He telephoned to say not only was he lost in London but had forgotten to bring a pair of trunks so was not coming as he knew he would have to take his trousers off. He rang off before I could tell him we had plenty of dressing gowns and towels. A patient was arrested for GBH while face down on my couch by two slightly embarrassed members of the police force. It turned out he'd found a dealer trying to sell drugs to his teenage daughter when he'd collected her from school. It appeared the dealer might not be able to ply his trade for some time. The Kray brothers were exemplary patients and on one occasion, just before Christmas, they asked me if - given a substantial amount of money - I would go to Hamleys for them and buy toys for an orphanage they supported. I did.

Bernard and I were always happy to be remunerated in kind often receiving theatre, opera, or ballet tickets in lieu of fees. My family were on occasion less than enthusiastic when rather heavy grey hued pies, or weighty fruit cakes were proffered by OAPs. On one sad occasion it was a wedding cake: the bride groom, having arranged a joint account had emptied it and scarpered two days before the big day.

The 'in kind' remuneration did cause me a problem following, I am thankful to say a one and only, but no less unforgettable, visit by the Tax authorities who arrived to investigate the Downs House books. In their view racing and equine sports were the pursuits of the very rich and therefore ought to be extremely profitable: what were we hiding? They went through all the accounts, line by line. They could find nothing wrong with the business books. Two days into the investigation I was summoned to appear before a tight-lipped senior investigator who informed me he knew I charged a certain amount per patient, yet my appointment diaries did not balance - neither the London nor the country one - patient appointments to income was incorrect. There were more patient appointments than entered income: had I been taking cash and not declaring this?

He rambled on: criminal offence, mutter mutter, fines, even custody. When I could get a word in edge ways I explained I could easily account for the variance. OAPs often knitted me socks or jerseys, and others gave me potted plants or cakes. Dr Watkin and I treated injuries sustained by cast members involved in all the Andrew Lloyd Webber shows, also saw performers and support staff from the Royal Opera House and Royal Ballet:, many of these gave us tickets to the theatre, opera or ballet. The Lebanese brought caviar, the Rothschild's paid in fine wine, Barbara Cartland would proffer her latest novelette, always a paperback, never a hardback copy! Others, for example Katie Boyle arriving to have her dogs treated, was guaranteed to leave a tray of smoked salmon. And David Guider, an orchestral conductor brought cakes from Fortnum's.

The tax man was not impressed and there followed an hysterically funny two days as every single set of patients' notes for the previous seven years were scrutinised and the value of the 'in kinds' argued by the investigative team. By some miracle, at the end of the investigation the Tax man owed me money!

With the amusement of London and aggro from other professionals in the country, why was I trying to keeping things going in both? Life was becoming, for the first time, exhausting. And worse - I was not enjoying it. I got to the stage where I was debating whether to call it a day, and sell up.

Fed up with life I departed for a Greek island, slept in the sun, ate a lot of Taramasalata and came back feeling a bit less jaded. On my return, following a session at Martin Pipe's Pond House Racing Stables and while flying back to Downs House in their private helicopter, the flight gave me time to consider my life style without telephone interruptions. Eventually as we flew above the English country side I started chatting to the pilot and we both agreed how privileged we were to work for Martin.

Thinking it through I was shocked to realise the number of people I would let down if I gave up: not just my family but also all those who were supporting Downs House and backing my ideas. I realised I must prove, as I had set out to do, that Physiotherapy was viable for animal injury. It would be cowardly to pull out. I needed to continue, despite more often than not, feeling I was pushing a steamroller uphill. I thought of Martin and how he must feel with the negative publicity he was receiving at the time because his training methods were deemed unconventional. Such adversity causes people of a lesser character to call it a day.

I realised I had been offered a unique opportunity: invited to work for a trainer who was doing something that had never been done before in the racing industry, taking, in most instances, horse failures and retraining them in a manner that enabled them to win.

There was so much still to explore. Working out what was required to combat and repair a horse's injury was a new, ever changing and exciting field and at Downs House several inmates described as write-offs were improving. At Martin's, Carvill's Hill had arrived as 'finished', his racing career over, yet following a patient, carefully tailored, individual training programme he recovered and went on to win the Welsh Grand National.

I can honestly say, that while there are many, people without whose help the acceptance of Physiotherapy for injured animals would never have become recognised by the veterinary profession, that it was working for Martin that kept me focused. A man who leaves no stone unturned, he always wanted to know 'why?' His questions and support over the years have encouraged me to learn more: to delve, to research, to dissect, to search for facts, until questions asked can be usefully answered.

Martin's father demanded a very high level of security at the yard. His orders to me were, 'Yes, make notes on every horse but hand them into the office before you leave. Do not keep copies, and do not discuss anything you do here with anyone.'

Because of this level of security I could never be certain if the name on the stable door was necessarily the name of the horse within. And while my memory for names has never been outstanding I rarely forget a case. In 1994, I remember glancing at the runners for the Grand National and noticing Martin's name rather than recognising that of the horse. Watching the parade his horse did seem familiar, then toward the end of the race I shouted to Penelope, 'Come and watch! I think Martin's horse will win if Dunwoody can keep it going from the elbow.' It did win and I remembered: Miinnehoma had spent a considerable time at Downs House recovering from a severe pelvic injury.

Staff

I did not have much time to be domestic although cooking was therapeutic. The house survived - just - and was cleaned by Marlene Price from Lambourn, who understandably was struggling. One day she heard on the local grape vine that a Mr and Mrs May were looking for a job: they were leaving the de Savory family. Both had been in service all their lives.

Martin Pipe. Shared goodies

Remembering my training at Miss Randall's, particularly the protocol required when engaging a butler, I was mentally ready to interview them, but when we met *they* interviewed *me*. Luckily, for *me*, they liked the place. Both were proud of their household knowledge, 'Mrs May is good with silver' he said looking at some rather tarnished wine jugs. 'Mr May is good with shoes,' she volunteered peering at rows of dusty boots. Over a cup of coffee, in the drawing room rather than the kitchen, they agreed to come and work at Downs House.

They were a Godsend, becoming a vital cog, always to remain just on their side of the fine line between employer and employee rather than becoming family members, although in the face of any local criticism we became fiercely protected as 'their family'. The shoes and boots were cleaned; missing buttons reattached as if by magic, everything that could be ironed was ironed, the cars shone and were fuelled. It was almost as though cookie and amah had resurfaced. Arriving in 1987 they remained until we left in 1999.

When we moved to Exmoor I offered them - as a thank you - a holiday. They could go wherever they wished: touchingly they booked a holiday at Butlins in Minehead, about 5 miles away from our new home and popped back to visit in order to see that all was well.

I am afraid Combeleigh was a disappointment: much smaller than they expected - and there was no dining room - just an 'eating-in kitchen!' Their little car just made it up the very steep drive as they drove rather sadly away but I am glad to say we are still in touch.

Maintenance in a stable yard is full time occupation, the inherited Roy retired and was replaced by Ed. He turned up more or less daily: mended boxes, taps, drains, roofs, and fences. After about five years he appeared, one morning, wringing his cap in apology saying he needed to be off for a few days. When there was no sign of him after two weeks I made enquiries only to discover he was 'holidaying' in Princetown Prison on Dartmoor. It was impossible to discover the exact reason other than he'd been accused by a family member of a crime: apparently committed years before, and eventually proven to be false. Nevertheless he was sentenced.

While resting in Princetown - awaiting retrial after which he was acquitted - he built, out of used matchsticks a replica of Downs House. It was delivered by his sister who had flown over from America to visit him. She arrived in a chauffeur-driven limo with the model carefully packed in a large box. Mounted on a board about two foot square it was perfect down to the last creeper, window, door, gutter, and fire escape.

I rang the Prison Guvnor to say it was a remarkable achievement and learnt to my horror that the authorities had been so impressed it had been on display. Several of the inmates I was told had been very interested: 'I should think so' I said. 'How soon do you expect me to be burgled?' After a short silence he said rather sadly, 'Perhaps it might be a good idea to check your security'.

Downs House made in Princetown prison, from matchsticks, by our one-time maintenance man Ed.

Manton, Shadwell and Dubai.

Shortly after training the first five home in the Gold Cup Michael Dickinson moved to Manton an old training establishment just outside Marlborough, to train for Mr Sangster. He came to look at our pool. After watching a horse swim he announced: 'When there are swimming races for horses I'll swim mine.' Then he asked if I would consider giving the Physiotherapy if, and when, it might be needed at Manton. Antony Stirk, his newly appointed vet, believed it would be a good idea. A suburb diagnostician, Anthony, is amongst those needing to be thanked, as Physiotherapy was not even mentioned during the veterinary training of his generation, yet he was always open to suggestion and working with him I gained much vital veterinary knowledge.

The Manton time, however, was not really a success for anyone and eventually Michael - quite rightly - fired me when I told him I simply could not mend the horses as fast as he was breaking them! One of the many problems were the new, all weather, wood chip gallops: not only were they very loose but no one realised differing types of wood chips offer a differing resonance. Lay 100 yards of one type then 100 yards of another, and the variation of impaction force between the two, at gallop, can be catastrophic. Adding to training problems was that all the turf on the grass gallops, which had not been disturbed for several hundred years, was, following a visit from an American turf expert lifted and re-laid. This resulted in the underlying down-land flints breaking through the surface: flint cuts are incredibly difficult to heal and it took months of painstaking flint collection before the gallops were safe to use.

Michael was dismissed shortly after I was, yet Anthony survived for longer before he too found himself 'no longer required.'

We gave a farewell party for Anthony and his wife Maxine. Miraculously the alcohol stocks lasted out for Max had invited so many people she had forgotten to mention, and the numbers were considerably more than had been catered for. I distinctly remember grasping a clergyman friend of theirs by the collar when I realised the salmon I had cooked was not going to cope and saying, 'We're in a similar situation to the loaves and fishes story, please come to the kitchen and help.' He did, redistributing the salmon and disguising the miniscule portions with generous slices of cucumber.

The Manton episode was not all bad as far as I was concerned and one thing leads to another. Michael knew Angus Gold the racing manager for H.H. Sheikh Hamdan Al Maktoum who invited me to Shadwell. Angus asked would I visit when needed and explain to Dennis O'Brien, who was overseeing the yard containing the resting and injured horses, how they could be helped. I could, he told me, order with-in reason, appropriate therapy apparatus. Eventually Angie, Dennis' wife, attended one of the Equine Sports Massage courses run at Downs House enabling her to continue to give the therapy required in between my visits.

My first visit was the start of a long and very enjoyable association with Richard Lancaster the director of the Shadwell organisation. The work was not confined just their TB horses but also included the endurance Arabians; when I joined Shadwell I knew nothing about Endurance Riding and told Richard if I was to be usefully involved I simply had to take part in an endurance race to gain experience for I did not feel attendance at the first Golden Horse Shoe ride over Exmoor many years before had taught me much, other than that the shepherding ponies of Exmoor farmers were incredibly fit. I remembered they had escorted the riders over a boggy area, the Chains, then for amusement ridden on to the finish at Welcombe Head, there joined the competitor's bun fight after which they hacked back to the moor.

As usual Bernard had a solution. The premier French Endurance race was about to take place, it started in the village near his father's French home. He would find me a horse trained locally, we would fly out, stay at the house, and I could take part, 'hors concourse,' to gain the necessary experience.

Endurance rules were not as stringent as today, no set distance times, you really did race. The Bernard idea seemed too easy and the visit became an even more enticing prospect for, when treating him, I told the Baron de Rothschild of the plan. 'Oh,' he said, 'you will be flying to Bordeaux, do go to the vineyard, I will arrange for you to visit the museum of wine I have built at my home'.

Bernard had gone ahead, I flew, clutching my saddle, to France two days before the ride, a car was waiting at the airport and I was whisked silently away through a rolling landscape of farmed fields, then these changed to be replaced by acre upon acre of the vineyards belonging to the Chateaux Mouton estate. The visit was an unforgettable experience, a section of the cavés, the original storage area for the Chateaux wine, had been re-designed to house the museum. In the first chamber, mounted on marble stands, there were three preserved heads of a huge breed of horned sheep, each wearing a necklet of a differing gem stone thus demonstrating the unparalleled excellence of Rothschild's Chateaux Mouton.

My guide pressed a button and a wall slid back, before us in a vast cavern, arranged in seemingly endless rows, lay cask after cask, the heady scent of fermenting grape pervaded, then as eyes became accustomed to the gloom, at the far end of the cave, seated on a long bench type table, a small, exquisite statue of Bacchus gleamed, fashioned, I later learned, from pure gold.

Walking between the casks we arrived to view him at close hand. 'This is where the tasters work' explained my guide. The wood table ran the full width of the end of the cave, below were small drawers, each dated, each contained a single copy of an individually designed label, one for every bottling from the very first to the present day. With much reverence that designed by Picasso was offered for inspection, with even greater reverence his original sketches were shown.

What else I wondered, senses reeling, as we moved toward an entrance, this proved to be a double panelled, security door. The ballroom sized room beyond was filled with show cases, each enclosing wine related items, the overall magnificence was almost too much to appreciate, bejewelled loving cups, simple peasant horn vessels, Roman Glass, every shape and size of wine container, jugs, bottles, pictures, statues, tapestry, an endless, breath taking array.

Passing out from the temperature controlled atmosphere of the museum it was chilly and it became apparent we were deep underground, 'The wine requires this temperature' I was informed. Silent figures, tending the wine glided by in the gloom, rack after rack of bottles, then a caged area, each rack it was explained, held the wine from an outstanding vintage with samples preserved both in normal bottles and jeroboam, 'Monsieur le Baron holds the key'.

The car sped me to Montcuq following a visit it was unlikely I would ever have made, had circumstances not necessitated an attempt to learn, first-hand, about Endurance riding.

On joining Bernard it was back to reality when I learned there was a British Team competing. I realised not only was I inadequately prepared, but so apparently was my horse. Its charmingly mad American owner, who had broken her leg, hence the spare mount, had been unable to find a local rider to get it fit so in lieu of ridden work she had been galloping the animal, attached to a buggy, across the French countryside.

The town of Montcuq, venue for this particular ride, is built on a hill, with half a mile of near vertical tarmac leading to the start. 'You must gallop down, to get away early from the start is good' I was informed by the American.

There appeared to be around 200 horses competing, the town square, containing tented stables, was buzzing, I noted most of the European riders were happily partaking of local hospitality. Not so the Brits, sighing inwardly I was driven to the farm where they had elected to stay. Nothing was right, no RULES, no vet inspection, no speed restrictions, they had not found a clean place to eat, as for the sanitary arrangements. . .

Bernard suddenly changing allegiance from adopted French, to being very British, suggested they all come to supper, all being, riders, grooms, hangers on, twenty in total. I began to realise why Jennie, his wife, had vetoed the trip.

'There is plenty of rice, you can make a chicken risotto', 'thanks I am supposed to be riding in this B***** thing, how can I go to the briefing, cook for and entertain that lot, I would much rather join all the other riders to eat, even more importantly, drink with the Mayor'. His silence suggested this was not to be.

While he went in search of chickens I foraged in the storage area for rice, his elderly father, a permanent resident, lit the Calor gas stove and filled a large pan with water. Before the rather dubiously coloured water even began to warm the gas ran out. Family domestic on Bernard's return. The chickens he had procured were of the typical French peasant variety, skinny, limp, pale and uninspiring, but there was a plus, they were cooked.

Eventually the water heated and I poured in the rice, it seemed unusually active; I soon realised why, it was weevil infested, the occupants disliking the heat were trying to escape. Giggling weakly, as they rose to the surface I scooped off as many as I could, who would know?

Despite being by the stove the air was becoming decidedly chilly; the house was not really a house but a huge barn, sleeping quarters having been created by boxing in an area where the slope of the roof was some ten feet off the ground before continuing downward. Other than his father, who sensibly had a series of ladies to stay during the winter, 'to help me' he explained 'keep warm', the family only visited in summer, then with the great doors open to keep cool they sat inside around a long refectory table which served their various needs.

It was November, the bottom of the great doors sat well above the ground and a freezing wind was wandering in through the gap. Noticing a fireplace of sorts I suggested it might be sensible to try to create an illusion of warmth by lighting a fire, no dry wood, more family stress.

The Brits arrived, huddled round some slowly smouldering logs, ate, drank and left; eating by candle light had meant it was impossible to see the contents of the risotto. Plenty of wine probably salvaged the meal, I went to bed fully clothed.

The wind dropped during the night and by 8:30 am a melee of fresh horses filled the square, directions were shouted in a variety of languages indicating that the route was marked with orange tags, not easy to spot amid late autumn colours. Someone fired a pistol and we were off, galloping downhill on tarmac caused several early falls, to my astonishment my horse survived probably because I was so frightened I just held onto its mane ignoring the reins.

Off tarmac and onto grass was a relief, as the morning wore on so the casualties increased, lame horses, exhausted horses, all being dragged by their riders to the nearest road, there to wait while hoping some form of transport would appear to collect them or, the most popular ploy, walking to the nearest village where they, the riders, could replenish lost fluids while their horses recovered.

Beginning to feel, even if my horse were able to continue I would probably have to ride standing rather than sitting on my saddle on day two, on glancing down I realised my horse had stopped sweating, obviously it suffered from anhidrosis, a condition that does not enable a horse, when over-heated, to sweat. End of the ride for me, I joined the other casualties by now, in both number and appearance, somewhat resembling Napoleon's retreat from Moscow. The American owner was not amused by my failure; subsequently I discovered the horse had always failed after 40k, the exact distance we had covered!

Hoping the experience might be of some use, after consultation with Richard, I was dispatched to Dubai; jetting out on an Emirate Airline flight, at the front end of the aeroplane, then collected and taken to a hotel so luxurious one felt the story tale magic carpet of the Middle East really existed.

The endurance horses were stabled and trained in the dessert, the main problem I was faced with on arrival was the number who had become 'stiff legged' behind. The hock, although made up of a number of small bones is designed to move freely at one only of the internal joints, the others are stabilised by soft tissue structures. A request for soft tissue scans of the hocks of those affected with lack of hock flexibility was implemented, the scans pinpointed inflammation in a number of the tiny, internal, supporting structures. The very open minded American Vet, Martha Misheff DVM, injected these with considerable success and the training programme was modified.

Camping in the dessert with the horses, sleeping on priceless Persian rugs spread on the sand in the tented homes of the dessert Arab, or under the stars, was memorable and an experience for which I shall always feel indebted to Sheikh Hamdan, for women, in Arab culture tend to be kept behind the scenes but I was allowed to live alongside his horses under true dessert conditions.

Following this visit, the first major test was a ride in Ireland sponsored by The Boss (Sheikh Hamdan). I joined his team, using massage at the check points to help reduce heart rates, also working in the evening to ensure both horses and riders were not muscle sore when starting out on the second day.

Sheikh Mohamed had also brought a team, he rode himself, not only completing the course but with his adjudicated the winning ride. Family rivalry ensued, agents searched worldwide for the oldest pure bred Arabian lines, those selected displaying the qualities considered to be required for endurance, Arabians arrived from France, Russia, Poland, the USA.

Re-training of the eye was required as few of the imports displayed the conformational characteristics prevalent in the UK where horses, originally imported by Lady Wentworth, stemmed mainly from those Arabian lines used for ceremonial occasions.

HH Sheikh Mohamed Al Maktoum is a very remarkable man displaying an amazing animal empathy, I was privileged to be invited as a guest to the first Veterinary conference he arranged in Dubai. During a stable visit, as he moved down the central corridor of an American barn, every horse came to its door, nickering, trying to be noticed, to be caressed by him as he passed them.

I know, he is sympathetic because I have witnessed it, if his horse falters during a ride he dismounts and he leads it in to the next check point despite the personnel travelling in a fleet of accompanying vehicles.

The hospitals he has built for all animals, not just horses, in Dubai are second to none. I was enthralled to see a camel skeleton, watched spellbound as a hawk had a femoral pin inserted after breaking a leg when flying for him. I expect there are other places where you can watch a baby camel born but certainly not under conditions that would put most UK maternity units to shame. Where else I wonder, are the harnesses of racing camels investigated for comfort and not just horses, but racing camels and birds of prey so well cared for?

As well as hospitals he has funded research programmes whose work has benefited the welfare of the horse internationally particularly in racing and endurance. It is largely due to work, originally stemming from Dubai that knowledge of electrolytes is now common place, people have very short memories it is not so very long ago that their significance was unrecognised. I suspect, rather as with Her Majesty the Queen, that his horses are a pleasurable and welcome relaxation from affairs of State.

Many people accuse Sheikh Mohamed of only wanting to win, I would dispute this, in my experience he is a man who cares deeply for his animals and will go to all lengths to ensure the health, welfare and comfort of those he owns, no matter what this takes.

Muscle recovery

In order to comply with restrictions imposed by the Veterinary Act no horse was admitted to Downs House without the agreement of its own vet who had in turn referred the animal to a local vet in case veterinary intervention was required while the horse was in the yard, all had also had a blood test, no point in admitting a horse carrying a virus or was suffering muscle damage secondary to 'tying up'.

In the early days, from a therapy point of view, I confess we continued experiment, this the only method to discover the best way to resolve the problems with which we were faced.

Despite my personal certainty, backed by successes in the human field, that addressing muscle function was vitally important, (if you do not want to lose it use it), no one had explored this premise in injured animals. Charles Strong had treated muscles electrically but no one had tried active, controlled activity before; it was a huge learning curve, often we were near despair when a horse that should, to all intents and purposes, have been recovering remained agonisingly static showing no appreciable improvement, then joy of joys a break through and it was suddenly possible, when they were being worked in long reins, to see the underlying latent power we had been trying to regain.

Every injury is multifactorial and impossible though it is to comprehend every cell of the trillions within the body is in a state of constant communication with its fellows. Damage to any body structure, bone, joint, ligament, tendon, organ, interferes with this communication, thus any problem, however minor affects the whole. Perhaps comparison with a computer virus makes it easier to understand, one minute the computer is doing every-thing you ask it, then no longer responds to command, programmes cease to function as expected.

If muscles cease to receive their constant, anticipated stream of commands, secondary to curtailment of information and due to the fact muscle tissue is programmed to be economic, affected muscles close down some of their contractile segments with resultant loss of power, this leads to impaired function within the section of the body they control and increased stress, often resulting in secondary injury, in other areas.

Electrical stimulation can help in cases of muscle deterioration but muscles work in partnership, there is a need for an equal and opposite force to ensure smooth movement, injury to one muscle also affects its partner. When using a muscle stimulator it is difficult to be certain you are influencing the partner muscle adequately, if at all.

A further consideration when attempting to re-establish lost power is that muscle requires to be loaded in order to recover pre-injury efficiency necessitating an increase in demand while working. In the human model this is easy, resistance can be selectively incorporated into exercise programmes. Devising similar situations is not so easy when working the horse.

Originally there was an exercise flaw in human gymnastic apparatus, James Hunt the Racing Driver, son in law of Rosie Lomax and a fitness fanatic, was one of the first people to realise many gym circuits and exercise programmes only targeted one unit of a muscle partnership, for example bending the elbows, working against a weight attached to a pulley, was used to strengthen the biceps muscles, but when biceps ceased to work the weight returned to its starting point, straightening the arm as it did so because the apparatus was not designed to offer resistance for the partner muscle, triceps. We discussed this in some depth while I was treating him; valuable, thought provoking information that caused me to look very hard at the programmes I utilised for the horses.

James solved the problem for the human model as he found 'push me, pull me' type apparatus in the USA, the exercise machines ensured paired sets of muscles worked equally.

I decided we needed to devise a method of using weights when working horses, hackney trainers used circular, weighted pastern boots, loading all the limb muscles equally while I wanted to try to target only the weaker groups.

To achieve a varied placement of weight, to ensure resistance, woof boots were the answer. Weight boots were created by removing the padding and replacing this with lead shot, bless Billy Morris for providing several pounds of No 5 shot. The amount of shot used varied the weight, 4oz, 6oz, 8oz provided a useful range. Once these were made a boot could be attached to the weaker limb for a given time period daily, applied when the horse was exercised in long reins or was on the walker. Dependant on the groups targeted the weighted section could be placed on the inner or outer aspect of the lower leg. Not ideal but better than nothing.

Another method was to have the horse shod with a weighted shoe attached to the affected limb. Garry Pickford achieved this by riveting a second shoe to the inner rim of the normal shoe, its size and placement ensuring the frog and bulbs of the heels could function normally. The weighted shoe obviously affected all the muscles of the limb complex but I reasoned that there would be general muscle loss after tendon injury, this was confirmed by measuring around the forearm of the affected limb when a reduction of up to one inch in circumference was common. Similarly hindquarter injury affects all the muscles to a greater or lesser extent.

I already knew following injury in a human patient, that persuading them to wear a weight around the ankle or wrist following muscle loss, worked far better than suggesting an exercise regime, a patient will always do the exercises prescribed for a few days then give up or forget, if asked to wear a weight, for increasing periods as they indulge in normal activities they are continually exercising weak muscles and most importantly building these in the correct balance for normal, daily, activities.

In many horse patients, admitted for a limb problem, roach backs or poor general muscling along the back was also common. One day, after eating some excellent loin chops, supplied by Ron Thomas from a Welsh mountain farm and wondering why they were so meaty, I had a sudden thought, meat is muscle, mountain tracks zig zag, these sheep zig zag up mountains, why not try walking the back cases diagonally across a slope? It worked, but why? I suspect because the horse is mentally programmed to keep the vertebral column straight. When walking across a slope the vast weight of the abdominal contents slips to the downhill side of the body creating a slight vertebral concavity on the uphill side, in response, the muscles sited on the convexity (down-hill side) automatically contract to pull the column straight.

An interesting feature associated with weak equine muscles is once you have persuaded them to work they appear, although this is not scientifically proven, unlike human muscle, to click into a rebuild mode of their own. Perhaps because the horse is a prey species?

Gradually our recovery rates improved, there were enough funds to buy a small treadmill, but what was it doing? In order to try to see what was happening I used Tigger our lurcher. The belt began to move and he nearly tipped onto his nose as the belt took his legs backwards, he hastily moved his legs forward only to find they had gone backward again without his knowledge. He then froze and would have got his front feet trapped if the emergency cord had not stopped the belt. What had it demonstrated? On the tread mill the legs need to be advanced actively but the belt takes them backward with little or no muscular effort on the part of the exercising subject. Useful experiment.

As forward movement of the horse is resultant from the power generated from the backward thrust of the hind limb, the tread mill is not much help, the power muscles are not recruited. Checking with Professeur Dr Auer in Switzerland, whom I knew used one for investigation of respiratory function, I asked if work on the treadmill mirrored over ground muscle recruitment, I learned it did not!

Was my impulse buy a waste of money, possibly, but then discovery that it was very effective if used for horses that had been lame and habitually moved with a one, two, three, hop, rather than a normal stride. On the tread mill, in order to keep balanced, they quickly learned they must take even strides leaving out the hop. Two or three sessions were usually sufficient to re-establish the correct movement sequence in the brain, this discovery, to a degree justified the expense. Over time we realised there were several other benefits, due to the way the hind limb is lifted off the belt, prior to advancement, the loin muscles are recruited, at slow paces active muscles had to work in their middle range so it was useful for recruiting slow twitch muscle in horses predominately endowed with fast twitch.

Interval training or exercising the heart, its self a hugely important muscular organ is important in any fitness regime but despite claims the treadmill could be used for this we found, probably because the model only enabled a fast walk, once the horses became accustomed to the work it was not as effective as swimming.

Trainers various

Stan Mellor began to use me shortly after I began to work in Lambourn, still very conscious of being a new face on the block I was careful to try not to intrude when I visited a yard, one evening when I reached Stan's I found the office door was firmly shut, this was unusual, it sounded, from the muffled voices from within, as though a momentous conference was being held, or did I detect the tempo to be one normally associated with a real argument? Eventually, and with some trepidation, I knocked, Stan bellowed 'Come in!' Stan and the Head Lad, Eric, normally in perfect accord were both red in the face and obviously furious with each other. What had happened?

The rapport between head lad and trainer is, as eloquently described by Corky Brown during an interview, rather like a marriage, when pressed he did add 'But in every marriage there are moments of discord'. This was obviously one of those moments. As I waited for orders Stan suddenly said, 'You win, the dam thing can go to Newbury'. It transpired that two horses, both nervous travellers, were due to race on the same day, one locally the other in the North. The Mellor's kept a donkey to accompany and calm nervous travellers, the quarrel had apparently started as Stan and Eric tried to agree which horse needed the donkey most! As the yard probably had its shirt on one of the runners and Eric knew which he was determined to win, hence the discussion. I offered Mokey, I was certain he would love to be of use and yes, he was up to date with all necessary injections. He moved to the Mellor's and remained until it was discovered that if sharing a box, he refused to allow his companion to eat until he'd had his fill: he got fatter and the horse got thinner.

Stan's wife Elaine, a notable jockey and one of the first professional women to race ride, became a great friend and through her I met her great mucker Brook Saunders, also race riding but training in Epsom rather than Lambourn. Shortly after we met I was surprised to be summoned by Ron Smyth one of Epsom's elderly, traditional, trainers. Time and date organised I drove to Epsom, then following a fortifying glass with Brookie and feeling somewhat apprehensive, for Ron's reputation preceded him, I set forth. After negotiating his

Alsatians we met in the main yard and he showed me the horse he wished me to look at, then left me with a lad to continue his evening stables round. After about 5 minutes I told the lad to rug the horse up and set off to find Ron, 'Mr Smyth I am sorry but really cannot find anything wrong with that horse', 'Good, there is nothing wrong with it, now come and see the one I need some help with'. I had passed the test, he was a pleasure to work for and it was a sad day for racing when he retired.

Elaine was good fun and several times, during the winter, we took small groups to sample the jump racing in the south of France, staying in a Pension overnight, lunching with one of the local trainers on *Foie Gras* washed down by locally produced wine, then on to the races and home next day. On one occasion Edward Gillespie, who had just begun to manage Cheltenham Race Course, was a member of the group. Some of the races included a variety of obstacles rather than just plain fences, he was very enthusiastic about this and the trip undoubtedly sowed a seed, one that eventually resulted in the Cross Country race at Cheltenham.

Dr Vincent O'Brien, one of the many trainers I had the privilege to work for, was as meticulous as Martin Pipe. Flying over, sometimes in company with Lester Piggott, the car would drop us at the back of the house, Lester would get into another vehicle and go straight to the gallops but I was usually waylaid by Jacqueline O'Brien, who would shout after the disappearing car group, 'You will need to wait for Mary, Nora is more important than the wretched horses if you want your lunch'. Nora ruled the kitchen and suffered with her back but however bad it was there was always an Irish soda bread loaf waiting for me, 'To take across the water for they do not know how to bake over there'.

To sit, metaphorically at his feet and listen to Dr O'Brien was an unforgettable experience; what a memory, his knowledge of pedigrees, breeding, performance, was unsurpassed; visits became not just a therapy exercise but also an unbelievable learning curve, for the information proffered by probably the greatest trainer of the 20th Century was unique; I shall always cherish the memories of those visits and the kindness shown.

Nora must have spread the word for I was invited to visit the local convent at Thurles and treat the nuns; on several occasions this in conjunction with visiting Bally Doyle then came a time when the O'Brien's were away, I was needed in the yard but because of the troubles they did not feel I should stay alone at their house. 'Not a problem' said the Mother Superior, 'We will feed her in the evening and she can stay at Henrattie's Hotel, the wife was at the school as a girl and is a good woman'.

It was a while since I had been to the Convent, when ushered by a Nun into the outer parlour, the walls hung with pictures of your progression to Hell should you Sin, I thought she looked different, so did all the others I met as I was escorted through the inner parlour, last supper, crucifixion, empty tomb, to the nun's quarters. It transpired that they were no longer an enclosed order, freedom had sent them scurrying to the local haberdashers to purchase shoulder pads! We ate well, the food produced by The Brothers from a neighbouring Monastery. The mattress at the Hotel was interestingly lumpy but the breakfast outstanding.

Michael Stout, training at one of the main yards in Newmarket, was the first to put in an oval pool incorporating a straight section, this enabled new swimmers to look straight down the pool to the exit, giving a focus for escape; nearly all learned to swim correctly after negotiating the straight section rather than if introduced in a circular pool, first time swimmers often climb using their front legs only, others kick side-ways behind, both actions can injure backs but a horse that learns to swim using all four limbs will keep its back straight even on a circle.

When we first started swimming horses we were surprised at the effort required and the rise in heart rate, a feature often ignored. To breathe and supply the oxygen required for muscle activity over ground, the horse relies primarily upon diaphragmatic action rather than using rib movement to increase the size of the chest cavity to enable lung expansion.

We began to realise horses are unable to breathe naturally when swimming, ex-haling or breathing out almost impossible. Luckily, Dr David Snow, working at the Equine Research

Station in Newmarket, with whom I was doing some muscle investigation, was happy to attempt to measure respiratory function and heart rate in a swimming horse then endeavour to calculate fatigue levels. Resignedly Sir Mark Prescott agreed we could use his pool and one of his horses. At the last moment, apprehensive lest something go wrong, we used a hack rather than something in training. With various electrodes and a heart rate monitor attached the swimming team persuaded their charge to enter the pool. The effect of the heart rate monitor and its associated straps slipping, then ending somewhere around the horses balls, had an electrifying effect, the handlers lost control but fortunately managed to prevent the horse going over backwards, after two terrifying circuits the horse had the sense to leave pool by the ramp.

As the horse emerged David dived in, more concerned at the fact his heart rate monitor was at the bottom of the pool than that the experiment had been a total failure.

When Downs House was conceived I had never intended that horse patients be confined to Racing Thoroughbreds alone, but the difficulty was spreading the word to reach those who needed help; advertising, hideously expensive, did little or nothing to fill boxes. Television coverage of horse events was not commonplace and although Downs House had featured this was always associated with racing then I met Vicki Latter.

Vicki was the New Zealand rider based with The Princess Royal at Gatcombe, her horse, Chief, had bruised a foot and she brought him to swim. Vicki was attempting to organise the NZ riders based in the UK and I was invited to go to Badminton in case any of the competing Kiwi's needed help. After finishing the cross country, Horton Point, Mark Todd's spare ride was not comfortable in front, this was when roads, tracks and steeple chase were all included on the cross country day.

Discussion between the Bevan's who owned the horse, Toddy and Wally Neiderer the NZ vet resulted in my being asked if I could get the horse sound overnight in order to pass the trot up the following morning. I knew Wally would never allow pain removal if he felt it could be dangerous so I agreed to try, he had diagnosed mild bruising in a tendon sheath and considered it would be safe for the horse to show jump, but knew that the mild head nod indicating discomfort, even though only visible after a sharp turn and then for just one stride would be spotted by the eagle eyes of the Ground Jury.

At a three day competition the horses are inspected before the competition starts and on the morning after the cross country phase when any sign of lameness, however minor, results in their having to withdraw from the competition. As our discussion ended the loud speaker system announced Horton Point was in the lead. Reputation on the line! Having first requested that I be allowed to do whatever I wanted, without any outside interference, I got to work. I have never been happy with standing in ice, it can be useful but I prefer cold hosing followed by specialist electro therapy designed to pump away excess fluid, the pressure from which, particularly in a tendon sheath, is often a cause of pain.

By 10 o'clock that evening the horse was sound at trot and remembering my gypsies I wrapped the leg, much to the horror and amazement of all involved, in a cabbage poultice. The horse was a little stiff next morning but sound, the leg was clean, no heat, no filling. After a good body massage he moved freely in hand, then followed an anxious half hour, would he nod on turning as he had on the previous evening; a sense relief when he passed inspection at the trot up, that afternoon he and Toddy went out and won Badminton, this certainly helped spread the word.

It is now accepted that by using electro therapy, rather than relying on chemicals, you can remove pain, this a feature associated with shock wave therapy. Personally I am unwilling to remove pain lest removal might compromise the functional ability of the horse. Even worse is the worry that by making the horse sound, having removed guarding pain, one might endanger the rider. A rider instinctively knows if all is not well, and pulls up, but if the horse cannot tell the rider, because they have no pain and responds to an unrealistic rider command falls can happen, it would be terrible to mask pain and then see the rider suffer a serious, possibly fatal, rotational fall.

The showing world began to use us because of Bertha, she arrived after her owner had seen one of our Christmas cards - sent when we were resident at Downs House - in the home of a friend. We had, at the time, tried to make the cards amusing and this particular one had featured a cartoon carthorse named Adolphus. Inside was printed one of my sad efforts at verse. On the front he was depicted, miserable head down. On the back, recovered, holding a sprig of holly in his mouth:

Adolphus had a hurtie,
It made him rather sad,
They said Downs House for you,
He thought they must be mad.
They gave him sun and swimming
He did not feel so bad.
And when the visit ended
He was a happy lad

Bertha's owner thought if we were mad enough to advertise thus we would cope with Bertha, she turned out to be a large, self-opinionated, show cob. Qualified for the Horse of the Year Show she was becoming contrary and her owners felt she needed a change of scene and some sweetening. She took over the yard, if any of her meals were late she screamed and beat up the door of her box, she swam very splashily, trod heavily on nearly every ones feet, causing considerable damage to staff toes, nipped anyone stupid enough to pass too close to her box door, got so much sand in her coat in the rolling boxes that she had to be brushed, tied up in the box in which she had rolled, to restore the sand.

Swimming certainly tuned her shape and she set off for London looking really good. She was amongst the few selected to go into the main ring after the preliminary judging and her owners were ecstatic. When it was time to enter the indoor arena for the final judging she peered through the entrance, did not like what she saw and planted, a performance that ended her showing career, but until she went to her paddock in the sky, we always received a Christmas Card.

A Christmas card from Downs House

Aldolphus had a hurtie
It made him rather sad
They said Downs House for you
He thought they must be mad
They gave him sun and swimming
He did not feel so bad
And when the visit ended
He was a happy lad.

The card achieved more than any costly advertising

The Seasons Greetings
from all at

Downs House

General Expansion including overseas assignments.

I have often been often asked, 'Why did you not work with the Brits?' In the mid 1980s the British riders were uncertain whether Physiotherapy, a completely new idea, would be of help at competition - neither did the riders see any need for structured team training. Their attitude at the time tending to be: the Brits rode best across country. Anyone could ride a dressage test, for heaven's sake all you had to do was a few circles in a flat arena. Show jumping was easy.

When it became apparent that to win help could be useful, Mark Phillips and I were invited to go to a European Event with the British Team: he to discuss training and I to offer massage and therapy to both horses and riders. After we returned to the UK, having done our bit, neither of us heard anything. Three months passed before Mark telephoned me and said the Americans wanted him and he was off. The Kiwi's, however, decided I could be useful, asked would I go with them to Atlanta for the Olympics. I accepted without a second thought.

The NZ squad were one of several teams who decided it would be best to acclimatise horses and riders for several weeks before the games started rather than fly in, compete and fly out. Riders and horses and grooms were flown to the USA and based at a polo ranch. This was ideal - a ranch in the true sense of the word - so plenty of room to exercise, and separate accommodation for all. The only question was how do you keep riders, used to riding a minimum of six horses a day, amused and fit with only one horse to exercise? The ranch owner took care of this, arranging baseball games against scratch local teams, water skiing, and gave endless parties.

Flying in a week before everyone was due to move to the Olympic venue I was met at the Airport by the Chef D'equippe, who told me: 'The horses are sound bar one, but half the riders and grooms are injured.' Water skiing was the culprit. On a lake it's difficult due to the tight turns required and a number of knees and low backs needed repair. The horse casualty, Mark Todd's ride, appeared to have an injured stifle, and this proved to be the case when Wayne McIlwraith - a New Zealand vet based in the USA - arrived. He was a pioneer in joint disease and was able to look inside the stifle joint using an arthroscopic camera. Investigation showed a meniscal tear, and sadly this precluded Todd from competing although he stayed with the team giving help and encouragement. The night before we moved to Atlanta the Kiwi's decided another party was required before every one became serious, not only as a thank you to their host, but to entertain as many of the other teams as they could find to invite. Somehow a Māori band was discovered and imported. Fiona Tibone, team cook and general factotum, produced food for around a hundred guests. The dancing, as the ranch owner pointed out next day, had flattened an area nearly large enough for another polo ground. One departing guest managed to wedge his car between two trees and was found next morning, unhurt but fast asleep in the driver's seat. Everyone involved moved to the horse park more or less prepared and with enough sound horses and riders prepared to go for Gold.

I knew Doug Hannum, who treated the USA squad, having taught several seminars at his equine clinic in Virginia. He gave me a great welcome when we checked into the Olympic venue and was kindness in itself: not only was he a past master at unravelling red tape - ensuring the Kiwi team always had sufficient bedding and hay - but even more important, he always had a source of good, hot coffee on hand, no matter the time of day or night.

Rolex was sponsoring the horse section of the games and as the NZ team were among the Medal winners: Blyth Tait winning individual Gold and the team Bronze, the entire squad was invited to a celebratory function following medal distribution. On arrival we stepped back in time to the era of *Gone with the Wind*, rows of chairs were arranged on the grass in front of a replica of Tara. I am not certain if Rhett Butler or Scarlet O'Hara were around! We were directed to sit and watch a re-enactment as Unionists fought Confederates; eventually the battle ended, tables appeared and the soldiers, re-clad as servants, laid out a meal.

I suppose the set and the actors must have been hired for a given time period for we were still eating when several lorries chugged into view, their crews leapt out and began to disman-

NEW ZEALAND OLYMPIC THREE-DAY EVENT TEAM
ATLANTA 1996-WINNERS TEAM BRONZE; INDIVIDUAL GOLD AND SILVER

tle Tara and to pack away the chairs we were sitting on. The food and the tables also disappeared. No one was given a Rolex watch despite the rumour these would be handed out with supper!

Doug and I both met up regularly at International Events and subsequent Olympics, both having developed our own methods to keep our team horses sound. Doug would arrive loaded with therapy gear, while mine fitted into a small case. And you could buy cabbages on arrival, also Sauerkraut, the latter second to none for taking the bruising out of a foot. On one occasion, when a group were discussing therapy, in the canteen, the following comment were overheard: 'The Americans have a 747 of therapy gear! All the Kiwi's have is an old woman and a bucket.' Probably, because the Kiwi's really understood preparation and fitness, I had less to worry about and gypsy lore certainly got rid of bruising!

It seemed a pity to turn down the invitation to work with trotters in Los Angeles, I could easily hop across to the Caribbean on the way home and see my younger son, by then settled firmly in the Turks and Caicos. I knew nothing about the owner who had invited me and even less about trotters but things boded well when a first class plane ticket for the round trip arrived. A stretch limo met me at the airport. I'd had no experience of such transport and wasted the journey for, after being ushered into the back, the dimensions seemingly as large as a good-sized room, once the door was shut it became pitch black, and deeply shaded windows blocked out even the glare from the street lights. I had no idea where anything was: light switch, TV, fridge, drinks cabinet! I knew they must be there as I had seen the inside of similar vehicles in the odd James Bond film. At the hotel I was taken to my suite and on the desk lay a note directing me to order whatever food and drink I wanted. I was informed that a car would leave for the stables at 9:00 am next morning. After a light repast, washed down by a Whiskey Sour, my favourite drink when in the USA, I eventually fell into a huge, comfortable bed, rounding off a VIP day.

The owner, a tall dark haired man probably around 35 years of age, dressed Cowboy designer throughout, was waiting in the foyer next morning. Chauffeur driven to the stables it seemed only honest to explain to him that while I knew a bit about most disciplines in the horse world, trotters had not featured. Remembering the sled dog ride, (surely not so different?) I asked could I drive a pony. I felt I would be of more use if I had actually experienced what they needed to do.

The grooms did look rather dubious as a pony was harnessed. Shown how to perch I was given the reins and was led out then loosed on the trotting track. No problem it all seemed too easy at first, a nice sedate circuit of the track completed I thought, why not a second then pull up? As I gathered the reins firmly after the second circuit, expecting to come from trot, to walk, then to halt, we accelerated. Unfortunately no one had told me the harder you pull the faster they go! With no other competitors to avoid the pony flew. I thought I would die - apparently I broke the track record - before eventually a car appeared along-side. 'Drop your reins. DROP YOUR REINS!' My brain said, if I did I would fall off: nothing else to hold onto. Eventually exhaustion took over, my arms sort of collapsed, and we slowed down.

Despite the fact that in the training stables, as in Martin Pipe's yard, nothing was left to chance there were several techniques that I felt could be utilised to improve performance. For example massage followed by limb stretching had never been tried. Introduction improved stride length by one inch in several ponies, enough to make a big difference in a race. Working on a small inclined tread mill, already in situ but never used, improved the loin musculature in ponies with roach backs.

Conformation and muscle requirement were totally different to those I was used to working with: the ponies needed to lean into their breast harness to pull the vehicle, but a high head carriage appeared to be essential. Balance demands, when cornering at speed, contributed to a number of injuries, these manifesting across a wide range of muscle groups. Leg injuries were sweated, same principle as a cabbage leaf, but the ointment used was even more effective. Wheel collision between carts, particularly when overtaking was not unusual when novices were training, but it was catastrophic often injuring both drivers and horses. It was a really interesting visit marred only by the fact that I never got paid!

On the final morning of my visit the owner appeared in the yard much later than planned and distinctly shaken. He was driving an old banger rather than being dropped off by a chauffeur. Almost in tears he explained he was broke. He'd made his money in electronics working in partnership with a life-long school friend and they held a joint bank account with his partner managing all their finances. On the way to the stables that morning he'd called in at the bank to collect my dues only to discover the account was empty: no bills had been paid for six weeks and the bank had foreclosed, freezing all his assets.

Fortunately my plane tickets were paid for and I had packed, taking my case with me to the yard ready to fly out in the afternoon.

Herbs and alternatives
I flew to Providenciales, an island in a group known as the Turks and Caicos where my younger son worked as a doctor.

Not horse minded as a child he had married Camille, an American who could not live without one. Relocating to the islands she had discovered and rescued a number of feral animals, broken them in and was running a very successful business taking visitors out to ride on the many unspoilt, empty beaches, and encouraging those responsible enough to swim with their mounts in the sea.

The local peoples, the TIs or Turks Islanders who call themselves 'Belongers' and are descendants of slaves originally transported from middle Africa and dumped when slaving fell into disrepute between 1810 and 1833. Many of the islanders still had knowledge of herbal medicine: how else could they have survived? I had always felt that with the integration of western, chemically based ideas this information would eventually be lost and longed to glean some knowledge. Many TIs were suspicious of the relatively recent 'white' invasion, but Sam had treated several and after lengthy negotiations using Steiner - one of the boatmen - I was informed a lady called Stella Harris, 'Would talk to Dr Sam's mummy'.

The settlement where Stella lived lies at the north end of the island, an area remote from the tourist hotels: the shore rocky rather than sandy. Small churches, of which there are many, are the only concrete buildings, local people still tending to live in corrugated huts, for despite the opulence of the tourist areas life is still primitive for most and their only income is derived from selling the fish and lobster they catch.

On arrival I was directed by a small naked child to a dilapidated heap of tin on the outer edge of a group of corrugated shacks: the heap turned out to be two huts, Stella's home. I hesitated, then looking in through a gap rather than a door, I saw a small, wizened, elderly coloured lady dressed in a grey caftan-type smock and wearing a green, brimless, circular hat. She was sitting on a bed with a metal spring base, sewing. I knocked, 'Steiner' [the negotiator] says you might talk with me'. 'Is you Dr Sam's mummy?' 'Yes.' 'Come in, come in. Sit by me; my hands is busy but my mouf is not.'

I offered a tin of shortbread biscuits. 'You know these my favourite?' 'No.' 'Who tell you?' 'No one.' A small silence. 'You can see,' she said, almost to herself.

The first hut served as a living, sleeping, cooking area, the second as her pharmacy, there she mixed a wide range of potions, both liquid and powdered prepared from the from ingredients derived after boiling, storing and drying carefully selected plants, roots and berries. The varied scents, which swirled from pot to pot, jar to jar seemed very similar to those I had experienced previously in a Middle East spice emporium.

It was the first of many very special meetings, Stella had been taught herbal lore by her pa, he by his ma, the knowledge handed down thus since the first, enforced settlement of the islands, over 200 years previously. I visited her each time I went to the island to see the family and learned so much.

A great deal of the information, particularly regarding the time to gather plants, roots, fruits, leaves, how to dry and mix them, also the use of sweats, was remarkably similar to that I had gleaned from Romany acquaintances and would subsequently discover were also comparable to the plant lore of the Cherokee Indians.

On one visit we discussed the use of Aloe Vera of which there is a mass on the islands; it had recently become the 'in thing' in Europe and when I told her it was being drunk, she nearly fell off her seat. When she recovered enough to speak she said, 'Why you think it got spikes, silly girl.'

There are over 240 varieties of Aloe Vera, each with a slightly different chemical make-up. To me this reinforces the necessity to be extremely careful in the choice of all medicinal plants, for if one is beneficial it may well have a first cousin that is poisonous: something certainly applicable to fungi.

On what was to be our final meeting Stella told me her time was near; that her dead husband had told her he was tired of waiting. 'In a dream?' I asked. 'No dear: he around all the time. Only good thing is, he don't want no meals no more.' She roared with laughter.

As we talked she pointed to a bungalow-type structure, obviously very new and constructed from concrete blocks. 'I had that builded for my son,' she informed me. 'You want know how I got 'nough money?'

She described a potion - I suspect a cream Viagra judging from the fact she ended by saying, 'They use; they up for tree days; the men very happy. They pay me well.' I could only giggle inwardly as I thought of my son trying to promote birth control at one end of the island and Stella encouraging the opposite at the other.

She died about a month after we had been together: death prediction is not uncommon amongst those whom, we in the West, describe variously as natives, uncivilised, or third world inhabitants. I had first met it in Malaya when bidding goodbye to a Leprosy patient, one no longer considered infectious following drug therapy and who was returning to his village. 'I am glad to die at home. I will be gone by the third quarter of the next moon,' he informed me, after thanking me for his artificial leg. 'Remember to get someone to send the leg back, when you do not need it any more.' I said, half joking. Then remembering his religion, 'Do you need it to be buried with you?'

'No, I have mine here.' He indicated a brown package.

Memory flash: I had been summoned, shortly after starting to work at Sungei Buloh, to assist during an amputation, and arriving late I had not realised the patient had been sedated using a spinal rather than general anaesthetic and had to swallow hard when he asked, as I passed, 'Has doc started cutting yet?' A Holy Man was waiting outside for the leg, to remove it for mummification in order that the whole body could, when the time came, be buried as one. This was that very patient off home now with his preserved leg under his arm. News came that he had died on the exact day he had predicted and subsequently his artificial leg *was* returned.

Acu Medicine

In many cultures as medicinal information has been handed down by tradition rather than being recorded in text, the result is that much has been lost or mislaid. One example, which includes herbal use is acu medicine. These methods only resurfaced in Europe in 1800s when the benefits were described by French Missionaries returning from China. There, acu medicine, is documented as having developed 3,000 years ago but a discovery in 1991 poses several questions. Had acu knowledge been present in Europe 5,000 years ago, perhaps having travelled from China, or, did it go from Europe to China. If European why was it lost for centuries? These questions are reasonable following the discovery, in the Otztaler Alps, of a preserved male corpse, lying where he had died some 5,000 years previously. His skin appeared to be tattooed, and these marks were subsequently identified as being identical to the acu points used for arthritis in knees and low backs. X-ray evidence confirmed he had suffered from arthritis in the knees and low back.

The Chinese Texts are very specific, detailing the points that require stimulation following diagnosis in both humans and animals and I have always been amused by the fact that the chicken has rather more points than the horse. Over the years I have observed treatment by acupuncture but never considered I was suitably trained to practice the methods.

Leeches

There are of course medicinal animals as well as plants. Healing wounds in many of my horse patients was still a major problem. The Low Level Laser helped heal small cuts, these usually caused by the edge of a shoe clipping a leg, but unfortunately due to modern, glass-like tarmac surfaces, young horses often slipped on the roads however carefully ridden. Some fell onto their knees, skinning them and creating large open wounds. These were a major headache, not just to keep clean to avoid infection - difficult in a stable however well bedded down and skipped out - but because it was essential to try to prevent the growth of the wrong kind of repair tissue, in horse parlance known as 'proud flesh'. This is a tissue type that does not conform to the original, over growing and creating large areas of bleeding, unsightly flesh that does not grow a skin covering.

Even without proud flesh a problem can occur if the area heals too slowly as scar tissue develops. This results in considerable loss of elasticity in associated soft tissue and reduced movement in the joint, lying below the scar.

Moaning about this to my medical son after re-dressing an unresponsive knee wound on a two year old filly I asked if there was anything he could think of, however unconventional.

'Try Leeches', he said. 'Leeches!' I queried in some surprise. I had met my first after an expedition into the Malayan jungle when on removing my boots I had found several families dining round my ankles.

I made a tentative enquiry to the only leech farm I could find. Located in South Wales the farm breeds leeches of all kinds in order to extract and analyse their bio chemical components.

I explained my problem: a young racehorse with knee wounds that refused to heal. Unfazed they enquired, 'How many do you require?' After describing the wound and following the subsequent discussion I settled on four, but was advised to have one extra in case of *a calamity*.

'Not April the first is it?' asked our postman some two days later as he handed over a small brown-paper parcel marked: LIVE LEECHES HANDLE WITH CARE.

I had no antique receptacle in which to put them although I had seen a photograph of Leech Jars in the Medical Museum in the Apothecaries' Hall. I wonder what Mr Noah used: did leeches feature amongst the creatures who went in, two by two?

The best readily available home for them was a large glass jar, ex Heinz mayonnaise. This was filled, as instructed, with sterile water. When shaken from their damp linen bag, the five medicinal variety, *Hirudo Medicinalis*, swam slowly around, then, looking like strands of exotic seaweed, settled at the bottom of the jar in a vertical pose.

My Malayan memory was of tiny, thin, brown worms about half an inch long. These were quite fat, at least two inches long, beautifully coloured, yellows, blues, greens, browns, seeming translucent they shimmered like petrol on water. It was decided to allow them to relax and to introduce them to their host meal later in the day.

Between placing the order and their arrival, too ashamed to ask the purveyors why the application of their product would help healing I had done some research. I discovered leech sustenance is whole blood and in order to insure a good, uninterrupted meal, they excrete, through the rim of their triangular shaped mouth a chemical cocktail containing an anti-clotting agent when attached to their host.

In living beings blood loss is a disaster so should damage occur to a blood vessel wall there is an inbuilt ability to seal the leak by clotting. However, as blood is the porter liquid of the body, reduced flow is in some situations disadvantageous.

In the 1980s there was emerging a new medical art, micro surgery and those performing this revolutionary work desperately needed blood to flow rather than clot after they reattached amputated bits from a body. It was this requirement that had rekindled interest in the leech and its use.

My purchases were, I hoped, going to re-establish blood flow to promote healing.

The patient and leech-containing jar were moved to the wash box: action stations, and off came the dressings. Slight pause, how does one catch a free swimming leach, from a large jar with a rather small opening, small enough to allow careful entry of the catching hand but preclude rapid removal if squeamish on contact. Then, when caught, how does one attach the captured specimen to the knee of a probably reluctant, certainly unpredictable two year filly?

Unlike most medical preparations, for example pills or cough mixture, there were no accompanying instructions: leeches handling of. . . attachment of. . . disposal of. . . Not one of the staff, who had gathered to witness yet another of their boss's crazy ideas, was anxious to try. Rubber gloves perhaps? None in the box. Forceps? Yes, they *had* been around but no one was certain where they were. The leeches continued to sway in a rather bored fashion. I hoped they were hungry or my experiment was doomed.

My original concern, unpredictability, saved the day. The filly, tired of everyone around her apparently doing nothing decided on an escape attempt. In the ensuing flurry the jar fell over and broke, and there they were on the floor. No longer squeamish I grabbed one: at £5:00 each they were expensive. Hoping I had chosen the correct end I pushed it against the edge of the wound. Immediate attachment. It seemed a shame that number five (*in case of a calamity*) should miss a meal and soon all were busy. It was fascinating to watch as the wound changed colour from dirty grey to healthy pink.

After about 15 minutes during which each swelled to the size of a giant slug, they self-detached, falling to the floor and lying somnolent. By now, armed with a pair of barbecue tongs, I found collection was easy. They were scooped up and dropped into a new jar within which all five sank to the bottom.

What now? How does one dispose of a used, redundant leech? As far as the farm was concerned they were of no use as no longer sterile.

Further research was enlightening. They could be cleansed if put into a salt solution, the principle being absorbed saline, just as in the human model, would cause them to vomit. It was decided to try but the result was so disgusting and the paroxysms suffered appeared so agonising that rather than flush them down the drain they were tipped into the garden pond: a natural habitat after all, and left to their own devices.

The farm continued to supply leeches when needed and a number of cases responded favourably. It transpired my initial enquiry had been their first animal-based request and after I sent them a photographic series depicting wound healing, accompanied by a short description of the case histories it was published in the *Leech Society Journal*.

To my astonishment publication was followed by an invitation to present a paper at the annual Leech Society gathering.

Not an invitation to turn down for several reasons, not least because the meeting would be held in the Apothecary's Hall. This stands on the site of the original - rebuilt in 1672 following the Great Fire of London. Accepting the invitation would enable me to visit this famous building, not normally open to a member of the public. I knew the library, containing a wealth of Herbal knowledge was unsurpassed; and housed in a museum there was a fascinating collection of early medical tools amongst which were several jars marked: Leech.

The Worshipful Company of the Apothecary's is one of the oldest livery companies, first records appear in 1180 when apothecaries were members of the Guild of Peppers. Then around 1345 the group became linked to a new guild: the

Grocers Company. Down the years the Apothecaries achieved recognition as an individual group and a Royal Charter, granted by James I in 1617, enabled a split from the grocers. Shortly after this in 1673, they created the first herbal garden on record: the world famous Chelsea Physic Garden. Obviously a group not easily satisfied with their lot they challenged the medical monopoly of the Royal College of Physicians throughout the 17th century eventually being given the right to practice medicine. Thus Apothecaries were the forerunner of today's medical practitioners, and their history takes us full circle, back to leeches and the re-emergence of herbalism.

Arriving to lecture I noted a large number of jars arranged behind the speakers rostrum. I suppose it was appropriate that many delegates had arrived accompanied by a live example of their favoured variety, and there were a fair number for worldwide over 650 differing species of Leech have been identified. The receptacles had been, or were being, reverently placed on long tables thus acting as a backdrop for all lectures. I was glad to observe that all the jars had securely taped, butter muslin type covers, rather than lids with punched air holes for the species have a tendency to evacuate even through very small apertures and I was not certain how I might react in front of such a distinguished audience if a passing escapee decided it required a meal and chose me.

As I rose to speak, glancing at the seated rows of solemn faced, elderly delegates, gazing with rapture at the back drop of their jars I realised the light hearted opening, a recently discovered verse, that I had clipped to my serious, science based notes, would have been totally inappropriate:

I'm just crawling along the forest floor,
Any likely leg I will not ignore,
I'm after your blood so you'd better look out,
Cos once I start sucking I don't hang about.

I admit I was slightly nervous throughout, but no one escaped, and luckily all went well. The slides were the right way up (some projectors turn the slides and this can be confusing). The questions asked were appropriate, and I was royally applauded and left after lunch clutching a pass, one allowing me to use the library whenever I wished.

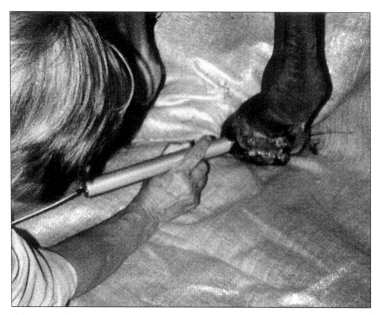

Above: A deep wound through the heel bulb. Healed by a combination of laser and leech.

Below: A knee wound

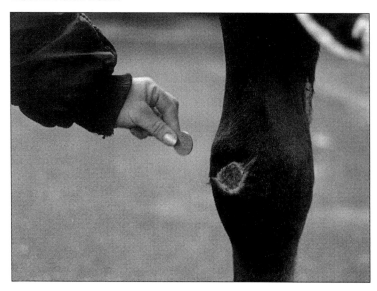

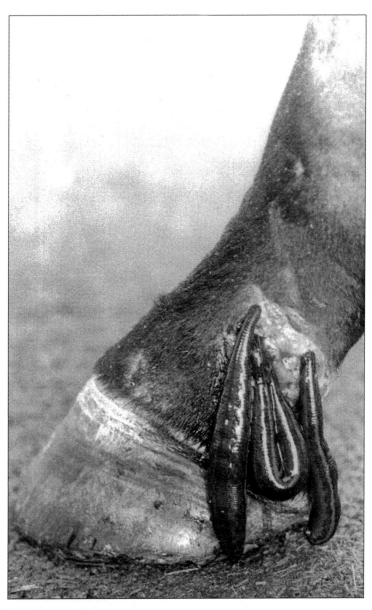

Lasers and leeches. old and new combined achieve perfect healing

Slugs

A telephone call from a Vet in Ireland regarding a problem with a horse was about to end when she said, somewhat hesitantly, 'I understand you are interested in old time cures. Could I ask you, have you ever heard of using a Black Snail to cure warts?' I had not and begged for more information. The vet explained that she too was intrigued by past methods of curing and while discussing these, with an elderly healer from the bog in the south west of Ireland, an area both devoid and suspicious of antibiotics, he had told her that Black Snail slime, wiped over a wart would kill it. She had tried this with apparent success on several horses with sarcoids - wart like growths. Foolishly, in my excitement, while scribbling down everything she told me, including the fact these snails were found in boggy areas I failed to jot down either her name or telephone number for had I been able to make contact I would have asked for photos, even arranged for a jockey to bring one back in a racing bag!

Frustrated and having failed to get any information from Google I did approach a jockey from a local yard who was about to go over to Ireland to ride and was staying on, in the south west, for a few days with his family after the race meeting. With just the area described by the vet and giving him a small plastic container I begged him to bring back some Black Snails. He reported, on return, that no one knew of any Black Snail.

With no hope of tracing the vet, I decided if anyone knew about the snail it would be Jim Marsh now retired to his Irish home. Jim was the Vet who, in Malaya all those years ago, had suggested I should try giving Physiotherapy to injured horses. 'You are as crazy as a bat,' he offered when I telephoned and explained my needs. As luck would have it one of his daughter's was a wild life photographer for television, and she would certainly find someone who knew!

A slug is, after all, only a snail without a house on its back and eventually it became apparent that sometimes, in remote areas, slugs are referred to as snails. The black snail turned out to be the black slug *Arion ater*, a great slug, because on reaching adult maturity, its length can vary from 10 to 15 cm.

Once I had a name I could start research, pages of helpful information arrived from people I contacted including the fact it was documented that 'their slime is rubbed on the skin as a folk remedy to treat warts, burns and injuries,' also that the practice was still current in some parts of the world: southern Italy for one. The slugs could be found on boggy upland areas and were easily recognisable because when disturbed, rather than curl up they 'start a slow deliberate rocking', which might be better described as a hula, hula wiggle.

I went and saw Phil Browne, a very supportive vet, and told him of my excitement at discovering an ancient sarcoid cure: one which might be worth resurrecting. There were several horses with small sarcoids in one of the yards where I worked under him and he agreed I could try. The question was how to find my first specimen, several hours spent crawling about Exmoor was fruitless and I was in despair until a gardening friend whom I'd told of my slug quest telephoned: she thought she had found one in her Hostas. It was captured and awaiting collection in her garage! Poked, it wiggled as the research information indicated it should; it was black, fat, about 8cm long and its underside was coated with very sticky mucus.

I took surgical gloves with me for the handling. Of the three horses selected, one had a tiresome sarcoid behind the girth area which when chafed by the girth bled copiously, this had regrown following excision. The other two victims had small growths on their necks. To say the experiment was a stunning success would be untrue, yet to say it was partially successful would be correct. The girth sarcoid shrank following three slime applications and was no longer bleeding. The neck ones did disappear, but they were small and might have been healing naturally.

The reason it was not possible to continue treatments was because the slugs were nearly impossible to find and did not last long in their jars, despite care. And unlike the leeches I could find no one who bred them. I finally gave up after the head girl, Liz Welsh, who was applying slime on alternate days, telephoned to say, the slug appeared slime-less and nor was it wiggling. 'In fact,' she said, 'it's become sluggish.'

Animals other than horses

Gradually, entirely because of the fact Penelope managed Downs House so successfully in my absence, life for me became easier. An increasing number of 'write offs' returned successfully to their pre-injury discipline and others won good races - including the Gold Cup at Cheltenham. While being interviewed on TV in the winner's enclosure, the horse's owner kindly suggested it was due to the repair job done at Downs House that the horse was back in training. The BBC must have been short of newsworthy interviewees at the time and I was excited to be asked to join Libby Purves on her Radio 4 show, Midweek. A new experience: I would be in a studio, live on the radio, however it turned out to be rather boring, we - the invited - were more or less being directed to say what it was considered those listening might want to hear.

On reflection the experience could be summed up as somewhat comparable to my favourite Mrs Thatcher cartoon, depicting the Cabinet sitting round a table looking wary. The caption reads:, 'When I want your opinions I will tell you what they are.'

A few days later a goat owner telephoned and enquired, did I do goats? If so could I help one of her flock: a nanny goat who'd needed an epidural when kidding and was now paralysed in one back leg. The caller had heard the broadcast, and tracked me down.

I was not new to goats, when a child a 'delicate friend' named Fiona had been the proud owner of a goat cart. Children who were unusual were often described 'delicate' in my childhood, circa 1930s. No child was 'stressed' or 'unmanageable' as they seem to be these days. All the other local children were pushed around in a variety of prams, most, but not mine, having a crest or initials emblazoned on the sides, denoting the status of the occupant. Seeing Fiona sitting regally in her miniature goat cart, we all felt she looked infinitely superior to ourselves, crest or no crest. The memories were not all rose coloured because Fiona, having drunk the milk supplied by the goat - for breakfast, then considered to be safer than cow's for the delicate - was often sick. When my own children were small self-sufficiency had seemed attractive: two goats, Snowy and Pandora had arrived, both supposedly pregnant. Snowy produced Puffball, Pandora remained barren. Casting my mind back I remembered none had bitten or kicked. As I debated the goat owner's request all I could recollect were disastrous milking attempts; either hobbled, tied down, held down, the minute amount of grey milk extracted was certainly not enough for the needs of a family of six, and even when strained was rejected by the cat. The goats I had met had not been dangerous to handle and mentally I decided a three-legged one should not present problems. A date and time for a visit were fixed.

How useful Sat Nav would have been. Directions given to find remote country locations so often included such gems as, 'Remember to turn left after the second oak tree on the right,' forgetting that the tree blew down three winters ago, or 'I think the sign post says. . . ' leaving - if one is lost - considerable doubt as to one's actual location.

Juggling with a map, on a grey, damp, misty afternoon; I cursed poor directions. While in the hinterland somewhere near Reading, it was a relief to see a group of buildings more or less fitting the telephone instructions. I parked in the lane, resignedly pulling on long boots: there was mud everywhere, and no sign of human life but wafting from a somewhat dilapidated barn Billy Goat reek suggested a caprine presence. Squelching across the yard and banging on the door of a caravan resulted in the sound of a human voice, 'Enter!' As I yanked open the door I exposed piles and piles of what appeared to be shorn wool, and buried in the midst, was a woman, spinning.

Emerging, wool covered, she led me to the shed which seemed to be full of rather odd looking goats, each penned separately, many obviously pregnant. Some were wearing what appeared to be cast off human jerseys. Oh dear, another crank, I thought resignedly as we made our way to the where the patient lay.

It had been a difficult kidding, twins, one saved but an epidural and forceps had been required to remove the second which had died. After examining the goat it was obvious she had nerve damage. She could balance on three legs but collapsed if she tried to put weight on the fourth. The goat owner explained she was having to be hand-milked, as even propped up with a straw bale replacing the weak hind leg, she refused to suckle the surviving kid which at considerable inconvenience was having to be bottle fed.

I explained I could treat the condition using a Low Level Laser: there was no guarantee but I thought it would help. To be of use, treatment should really be given twice a day; perhaps I could pack, goat, kid and bottle into the back of my Land Rover and take them home. Silence.

I explained I had kept the odd goat, we had an empty stable, plenty of straw, and a helpful staff who could do the milking and care for the kid: all I needed was a bag of dry food. The lady asked what I would do if treatment did not work. 'Oh,' I replied airily, 'I'll telephone and let you know, but with the popularity of goat meat in the country these days I'm certain I could find a ritual slaughterer. They are very efficient and you would get enough to cover my fees: at least £25:00.' I was baffled by her slightly strangled gasp, and when she finally managed to speak she asked, 'Have you any idea how much this goat cost?' 'No'. '£3,000! She's from the very best New Zealand Angora line.' It was at the beginning of the Angora goat boom, and anyone with goats to sell was making a small fortune.

It was agreed I should, instead, visit the goat regularly and administer treatment, and luckily it recovered. The owner subsequently managed to breed some excellent animals. From their fleeces, which I learned were called coats, she spun yarn, this when knitted, resulted in socks to die for. Eventually other people breeding the goats - Jill King in particular - had cloth woven, this when made up and the garments displayed at fashion shows, appeared appropriately titled as *Goat Couture*.

Prior to my initial visit, as the nervous system of the goat was not a strong point I had returned to the anatomy books. Comparative anatomy is fascinating and I had wandered from nerves to muscles.

Information subsequently to prove priceless leapt from the pages. I quote:

'scalene muscle development in the goat stabilises the front of the chest and the front legs, allowing the animal to jump with safely from rock to rock, also to move at speed down the steep slopes found in its natural, mountainous habitat.'

Owners, riders and trainers of horses fear downhill work. Would targeting these muscles help? Where were they located?

Research revealed the site. Lying deep they span a small but vital junction between the base of the neck and the front end of the barrel-like chest (thoracic cage). By locking the two securely together they create a stable area for important muscles which attach the front leg to the body. The muscles are active, therefore building, if the horse is able to 'nod' at walk. Although modern texts describe the requirement for general core stability at length curiously, limb stability, despite it being essential for optimum performance, is rarely considered.

Read the books, discuss with trainers but I do not think you will discover an activity specifically designed to improve the scalene. They are essential: a horse is mentally programmed to remain upright and does everything to avoid falling. Because it is programmed to land on one front leg, if it feels a front leg is insecure it will instinctively shorten its stride, particularly at speed and when jumping. Trainers and riders avoid fast work down-hill, which obviously loads the front legs, for fear of injury.

How could this possible instability be addressed? Unrestricted the head and neck are designed to move up and down, this is something the feral horse does naturally ensuring the important muscles develop. Sadly, due to haste in order to achieve 'an outline', movement of the horses' head and neck is curtailed by the use of side reins, this effectively locks the deep neck muscles with resultant inadequate development. Ride on the buckle end at walk! Very boring but very necessary unless your horse has been raised on hills: 'As sure footed as a mountain pony,' is a timeless quote.

Not only did this first goat patient episode give me a new friend and ensure a supply of socks, but revisiting the anatomy books made me appreciate the essential stabilising role played by the scalene muscles: Off with the side reins!

Happenings often seem sequential, and shortly after recovering from the shock of meeting a goat that had cost far more than any horse I had ever bought, I was in my Wimpole Street Rooms when a call came from the London Clinic. They had a problem: would I go at once?. A space in the patient list enabled a quick dash up the road.

The prestigious foyer of the London Clinic was in chaos. The porter was cowering behind his desk, and an irate ward Sister, whom I knew from her cap to be ex St Thomas' hospital and therefore formidable, was arguing with a dark skinned gentleman in Arab dress of a fashion worn only by those of the highest lineage. He was surrounded by a large entourage, some of whom, standing line abreast behind their leader, were effectively blocking the exit. 'No!' sister was repeating. 'No! I will *not* have that thing on my ward.'

Expecting to be directed to a private room to see a patient I tried to skirt the group. 'I sent for you,' said Sister turning on me. 'You know about animals, get that thing out of here.' 'What thing?' I wondered. Then saw it: a baby goat on a lead. Obviously overcome by emotion it had laid a considerable number of pellets and was busy creating a small lake. It transpired the porter had actually seen the goat arrive but had thought he must be hallucinating: people did not bring goats into the Clinic. He had watched the group, goat included, get into the lift, and the ward receptionist had been no better. The baby goat, probably the equivalent of a box of chocolates in Middle Eastern cultures, was being presented to a recumbent patient as Sister chanced to pass while making her rounds.

I half bowed to the central figure who, by chance, I recognised. 'Translator please'. One of the group moved forward, remembering that as a woman I must remain humble, head bent, I murmured, 'It is not permitted for uncooked delicacies to be offered. However, providing the patient is not on any special diet, cooked delicacies; perhaps later?' I raised my hands in what was I hoped was an appropriate gesture. Rapid exchanges in Arabic followed; then with no real loss of face the goat was removed. History does not relate if it ever came back cooked.

Dogs and Cats and Other Animals

As word spread that physiotherapy helped injured animals a varied assortment began to arrive in dribs and drabs, the worst probably a badger. It was a dark wet evening and the bell rang at about 9:30, as the flood lights turned on I could see a rather small car, its female owner, leaning through a back door emerged in tears, 'Are you the person who mends animals?' 'Er yes.' 'I have hit a badger - it's in the car. PLEASE help me.' Badgers are not famous for their friendly nature when hurting, and I collected a pair of heavy gloves and a stout stick: if it were alive and tried to bite a stick between its jaws this might save my hand. It was still breathing but obviously unconscious. No sign of any wound, however its flea population was fairly evident. Drawing a deep breath and hoping God or St Francis would forgive me I explained that badgers were very family orientated. It was not dead, probably, if she took it back to the collision site, where I expected in time it would regain consciousness, a badger friend would find it and help it home. 'How much do I owe you?' 'Nothing'. Amazingly she shut the car door, started the engine and drove off after thanking me profusely. Some weeks later I met her in the village getting out of a rather new looking car, 'I went back next day,' she said, 'and it had gone. You were so clever to tell me what to do, but do you know, I have no idea why, but my car smelt so bad I had to change it.'

The next badger episode concerned one of our own dogs and prompted an experiment with magnetic fields. A small Jack Russell terrier, called Douglas, belonging to Penelope disappeared on a walk and was found badly injured several days later. We concluded, from the severity of the wounds, he had been attacked by a Badger probably having gone down or fallen into a Sett. We bathed the wounds with saline: I had no other ideas but had recently taken delivery of an electro-magnetic therapy system sent over from the States, considerably less cumbersome than that in Major Hern's yard, but still needing a mains electrical connection.

The effects of Magnetic Fields were not fully explained, in fact even now, 35 years later, the Jury is still out. It has been shown, using thermo-graphic measurement, that by subjecting tissue to a low frequency, alternating magnetic field, temperature in the targeted tissue is raised. Cells are agitated by the alternating current flow created as the polarity of the magnets change and this results in heat; the reaction of the body to any abnormal change in tissue temperature is to increase local blood flow, it is therefore correct to suggest that the secondary effect of exposure to an alternating magnetic field increases blood flow. Unfortunately, like so many 'guess therapies' there is, as yet, no scientific explanation to determine if the response of body cells to random magnetic exposure is always beneficial. Field work had demonstrated that some horses hated Magnetic Fields; cats rarely tolerated them, and some human patients complained of feeling nauseous during exposure: a definite contra indication to usage.

Out of interest, when Douglas was well enough to come and lie in the yard I laid a pad from the newly designed USA model on the ground, then activated the pads, everything at the lowest setting. I was amazed to see the dog make his way slowly and painfully from his bed to lie on the pad, where he stayed for about half an hour before returning to his basket. Given the chance he did this for several days then, for no particular reason, he stopped. He did recover fully but I have no idea if exposure to the Magnetic Field was entirely responsible for this although circulatory flow must have been enhanced.

Several local vets began to refer dogs: a number with back problems. Some were easy to handle; others unpleasant. After treating several dogs with neck injuries for the police, I could feel sympathy the handlers. Often there was a need for sudden, almost violent restraint - lest the person they were trying to apprehend was badly bitten - and this gave many dogs a type of whiplash injury.

The requirement to hone feral, rather than domestic instincts, made them unpredictable when in pain. One, brought by a charming female police handler, seemed so aggressive I treated it through the mesh of its travelling cage. I shall always remember begging her to be careful as the dog, when not on duty, lived free with her in her home. Several months later she telephoned in tears to say that for no reason, when on their way through her garden to the travelling van, the dog had attacked her. She had fallen backwards and been kept down for if she tried to move it leapt forward, grabbing her forearm, just as trained to do during an arrest. It had taken nearly an hour to slide off her belt then to thrust it toward the dog with her undamaged arm so that it grabbed the belt rather than her. The moment she managed to stand the dog's aggression had disappeared and he had become his usual, loving, companionable self.

Sadly the dog unit had considered he must be classified as unsafe, and she had been given permission to take him out over the Downs one last time before he was put to sleep. She wanted me to know as I had warned her he might turn, but she was devastated and had applied for transfer to another section of the force.

Subsequently I was asked to lecture at the Army's dog training unit at Melton Mowbray to discuss whiplash-type injury and to teach the handlers basic massage. Many of the dogs were destined for overseas service and the expressed despair, from some of the seasoned handlers, because due to quarantine regulations 'their friend' had not been allowed to return to the UK at the end of a tour of duty, was very moving. Thankfully that has all changed due to the lifting of quarantine restrictions and many dogs end post service life with the handler's family.

A number of accidents, often road traffic, involved a hind leg and this often resulted in dogs, who had grown used to getting around on three legs, refusing to use the injured limb following recovery. Owners do not like their dog to hold a leg bent and carried well above the ground appearing to be three legged so we had to come up with a solution. As there was usually muscle loss it seemed sensible to attach a weight to the injured leg. This was done by cutting a strip of lead, sufficiently long to wrap round the limb, masking it with tape, and attaching it like a bracelet around the lower part of the injured leg. To my delight the new sensation, achieved by the weight, encouraged dogs to straighten the leg and put their foot on the ground: first when standing then, when led, to move the leg, albeit in a rather snatch up, drop down manner. Most, after two or three circuits of the yard, would begin to use it normally. 'Miracle worker,' commented owners. Not so: the weight had achieved stimulation of temporarily dormant nerve routes - those transmitting movement messages, the proprioceptive pathways. The dogs kept the weight, with their owners told to use it daily for up to six weeks, and they were also advised to increase the wearing time periods.

Dogs with back injuries also lost muscle and trying to rebuild their backs was difficult. Wading rather than swimming was an option as was making them walk in long grass or through heather where they had to use back muscles to lift their legs rather than being able to swing them normally.

Quite recently, since moving to Exmoor a 'Please walk through heather,' dog returned with fantastic back muscles. Congratulating the owner I commented that she must be very fit. 'Walking with him on a lead, on the moor was a bore,' she said.'We both hated it. Then I got a ladder, laid it on the ground and led him up and down making him walk between the rungs.'

There is always a way of solving a problem, and I wish I had thought of that one at Downs House. Now all dogs with back problems are asked to ladder walk: the exercise known as 'The Lindsey' in recognition of its inventor.

I learned very early on to always travel with a muzzle in your therapy kit, I wish I had patented the 'Halti' as I'd needed to invent a similar restraint, Muzzles, Pekes and Pugs do not add up. Before designing our own 'Halti', it was only swift hand withdrawl that once saved my little finger. I had just been told by the owner of a Pekinese I was treating that it was saying, 'Good morning,' to me. However my gut interpretation of its noises proved nearer the mark, 'I will *have* you.' SNAP.

I was now seeing nearly as many dogs as horses, particularly greyhounds. One importer from Ireland reckoned if the dogs he brought over could swim the length of our pool they would be useful on the track. If they sank or emerged appearing half drowned, they were returned to Ireland! He obviously spread the word for large numbers of these charming dogs began to appear, most arriving by word of mouth.

Time to learn more. Off I went to spend time with Paddy Sweeney, a noted grey hound vet. I was dealing with muscle injuries, he with fractures but if you have seen the muscles, when the skin is retracted during operation, particularly on a hock, wrist or toe, it helps. Paddy had large, seemingly pudgy hands, and he always appeared with a whiskey bottle under one arm, this placed opened on a convenient table in the operating theatre. Despite the odd swig, if things frustrated him, he worked miracles with wire and microscopic pieces of bone.

It is often assumed that delicate work requires delicate fingers but I was taught to make Corn Dollies by the champion ploughman of England who had hands like spades but could weave straw into the most delicate of Welsh Fans.

Paddy agreed that a number of muscle tears occur high up on the inner side of the hind leg, in greyhound parlance affecting the 'Monkey Muscle'. He'd had difficulty treating these but agreed I could try introducing low levels of ultra sound, and luckily this seemed to help.

No dog returned from his kennels, following operation, to its trainer until tried. At the back of his garden he had built a small track, and the lure - a smelly bit of something very dead - was dragged over ground on the end of a clothes line attached in turn to an elderly, extremely temperamental, petrol engine. The main draw-back was that when he set up his clinic he had been in the midst of open country. Since then his property had become surrounded by a modern building estate, some of the back gardens even encroaching on the outer margin of the training track. What had been designed as a nice curve had become a right angled bend, and if the dogs failed to corner and went straight on they ended up in a chicken run. Paddy just laughed and had a good swig, but even when offered the bottle the chicken-breeding neighbour was not amused.

Eventually he was forced to move as complaints became endless, this mostly due to the smell. He fed horse flesh and the scent, on hot days, must be described as seriously pungent.

The greyhound world very rarely paid its bills: it was always, 'Of course we will settle up.' It had to be understood that the 'settling up' would happen after the dog they currently had in training, had won! Paddy and I enjoyed each other's company, exchanged a lot of ideas - both learning from one another's results, and eventually writing a pamphlet on the treatment of grey hound injuries.

A greyhound trainer Hazel Waldron, whose kennels were near Newbury began to send her injured dogs for day treatment. They arrived individually caged, row upon row, in a large van. Stupidly I had been so intrigued working with Paddy, dealing with the injuries I saw, that I had never taken the time to go to a track and watch dogs race. When Hazel's dogs came I woke up to the fact that, even having worked with Paddy, I really did not know enough about the physical stresses of greyhounds travelling, let alone racing, so visited the Greyhound Track at Swindon. Watching the dogs loaded, break from the traps, accelerate, then corner on the bends was a huge learning curve. It became a new interest, and it was both fun and relaxing to attend an evening meeting after a day in the yard. Rabbit and our head girl Jenny became owners, sadly neither had any marked success, but having two greyhounds living with us was very useful for studying practical anatomy and bio-mechanics.

Eventually I visited Hazel at her kennels and found her very forward thinking. Like Martin Pipe she was a stickler for detail: not all that usual in some kennels. During general discussion she indicated that she felt her dogs were showing an increase in injuries; she was seeing more lame than during her early years as a trainer. She volunteered the information that one of her problems was to find dedicated walkers, people who would actually take the dogs, on leads, for the long exercise required to keep them fit. Greenham Common, adjoining her kennels was ideal for walking the dogs, but as the local teenage population, originally anxious to earn and from whom she had over the years recruited her walkers, became less and less physically able she found her dogs were not building muscle as they should, and she felt were injuring themselves as a result. At my suggestion she came and looked at the horse walker, within a month a greyhound walker had been designed and installed in her kennels, and I helped monitor its use as an experiment. Eventually it became possible to settle on what appeared to be a beneficial revolution speed, and although the results can only be classed as field work, using

Greyhounds appeared

the walker resulted in an improvement in general muscle tone with subsequent reduction in the number of injuries in her dogs.

An invitation to attend a big, VIP evening meeting, at Wembley Stadium arrived. This gave entry into another, totally new world, an amazing atmosphere in the Stadium. Never before in my life, other possibly than when meeting and treating the Kray brothers, had I met such an interesting group, seen so many women wearing such magnificent jewellery, eaten food far superior to that on offer at the average race course, nor observed so many men betting with thick wads of £50:00 readies! New contacts, new dogs to treat as Hazel, who won the big race with an ex-patient, was very generous in her praise of Physiotherapy when interviewed after receiving the trophy.

I'd had no reason to know greyhound racing was an acclaimed International sport, nor that it was very big in Finland. Grape vine communication, following my Wembley visit, resulted in a call from a therapist in Helsinki. Would I go and lecture to the group of animal therapists she had formed, also discuss and suggest treatment for problems they were experiencing with their racing greyhounds. Unusually there was a letter, accompanying the invitation, from the University Vet School authorising the trip, giving permission for me to visit and treat.

I continue to be ashamed at an inability to communicate effectively, other than in English when working abroad, although even that was queried in the USA when I said fortnight instead of two weeks and cervical instead of pronouncing it servicaal. At the time I announced rather crossly, I had delivered a similar lecture in both French and German, made myself understood to attendees with no English in Italy, Spain and Sweden, but felt that I must apologise on my inability to speak American.

I telephoned to accept the Finnish invitation explaining I spoke no Finnish, I was assured that if I spoke slowly and clearly they would manage. They were a charming practical group to work with, their main concern being the number of grey hounds who, rather than presenting with common muscle injuries had suddenly begun to fracture hocks or wrists when racing. The group were concerned lest these injuries might be as a result of Physiotherapy given for muscle injuries, were they over building muscles, creating incorrect stresses on the skeleton?

All the dogs we looked at seemed in good order, other than being a little dull in their coats and slightly lethargic. Discussion revealed the kennel affected had changed from raw meat to an imported complete diet, prior to this the dogs had been fed the carcass of deer newly shot in the Forest. Blood tests showed the dogs on the complete, pelleted food, were very low in calcium. Supplementation, I heard later, had more or less resolved the problem.

Diet is a fascinating subject and I can always remember my father saying 'what you do not put in you do not get out'. Wild, rather than farmed Deer, are still able to move freely, they know instinctively what they lack and supplement by choosing the root, plant or bark containing what they need. Healthy, nutritionally balanced deer meat, fed to the grey hounds had obviously supplied everything required, it really was a complete feed.

Finland is a beautiful country, and after a few days in Helsinki looking at greyhounds I was taken North visiting several stables on the way and watching the horses race, without any apparent distress, on frozen lakes. Remembering my disastrous efforts in LA when trying out a new sport I declined to race ride, certain I would mistakenly choose a weak area and fall through the ice.

Our eventual destination was a Husky research station, the sled dogs were training in a lab, on a treadmill, in very low temperatures. The reason for our visit was because dogs had been experiencing shoulder problems and National teams had recently fared badly in competition. These teams were preparing to go to Alaska to compete in the Itidarod; while examining a dog in its harness to see what I could find I recounted my experience there, then not concentrating sufficiently and moving my hand awkwardly under the breast strap I cut right through my leather ski glove. The man-made fibre harness had apparently, in the extreme cold, lost all its plasticity, no longer moulding to allow the dogs free shoulder movement, rather becoming rigid with very sharp edges. Following this suggestion and on examining their records, it seemed the shoulder problems appeared to relate to the time when they had changed from traditional seal skin to man-made harness, easy cure, back to seal skin.

I know from Ran Fiennes, both friend and patient that many of the problems associated with the early man-made Arctic gear have been overcome and I am certain by now comfortable harnesses, made from man-made materials, have been developed.

The final new experience was to meet and spend two days with a farming family living on the edge of the Arctic Circle, luckily the ground was still frozen, this meant the mosquito had not hatched, I knew I would have been unable to cope with them, midges in Scotland were bad enough but those, Arctic hatched, are as large as small wasps and nothing deters their need for a meal.

It was intriguing to discuss the methods utilised for survival of humans and animals under the extremes of weather they experienced annually and to be shown, stored in a cave cut into a hill, farming equipment dating back from the time when the ancestors of the present incumbents had settled the land 200 years before, everything perfectly preserved, the dry conditions and low temperature providing a natural, controlled temperature environment. While in the cave I felt I had been somewhere where the atmosphere had been similar, *deja a vu*? Then I remembered, it had been in the wine caves at Chateau Mouton.

Despite modern, tracked, snow mobiles they still kept and used Huskies. One of their bitches had an unplanned mating with a wolf, the pups, around twelve weeks old, were displaying heightened feral instincts and paced like wolves. In the interest of conservation the family had kept the full litter and were going to try to keep them as a working pack. They hoped to be able to train the dogs to respond to command, then use them in the forest to track down sick or injured deer, these when found could be humanely dispatched by a bullet, rather than being left to experience a lingering, painful end.

Shortly after returning from his trip, the vet having suggested swimming following a back problem, a St Bernard arrived. Nearly as large as his diminutive owner the dog looked somewhat embarrassed by the bib he wore, necessary because of endless emotional dribbling as he strove to please. Reluctantly he jumped out of the back of his car, with an expression suggesting those around him were of no consequence - being infinitely inferior. We progressed to the yard, he meandered along the mat to the entry end of the pool, reaching this he took one look and sat down heavily on the ramp, just short of the water's edge. We tried everything, cajoling with words, pushing, pulling, even dangling treats, hung from a pole just out of reach. The swimming team were about to give up when his owner volunteered the information he would do almost anything for cheese, I fetched a week's supply from the house. He did stand up when the enticing scent from some over ripe stilton was waved in front of him but remained planted, we floated a lump, he stretched out a front leg, was it step in the right direction? Unfortunately no, for rather like a cat he scooped the cheese from the water and sat down to eat it.

Having wasted an hour of precious time I tentatively suggested perhaps the dog knew instinctively that being quite heavy he should not swim lest he sink. I really did not want to risk a drowning. 'I could hold him up: perhaps he will come in with me,' suggested his owner stripping off down to rather elderly, inconveniently frayed under-pants. Into the water he strode while the dog remained seated looking rather surprised. By now there were too many staff members watching, all of whom were becoming slightly hysterical: none of their comments nor suggestions were of the slightest use. It seemed politic to dispatch one to fetch and offer a large towel.

Over warming coffee in the kitchen and during conversation after I had explained there would be no charge: the re-clad owner proffered the information that he was the co-ordinator of all the AA rescue services in the area. 'Are you an AA member?' As a family we were. 'I will put your names on the Gold Rescue list.'

A letter of thanks with the AA reference to be used in case of breakdown and a photograph of the St Bernard, which I still have, arrived a few days later.

Physiotherapy treatment for animals was eventually accepted by the Veterinary Profession as a modality both useful and effective, although the profession reserved the right to insist that a therapist must have been given permission by the animal's vet prior to treatment rather than as in the human field where direct referral is permitted. To the small group working with animals this was a break through and animal physiotherapy began to enjoy general acceptance. Possibly due to this the Physiotherapy Olympic Committee decided Equestrian Sports should be recognised and that an Animal Physiotherapist should join the committee.

I was delegated as the representative on behalf of the Association of Chartered Physiotherapists in Animal Therapy (ACPAT) and summoned to London to attend a meeting.

After the usual preliminaries: Chairman's report, minutes of last meeting, and financial report, all of which as usual took

The non-swimming St Bernard.

ages and were such a waste of time, the Chairman announced to the assembled group that a number of sports had been suggested as being worthy of Olympic recognition by the committee, and that after much debate, Equestrianism and Table Tennis [Ping Pong to me], had been invited to send a representative. Hearing this [and in hindsight I was being silly] I felt slightly let down. At the time Olympic ridden events hardly seemed in the same category as ping pong, slightly like comparing the Cresta run with ballroom dancing, but each obviously, in the opinion of the committee, worthy of recognition

I am not a debating type of committee member: I like short discussions and decisions based on fact. The atmosphere around the table began to deteriorate when, after being introduced, I was informed that on payment of a princely sum, as I was now involved in the Olympics I could wear the Olympic Rings as a brooch. I was shocked and, without thinking, said firmly I was not an Olympiad; there was no way I would wear them; surely wearing the rings was a privilege confined to the athletes? This was not at all well received, and looking round I realised everyone, other than myself, sported the brooch. I continued to speak out of turn when, under any other business, discussion began regarding the way to get rid of a vast amount of unused supplies lying in a warehouse. Bandages, Band Aid, Elastoplast, Tube grip, and every other kind of strapping, rubs, sweats, ointments, and pain killers, all donated as freebies by their manufacturers in the hope they would achieve free advertising. My comment when invited to give an opinion was, what a criminal waste, why not donate to overseas physio departments as they had nothing. When working with Leprosy in Malaya I would have given my eye teeth for such a hand out. There was further misgiving when I explained the Equestrian Physiotherapists for Sidney were already selected. I was sorry, it did not matter who had applied to go to the games, it was not just riders we were taking: the horses were coming too. The Physios needed to be members of ACPAT holding the dual qualification, enabling them to treat humans and horses.

'Do those selected have sufficient experience to go to an Olympic Event?'they asked.

'I think so: they have already done Barcelona and Atlanta.'

Silence. 'Are you going to Sidney?

'Yes, but with the Kiwis'. Consternation.

'Why are you here?'

'Because the British Equestrian Federation appointed me. I advise them.' I was, quite reasonably, replaced shortly after this meeting but continued, for several years to be sent a great deal of useful information regarding the results of human testing under varied circumstances including altitude training.

Writing Books

The publishers, Blackwell's Scientific who had agreed to publish *Equine Injury and Therapy*, were surprised by both sales and translation requests. Shortly after publication Jean-Pierre Pailoux, masseur to the French Equestrian Federation, called me and said he and Jean-Marie Denoix a French Vet were writing *Physical Therapy and Massage for the Horse*, 'would I like a copy.' 'Of course.' 'It is in French.' Remembering my first attempts at reading French, The Mouse Book, since when my French had improved, I said 'No problem'. Their book was fortuitous for the advancement of animal physiotherapy: Denoix was a known and respected veterinary anatomist. I could always telephone Jean-Pierre if I needed advice, he in turn would talk with Jean-Marie; to be able to discuss with other such far thinking individuals was an unexpected bonus. then I met Dominique Giniaux also a Docteur Veterinaire in France. He was interested in, and had begun to consider the use of osteopathy, and to practice acupuncture. He had just begun, when we met, to relate areas of surface tension or hypersensitivity to organ malfunction. We worked together on a number of occasions when I was in France seeing horses and he gave me a copy of his book, *Soulagez Votre Cheval aux Doigts* [et a l'oeil!]. In the preface Dr Jean Plainfosse says 'Le Docteur Giniaux a ouvert une Fenetre noveau.' Yes he did: a marvellous window for me.

Sadly he died young, before his time and many of the techniques he had developed were lost although Dr Struchan, a pupil, adopted some of his methods.

Following the success of *Equine Injury and Therapy* I approached Richard Miles my commissioning editor at Blackwell Scientific and suggested that the veterinary profession needed guidance, that they knew nothing about the benefits of physiotherapy. The only book was a French publication, part written by a vet, but it had not yet been translated. Richard accepted the proposal and *Physiotherapy in Veterinary Medicine* was the next book - a sell-out, but for some odd reason it was not reprinted, probably because I did not have it peer reviewed. Who could I have asked? The subject was a totally new concept.

Equestrian vision suggested a video-based on massage and Norfields, promoters of excellent magnetic wraps in the USA, were keen to contribute to the costs if I included magnetism. We went ahead, and to their surprise filming only took a day. Titled *Hands on with Mary Bromiley*, it has survived, elevated to CD status.

I think it was probably as a result of book publicity that I was invited to attend *The Woman of the Year Lunch*. This gathering was the brainchild of Lady Lothian; having been refused admission to a notable male lunch she became determined to create a similar event for women.

In 1955 she launched her first lunch at the Savoy Hotel. It was such a success it was decided to hold a similar event annually. Subsequently, and following glowing reports in the press, women began to go to extraordinary lengths to have their names included on the invitation list; for to receive an invitation was to 'have arrived'.

This attitude prompted the instigating committee to consider if there might be philanthropic benefits and a workable, charitable format resulted. It was decided to invite a small number of hand-picked guests, these selected from women considered to have made an outstanding contribution in some field. One would be invited to make a speech, another would receive a cheque on behalf of her chosen charity.

The chosen would be seated, in a rather Medieval Manner at the High Table, above the common mass. These lesser guests were also selected from those considered to have contributed to a cause: had served as war correspondents, ran clubs for the under privileged, were politicians, had shone in the literary field, in the theatre, the arts, medicine - the catchment sphere was vast. The only difference from the Top Table group was although having received an invitation they would have been invited to pay generously for the privilege of attending

The year I was bidden to attend, a blind lady 'Miss X' was to receive a cheque on behalf of the greater London Fund for the Blind. My pride at being invited as a guest rather than as a paying guest was somewhat deflated when, on arrival, I was grabbed by one of the organisers as I collected my name badge. 'Do you know why you are here?' she hissed in my ear.

'No, I thought I was invited because. . .'

'They have agreed to let Miss X bring her guide dog and you have been chosen to look after it.'

I was led to Miss X and introduced to both her and a golden Labrador. 'Was there anything I could do?'

'Oh yes, please. Take her out for a wee.'

Remembering a square of grass at the back, by the river entrance of the hotel I grasped the harness and threaded my way through the hordes milling around the reception room, glasses in hand, fighting their way to, and eagerly scanning, the table plans wondering where were they seated and which interesting person might head their table.

We made it outside, me in high heels and wearing the current fashion, a pencil slim skirt. I hopped gingerly over the railings and onto the grass and the dog followed. As she squatted, a mallard, which had been sitting happily in some reeds at the edge of the ornamental pond, took off. I was unprepared, and before I could apply restraint the dog leapt forward into the pond.

I let loose an unacceptable word. The pond needed cleaning, and as I hauled the dog back onto dry land, covered in mud, and slime it gave several good, Labrador-type, shakes. I too was now covered in mud and slime: the smell was truly awful.

Dragging the luckless dog I made it back into the foyer and thence to the nearest lady's cloakroom. I have never been certain if I was born lucky or luck favours some, but I recognised one of the attendants. In hindsight she was probably the loo cleaner rather than one of the 'Can I take your coat madam,' ladies. Years before she had been a patient when, as student I was working in maternity at St Thomas's. I had been somewhat apprehensive as to my reception when I entered the ward to which I had been sent in order to encourage the inmates - newly delivered mothers - to do arm exercises to 'bring on their milk'. My worst fears were realised, 'Wot abat me luv? I got gallons!' came a voice from a corner bed, causing giggles all round. Eventually she took pity on my inexperience and welcomed me loudly when I appeared next day, 'Come on girls, it's the milk lidy. Git cher elbows up!' I missed her when she was discharged.

A genuine Lambethian she was used to muck. As the dog and I appeared the smart attendants gathered their skirts close and moved away. She just shrieked with laughter and set to work with beautiful, pristine, pink towels. Some 15 minutes later, more or less presentable, both smelling strongly of Savoy soap, the dog and I re-joined the festivities.

Untoward happenings were not yet over. As I piloted Miss X forward, her dog met another also *en route* to its owner's seat. My charge obviously no longer smelt dog like, hackles rose in both before growls were followed by attempted conflict.

Guest drew back, leaving a fighting circle. As I struggled, 'Pepper works,' said a cultured voice in my ear. I turned to see Princess Margaret at my elbow. Snatching a pepper pot from a table she shook it hard, and considerable sneezing resulted, followed by immediate cessation of hostilities.

Wondering momentarily if the skill with which she manipulated the pepper pot stemmed from practice with the Royal Corgis, and why some people accuse the Royal family of being impracticable I followed her and parked Miss X and her dog correctly.

As International interest became apparent, invitations to lecture at Veterinary Conventions and veterinary establishments abroad began to arrive. One of the first was to teach in Belgium. Dealing with animals provides its fair share of amusing incidents and in hindsight this trip was no exception. The Vet who had requested I visit had been to Downs House with a group from Europe, all of whom had professed an interest in Physiotherapy.

In those far off days a secretary managed my life with some skill. She informed me the vets had offered to pay my air fare, put me up, and find interesting cases for a practical session, this to follow an illustrated (35mm slides) introductory lecture. Remuneration had not been mentioned. Why bother about a fee: it was a chance to visit and meet people from another country and undoubtedly to learn from the cases supplied.

On arrival I discovered the son of the house, aged five, had been sent to his grandparents, and I had been allocated his room. The night was uncomfortable as after several attempts to fit into a child-sized bed the floor seemed the answer. There was slight embarrassment all round when I was woken with an early morning cup of tea.

Why, I wonder are tea and the English always paired up? I simply hate tea: but when in Rome, do as Rome does.

With breakfast over, and on requesting that I view the patients to be treated it transpired we were taking some with us from the clinic and others would be waiting at the venue: not in Belgium but in Holland!

I had to draw a deep breath when, squashed onto the back seat with three occupied cat baskets and the trailer attached to the car - containing several dogs - swaying alarmingly as we sped toward Holland, my host asked if I could speak French. He was not certain if it had been explained, but the conference would be conducted in French. Hilarious. An eager group was awaiting our arrival armed with the usual trays of coffee and buns, seemingly identical at all conferences. Repairing to the lecture room, slides were loaded, and I did my best.

At the conclusion, the wife of the vet appeared, clutching specimen one: a large, very irritated tabby cat, whose voice, as it was carried to the treatment table, I recognised as that of a travelling companion.

My French was adequate to understand what had happened as the vet described the case. It had been in a road traffic accident, and he had operated, inserting a femoral pin to stabilise the break. Turning, he announced to the expectant audience that I would examine the cat and describe appropriate, post operative Physiotherapy. As I cast in my mind for an appropriate response, which in English would have been, 'Cats respond very badly to physiotherapy,' the cat bit the handler who very sensibly let it go. An intelligent cat, it had seen an open window and evacuated. Luckily Holland is flat, although on that day very muddy. An hour and several ploughed fields later we caught it: the operation had obviously been a great success, the cat was fully mobile, and physiotherapy was not required.

A pug with an inability to curl his tail, mercifully responded to treatment and there were satisfactory, appreciative gasps, as the curl returned. His owners had some English, 'He is named Golly' they announced. 'And here is the brother, Wog. Very English names we think.' This was rapidly translated by those 'with English' to those without, and all assembled roared with laughter, including several black students. No one appeared offended, in fact the general mood became very jolly.

Eventually with all cases examined, therapy suggested, questions answered, the group dispersed and we loaded the specimens, to return to Belgium.

Helping carry baskets into the clinic hospital I saw a very nice looking dog, curled, apparently deeply asleep, in its basket. On bending down to pat it I realised it was dead.

'Oh,' exclaimed the vet's wife. 'With your visit I forget, there was no time to take it to be burned. We use the crematorium, they just open a casket and add any small dead animals.'

I cannot remember how I reacted at the time, probably still-shell shocked from teaching in French and chasing the cat. On reflection, it seemed a remarkably sensible, even comforting approach, to have a companion with you, as you crossed the Styx.

We dropped off the dead dog - again a temporary back seat travelling companion - on our way out to supper, and before the swirling Turkish belly dancers whose act, accompanied a Bols enriched meal eventually numbed my senses.

Remembering the dog incident while writing, I fear such a departure in this country would no longer be possible due to European Rules, and their rigorous implementation demanded by DEFRA.

Italy
Conferences are usually held in really interesting places but when lured to Italy there was an unexpected bonus. I had been invited to visit a thermal pool in San Giuliao Terme, especially designed by a rheumatologist for horses and then to lecture at a veterinary conference in nearby Pisa.

Thermal spas were not new to me, Erna Lowe a travel agent, the first to specialise in therapy abroad trips, had sent me to visit Abano and Monte Grotto in northern Italy an area bursting with human thermal clinics, to write some advertising blurb for her. Prior to this visit I had done a great deal of research only to discover even Madam Curie could give no valid reason for the improved condition of patients suffering from arthritis, following immersion in the thermal waters. It was fascinating to recollect, while lying almost suspended by the therapeutic mineral elements, that their healing powers

Lecturing overseas

had been documented by civilisations over 2,000 years previously when the area, at the foot of the Euganean Hills, was described as containing 'waters of wellbeing'.

There must be a geological fault under the Italian Alps for similar mineral laden water bubbles out at the other side of the mountain range, emerging near the northern end of the Lake of Geneva, in Switzerland. These waters are a comparatively recent discovery. It was not until 1831 while fishing from the bank of the river Rhone that a fisherman, on falling into the river, found he was literally in hot water! These thermal waters, now captured at Lavey-Les Bains, fill three pools - two outdoors - and all maintain an ambient temperature of 69° C, rather warmer than in Italy. Lying back in a pool, beautifully warm, with snow shimmering on the mountains above has to be experienced to be appreciated.

The horse spa was beautifully built, an oval pool filled with the thermal waters as they bubbled out of the ground at 22-

Fellowship award.

23°C. I suspect these waters are the same as those of Monte Grotto and Abano. Unfortunately there were no case histories to refer to though several horses had fairly open knees but the spa director was not a vet and had no idea why the horses had been sent to swim.

One thing I did notice was the horses were less distressed than some swimmers I had seen in UK pools, and concluded this was due to the increased density of the water secondary to the high mineral content.

I made my way to Pisa and after I had finished my lecture at the conference was making my way to a poster session, when glancing up toward an approaching figure the shape seemed familiar. Was it? No, not possible. It was. It was Pavarotti! The wondrous Tenor there in front of me, in real life. I have no Italian, but 'Maestro, Bellisimo,' sprang to mind. I uttered these words reverently and half curtsied. He stopped, took my hand and kissed it, and saying something in rapid Italian, kissed my hand a second time before leaving me standing in a rapturous daze. I tried not to wash the subtly scented area: I had been kissed by Pavarotti. We were to connect again, under rather different circumstances.

Meeting a rich variety of people is the privilege of some and I feel I have been one of those. Amongst the vast eclectic group I've met in my life were a married couple: he of Swiss-German origin, she of Russian-German parentage. Living in the same town they had not known each other as children although brought up within the confines of a small ethnic group. Both families had Jewish connections. Written by her years later, the story - as Nazi persecution began - of a distressing departure to avoid transportation to a concentration camp makes harrowing reading, and particularly notable the sorrow of a small child who, with no idea of what was happening, had been made to free her canaries: birds she adored.

Meeting after the war, in Switzerland, they married, and during the ensuing years she had pursued her artistic career; he his music, before eventually moving to London where he formed and maintained a youth orchestra travelling the world to make music.

We had met through mutual connections. Their house in Sloane Street was immensely hospitable, the drawing room filled night after night with an international group of authors, artists, musicians, sculptors, and opera singers. They met, discussing innumerable subjects in at least four languages, and often a musician or a singer gave an impromptu performance.

I was surprised when told, by my receptionist, in the middle of a working day that a car was waiting outside: I was needed immediately, in Sloane Street. Enquiring from the chauffeur as we sped through London - Diplomatic Plates ensuring a clear passage - I learned that the new maid had hoovered up the current favourite canary. Canaries were a still a passion, it had never been forgotten that when forced to leave Germany the birds in the aviary had been loosed. The wife, never requiring silicone was naturally well-endowed, had a specially designed wicker basket woven, this secreted between the boobs enabling the favourite canary to travel, to Europe, America even Australia, undetected. As most countries forbid the importation of seeds the chauffeurs of the limos that met the travelling group - often an entire orchestra - must have wondered why on earth they were instructed, by the wife of the patron, to drive to the nearest pet store rather than going straight to the chosen house or hotel.

There was no sign of the canary on arrival, and everyone was in a state of collapse. No one seemed to know how to, or even had even had the sense, to try to remove the collection bag from the Hoover. I managed this and gingerly shook out the dust expecting to find a corpse. I was astonished to discover an alive but practically featherless bird.

A vet arrived and we discussed the bird. He appeared somewhat irritated that I had not already disposed of the naked creature and was all for a quick departure and purchase of a replacement. After all Harrods was just around the corner. The suggestion created such a level of hysteria that he shrugged his shoulders, said there was nothing he could do, and left. We made up a nest using a feather duster, and into this the luckless bird was placed. Why it survived I have no idea but it did, eventually growing shiny new feathers.

The downside of its recovery was, prior to being vacuumed, it had always remained silent during orchestral rehearsals or concerts, this became a thing of the past. As the conductor's baton was raised it would burst into loud song almost drowning the opening bars. It was taken back to the vet, and he deduced the effects of the vacuum incident had expanded its chest to such a degree that it had enabled a significant increase in both sound and volume. A three figure sum well spent I suppose, but one had to admire him for ingenuity.

Forbidden to attend rehearsals the bird was freed during the evening soirées. Nothing untoward occurred until one evening when a guest intimated he wished to sing. He assumed his usual pose, standing near the piano, handkerchief drooping from the left hand, he smiled as he took breath, before the first note was uttered the canary forestalled, unseen it emitted a warbling musical bubble of sound. The room froze in a mix of horror and anticipation, from his facial expression the great Tenor simply could not believe what had happened. At the third attempt he lost it, he was obviously still not certain if the sound was a practical joke, or if it was real. His tirade of Italian caused the canary to leave the picture rail, where it had been perching behind him, and fly to the window ledge, there it sat looking triumphant. With a bellow of rage he rushed to the window flinging it wide, the canary deemed it sensible to evacuate, he then collapsed onto a chair rubbing his shoulder, I was nearest to him when I heard someone say urgently, 'do something', not quite sure of the best approach I tried, in a mixture of languages, to calm him and offered a shoulder massage.

An hour later he sang, the sound filling the room, streaming out through the open window causing those in the street below to pause and listen.

Next time I visited the house an aviary had been built, it contained quail, it was explained, not only were they noiseless but their eggs were delicious.

For over 25 years, helped by Penelope and Rabbit we had offered a repair service embracing both animals and people proving undeniably that appropriate Physiotherapy - following injury - was viable, no matter the species. Other therapy centres were opened; ACPAT was up and running with a course specifically designed to train Chartered Physiotherapists in Animal Therapy, ably managed by Tracey Crook MCSP at the Veterinary School in Potters Bar, now transferred to Liverpool. Through the ITEC Diploma Course in Equine Sports Massage I ran at Downs House, past students were spreading the word internationally.

Not slow to appreciate a new market. manufacturers of medical therapy devices embraced the field: water tread mills were designed, saline and water massage spas made an appearance, and low level laser devices could be purchased by all. Many racing yards built their own pools, and some were employing rehabilitation experts. The veterinary profession began to study bio-mechanics and to plumb the depths of the musculo-skeletal system: this radically changing treatment protocol.

Rabbit had masterminded and extended the Flying Physio Scheme nationwide only to be slightly side-lined as it became, rather like the National Health Service, taken over by admin experts: luckily the organisation still appreciated the need for her expertise within the scheme.

Downs House had played its part, and we began to search Exmoor and the surrounding area.

5

Exmoor Relocation.

rought up in the West Country I had always considered
it would be good to spend the latter part of life there. Not
to retire: what *is* retirement? Certainly not sitting on a
beach watching the tide roll the pebbles in on one tide and out
on the next as appears to be the choice of some. Others who
having enjoyed a summer break end up relocating to the West
in order to keep their own horse, have a go at self -sufficiency,
and create a shortage of available properties with land.

Sadly for many, holiday memories may have offered somewhat limited experience in the ways of the area and its peoples.
Idyllic scenery is not everything and past memories tend to
tarnish particularly if a sea fret covers the country for days, or
the Atlantic gales sweep in at one side of a cosy cottage and out
the other. Roads are blocked by farm traffic necessitating
expertise in reversing - often for half a mile or more, and in
winter lanes are iced up as gritting only happens on major
roads.

We knew and were prepared for all of this. We just hoped, as
society began to change its boundaries, to be able to move back
in time and live companionably alongside the indigenous
farming community.

I had promised myself, after working in Exford for Frank
Mullins, way back in 1949, that one day I would return to the

area, hence the choice of Exmoor. Instow my childhood home was just too remote as we hoped for rehab horses from previous clients and communication with Taunton, the nearest large town was easier from Exmoor due to the M5 motoway which connects the area to middle England.

Berkshire had been the ideal location and yet the West Country is not a desert: it supports trainers, not least Martin Pipe, and also gives home to a cross section of riders, Event, Endurance, and otherwise. We decided we could down size to a unit not dependant on staff: at Downs House finding dedicated staff had become a nightmare.

Pelly and Rabbit viewed Combeleigh on a Friday, I saw it the following week, and with no further ado - despite the odd squeak from our solicitor cousin about surveys - the deposit was paid and Combeleigh with its barns, outbuildings and 90 acres became ours on Lady Day 1999.

Packing Downs House was a logistical nightmare. I was on my own, Rabbit was working in Ireland, while Penelope, the horses and dogs had gone to camp at Combeleigh while various alterations were made. One barn needed to be converted for stables and a lecture cum treatment area had to be built in another.

Bernard and I had parted before we moved although I'd agreed to train up to London to consult if needed. Thus for a while my weekly run became Berkshire to Somerset, rather than Berkshire to London. Eventually, a fleet of removal vans headed west, and their drivers eventually found the farm though horrified that after Taunton there were no street lights. A new owner took over Downs House and I moved down. Shortly after this Rabbit found a house she liked nearby, sold hers and moved too.

After arriving I began to wonder why I had given up a pretty smooth running life that had taken over 25 years to perfect! We were now living in a National Park and the Authority, having initially made happy noises about a 'much needed increase in the usage of local amenities' when first approached suddenly became far from helpful regarding the proposed business diversification on the farm. At the final planning meeting they suddenly refused permission for an outdoor, all

Combeleigh

weather arena, and for the extension of a barn needed for the horse walker!

As I re-applied for both of these, Foot and Mouth hit the country. It would have been too awful to have brought in a lorry load of horses from up country and then for a local farm to get the disease. The only thing to do was to shut down before we had even started and learn how to farm rather rapidly.

Clarence Stevens the previous owner came daily:, he had not wanted to sell but his wife had suffered a stroke and he himself was not well. He came 'home' most days often to collect water, as his new bungalow in the village of Cutcombe was on the mains and cups of tea - made with mains rather than spring water - 'Did not taste right.' On some days he described himself as 'Not feeling very workish today' collected his slippers and sat in his chair, a wing back still in situ near the Aga, waiting for a cup of coffee, I rapidly learnt Camp was the only acceptable brand.

Two other families of Stevens, first cousins to Clarence, lived in adjacent farms on down the valley to the west side, with a Mr Bawdon at Combeshead to the east. Tim Forster, still training when we moved, wrote to tell me how lucky I was to be living next to Harold Stevens, the nicest man on Exmoor; an outstanding farmer who knew more about the Red Deer than any one he had ever met. And so it turned out. Harold and Phyllis who summoned us to a meal shortly after we moved in, were kindness in itself. I cannot remember how the subject came up but sometime later, their daughter Angela Edwards, said to Penelope, 'After we saw your hands when you came to tea, we thought, those hands show they work: they will be alright.'

Rather than Clarence having to watch all his farm machinery being sold at Auction it was valued and we bought it. On workish days he introduced Penelope to every implement in turn, explaining the idiosyncrasies of each. The baler, requiring twine rather than plastic string, made eleven good bales, then a misshapen twelfth before returning to spit out normal bales once again. When it was time he mowed the grass with a precision not seen today as the huge machines sweep up and down often tearing, rather than cutting the grass. His rams continued to live in one field, waiting until the autumn sheep sales came round. He was delighted when our first Exmoor Horns arrived, despite the fact these had been chosen, bought by and dropped off by Harold Stevens following a local sheep sale. 'Can't farm on Exmoor with no sheep. Us don't want no Saturday farmers round here.'

Mr Bawdon and Clarence, despite having been to school together had not spoken for 40 years. Clarence told us they'd had a violent disagreement and Mr Bawdon had, 'Said a 'B' word.' When I went to introduce myself - despite a gap of 50 years - I recognised him as the person who used to come to kill Frank's pigs.

The Christmas before he died I took him a plate of dinner on Christmas day. He was waiting, seated at a long oak table, one that in former times had seated a family of at least 10. With a log smouldering in the open fire place, he sat knife and fork held pointing upward ready to dig in. As I put the well charged plate in front of him he looked down, sniffed, and asked, 'Call that gravy?' Then he set to.

Requests to see horses began to materialise. Martin Pipe asked me to visit his yard every week, and this was followed by a call from Philip Hobbs with a similar request. The vets in both yards gave me *carte blanche* provided, after I had seen a horse, they were supplied with appropriate notes.

Liz Welsh, about to become head girl to Philip Hobbs had taken a course with us, at Downs House, some years previously and became invaluable, reporting on performance, spotting problems early on, ensuring massage was given, magnets or weights were applied, when and if needed.

Robert Alner was not too far away and Arnie Sendall began to use me for his horses in training with Robert and Sally, notably Kingscliff, a lovely horse but almost too big and un-gainly for his own good. On good days he was unbeatable but on bad days, regrettably, rather indifferent. For me trips to the Alner's were almost a rest as Arnie would pick me up from a pub car park in Taunton in his automatic Mercedes and drive the one and a half hour journey to Robert's yard.

Arnie was a man of many talents, particularly well known in the gardening world and among his many prize winning successes were chrysanthemums and giant onions. As we chatted during the journeys I gleaned a wealth of horticultural information. One day, following a rather good lunch, I asked how things had gone at a flower show the previous week and he said rather sadly, 'Not good at all. They only gave me highly *condemned*.'

Following the all clear from DEFRA after the Foot and Mouth chaos resolved, normal animal movement had restarted and thankfully owners and trainers began to send horses to us. Jean Broadhurst and her partner Matt Archer moved their entire string to Martin Pipe allowing us to summer them. Blyth Tait visited, remarking it was hilly - 'like New Zealand' - and a rather broken purchase arrived shortly afterwards for repair.

Our Swedish friend Eric Du Vander, training the Japanese three day team, brought down a load of horses to be seen. Swedes often give flowers when they visit Eric but had forgotten to buy any. Shortly after realising this, he'd seen some lovely yellow flowers growing on a motorway bank, and stopping-picked a large bunch. Blue and yellow are the Swedish colours: there was a length of blue ribbon in the living compartment of the lorry, and the flowers were tastefully arranged by his groom and tied. Crises over, I could be presented with flowers when he arrived, he obviously did not know of the dangers associated, particularly to horses, of Ragwort! It was a memorable visit not only did his box just scrape through the final lane but it began to snow. Three hours and a broken towing chain later it seemed easier if he stayed overnight, flowers and all!

Comply or Die was sent in by David Pipe following a really tiresome fall, X-rays having shown mid back bone damage which needed time. Too intelligent for his own good he came partly because, very curious, he spent rather too much time on his hind legs attempting to see what was happening elsewhere. What this horse could not see through he tried to see over.

Both David and Martin felt daily therapy, coupled to time in a quiet environment was necessary if he was to regain full potential. The horse had lost most of his back muscle but was very receptive to therapy and tolerant of muscle stimulators. He behaved really well when worked in long reins, and remained a model patient until one day he decided he had mended. He imparted this knowledge to me by deciding to come off the walker on his hind legs, rising up gracefully with no sign of effort or loss of balance. He returned to Nicholshayne and David Pipe, giving the trainer his first Grand National.

I reinstated the Massage courses and we were becoming busy enough to keep the wolf from the door. It was with considerable pleasure and excitement that I watched the Exmoor Horns develop, under Penelope's care, into a prize winning flock. Lambing had been another new experience, and friends and neighbours guided every one through, often arriving as a result of frantic telephone calls to pull off a back to front lamb. Boiled fruit cakes - a receipt kept from the time when the children were small and people still had afternoon tea - proved a popular thank you.

Rabbit developed an enviable ability - after being shown how - to turn lambs, saving most. Unlike some breeds pure bred Exmoor Horn lambs are very slow to find the teat when born, and we failed to realise this until Sam, a Blue Faced Leicester ram, arrived and we saw that his offspring were up on their feet suckling within minutes of arrival.

Moving the sheep around the farm required trained dogs. Rabbit who owned a sheep dog but one only partially trained, set to. She devoured books, asked advice, attended training courses, and finally bought her first, bred to be a sheep dog, pup. She and Penelope both have border collies for farm work but Rabbit now trials her dogs: displaying a patience when training them way beyond my comprehension.

Word of mouth is the very best advertisement, and attending competitions extended the overall catchment field for patients: humans for Rabbit; dogs for me. The dogs included agility dogs, trial dogs, gun dogs, and of course hounds and terriers

Above: Comply or Die wins the Grand National

Below: Exmoor Horns from the Combeleigh flock

Prizewinning Exmoor horns from Combeleigh

began to materialise. Then as it became known that all animals, no matter the breed, were welcome - not just horses - injuries from an increasing range made an appearance including sheep and cattle.

Back to the anatomy books. Fortunately, when teaching at veterinary establishments I am often able, in between lectures, to sneak into the odd dissection lab, also sit in on operations, for even with modern computerised programmes nothing compares to the real thing. An in-depth, constantly refreshed knowledge of musculo-skeletal anatomy is, in my view essential in order to ensure successful outcomes for all those who offer Physiotherapy, rehabilitation or massage; my continual cry to students is 'never forget your anatomy.'

When at Downs House I had been able to brush up equine anatomy at the kennels of the Berks and Bucks Drag Hounds whenever I wanted. When we moved I was concerned I would lose this facility particularly because of a new raft of health and safety rules. Fortunately due to an exceptionally helpful and open-minded Huntsman, Donald Sommersgill, and because his kennels have the licencing required by DEFRA to euthanize, I can refresh my brain when needed: anatomy book in one hand, scalpel in the other.

Privileged to lecture to Vets and Students at conferences and Veterinary teaching establishments worldwide, had enabled me to keep abreast of all that was newly emerging in the field of equine orthopaedics; fortunately this is still ongoing particularly as Martin Pipe, awarded a Doctorate by the Liverpool Veterinary School, is generous enough to invite me to climb into the helicopter and fly with him to attend conferences of relevance. Amusingly, while finding lectures interesting, I have learned that most information is gleaned from discussions round the bar in the evenings rather than during the actual teaching sessions! The first invitation to lecture in Edinburgh embraced a unique experience: I suddenly realised I was teaching in the very hall, probably even standing on the very same platform as had my father and grandfather done before me.

One of the ideas - on embracing farm life - was to become self-sufficient, and this requiring varied live-stock: the bantams had come with us, and the yard pond could support ducks. To begin with all the poultry were free range, but - tiresomely - the local fox population made rather too many visits necessitating overnight housing.

During the spring of our second year it was with pleasure I noted a duck was sitting: sadly she hatched, not a duckling, but a chicken. It seemed best to ignore the situation, two or three days after the hatching the exasperated ducks decided the 'child' must do as it was told. Putting their beaks behind it they propelled the luckless ball of feathers to the edge of the pond and literally chucked it into the water. Rescue with a prawning net was not successful.

Over time the ducks fared less well than the bantams who mostly had the sense to take refuge in the nearest tree if a fox invaded by day. Following such a visit, left with one drake, I set off to a poultry sale. There, sitting in adjacent cages were two young ducks, each clearly labelled 'Call Duck' - just what was needed. I bought them, and of course they were, as described, ducks: but were drakes, not duck ducks. Identification had not been possible as they were too young to have grown the giveaway tail curl. Subsequently I reported this to the auctioneer, half pulling his leg about the trade descriptions act. It had no effect: one lives and learns.

I had not realised when I first went to see a horse for Tigger Pudd, nee Day, that not only did she breed thoroughbreds, selling some and training others for point to points, but she also ran a pedigree Jersey Herd inherited from her parents. Viking was an older member of the herd, and as her milk yield was beginning to drop she needed a good home. She settled in quickly and gave us real, rich, creamy milk in excess. But what to do with the excess? There is a limit to the amount of cream you can use or give away: butter is different and after crossly thinking people would given their eye teeth for such an offering during the war I stopped butter making and purchased a pig arc. I did say when I bought it that delivery would be difficult as it had to negotiate both a stream and substantial hedge in order to be housed in the orchard. Barry Fowler seemed unphased and managed to site the arc as requested although I gather his comments, made to friends following the exercise, were not perhaps 100% complimentary.

The arrival of the pig arc enabled the purchase of my first Gloucester Old Spot pig. Named Ellen she thrived on milk and barley but even then there was still spare milk.

Tigger to the rescue: delivery of a three-day-old unwanted bull calf solved the problem. Viking (previously quite happy as a solitary house cow) adored the calf and managed - although milked before he was allowed to suckle - to withold her cream giving us a rather dirty looking thin creamless liquid offering. This ability is not described in the books.

Ellen grew in size and obstinacy, - despite this and to my surprise - when she was old enough, I managed (using AI) to get her pregnant. She swelled and became even more difficult to move around from pen to paddock, collapsing and grunting, until one day when it grew near farrowing time, she suddenly changed, and became remarkably active, rushing around the orchard collecting materials and began nest building.

Books are excellent for information, but nothing beats practical experience: baby pigs need to be injected with iron very soon after birth; and I had not, despite pig book hints, anticipated Ellen's level of irritation when her babies needed to be handled for medication. As I pulled out the first, handing it to Gillie, a temporary helper, she erupted. Our combined leap over a substantial pig fence was sadly not caught on camera but certainly proved that an adrenaline rush really does enhance performance.

Most cattle were of course not nice placid cows, but generally irritated bulls. The first is memorable: an Aberdeen Angus lame in front, was out with 'his women'. His two rather stick-like, elderly retired doctors suggested he could, 'be a little tetchy'. After explaining I found it easier to see animals as individuals, preferably in a stable or pen, rather than in a herd situation they set off to bring him down to the yard. He must have been in a tetchy mood as the next thing I witnessed were his owners sprinting down the field. For retirees they seemed pretty nimble, leaping an electric fence before taking cover behind a convenient straw stack. It seemed prudent to join them.

Above: Ellen, resting

Below: With her babies

Luckily the bull decided to return to his cows, but left a small trail of blood, suggesting he might have burst a foot abscess for he appeared sound when going away. His owners were later kind enough to telephone to let me know this had indeed been the cause of his lameness.

Farm animals, unlike horses, are less likely to be able to visit, and this means travel. Most of the West Country is still truly rural with many properties well off the beaten track. One of the great joys associated with going to treat animals on their home patch is that nearly every call-out means seeing a new bit of country. I try to give myself plenty of time in order to explore and enjoy these beautiful remote areas, with some trips involving a drive through areas remembered from childhood. As you grow older familiar things are a comfort, and I can visualize my mother and her dogs in so many places: another bonus.

The first Red Devon Bull I met (belonging to Malcolm Hurd) was a totally different character to the Aberdeen Angus. His injury, involving a back leg, suggested he had slipped off a cow while serving her. He stood happily munching brewers grains while being treated and eventually recovered sufficiently to resume stud duties.

A farm on a remote area of coast I did not know, near Lee, was the home of another rather important Ruby Red Devon bull. The journey over was magical, one of those days when every colour seems enhanced, primroses were peeping from the hedge rows and it was fortunate there was little or no on-coming traffic as sudden glimpses of the sea, viewed through one of the many sudden dips in the coast line, were distracting.

I had not met Tony Sinclair before and he was not, from his voice, a Devon man. A relatively recent settler and breeder his cattle, all Ruby Reds, were his passion. It was obvious from the yard and buildings that care on the farm was exemplary. The bull I'd been asked to see was so lame they'd had to leave him out. It had been unusually wet and we slid down a near precipice to the field where 'Rocket', as he was called, looking very sorry indeed, was standing under a sweet smelling bush, staring out to sea. Why I have no idea, but I was immediately reminded of the story of Ferdinand the Bull. For those who do not know the story Ferdinand loved smelling flowers, and having the misfortune to sit on a bee when candidates for the bull ring were being chosen, he had leapt and snorted. This was mistakenly assumed by the selectors to be bravery and the wish to fight: then when taken to the bull ring in Madrid he just sat and smelled the flowers, upsetting the crowd and the Matador.

After a bit of prodding it seemed to me that Rocket had probably slipped, due to ground conditions, and jarred his pelvis. I agreed with the vet, that it did not feel as though there was a fracture nor did he seem sufficiently distressed for this to have happened. His pelvis looked remarkably similar to that of Malcolm's Devon bull I had treated, and it was his owner who had suggested I might be able to help.

We obviously had to try to get him up to the yard. He did not take too much persuasion following a food-filled bucket with rather more alacrity than I through the mud. Bedded down in deep straw he cheered up: even more so when a barren cow was brought in to keep him company.

Gentle exercise seems to work with cattle rather than full box rest providing there is no bone damage, and following laser treatment and after suggesting a forward programme, I left.

He had improved when I next saw him some months later, but was, I felt possibly playing to the gallery being a bit of a Ferdinand. 'Why stand on a wind- swept hill, even if it has a spectacular view, when you can be living comfortably in a barn?'

Tony and his wife Olive muttered about an account, drinking a cup of tea in their kitchen, and while eating a welcome ham sandwich, I tried to explain I really was not certain I had helped Rocket and, like my father before me, never submitted a bill if I did not feel I had achieved a cure. When I went to rub his head goodbye before leaving he demonstrated to me that animals inevitably have the last laugh. For his parting shot - after dropping a particularly wet turd - he swished his tail and turning, flicked a liberal coating of cowpat over both Tony and I.

Two days later four dozen Red Roses arrived from Rocket. This must be a unique one-off: has anyone else been so paid by a Ruby Red Devon Bull?

Such a payment is unlikely to be repeated giving a very good excuse to end a tale describing a few of my amusing and different experiences during a somewhat selfish, chosen Way of Life.

Edward Gaskell
publishers
DEVON

Also by Mary Bromiley

Equine Injury and Therapy
Physiotherapy in Veterinary Medicine
Equine Injury, Therapy and Rehabilitation (3rd Edition)
Fit to Ride
Natural Methods for Equine Health
Massage Techniques for Horse and Rider (2nd Edition)
Massage for Horses